# ENTREPRENEURSHIP
## *Made Easy*

Kingdom Entrepreneurship Nexus

by

REV DR MICHAEL APPIAH

The contents of this work, including, but not limited to, the accuracy of events, people, and places depicted; opinions expressed; permission to use previously published materials included; and any advice given or actions advocated are solely the responsibility of the author, who assumes all liability for said work and indemnifies the publisher against any claims stemming from publication of the work.

All Rights Reserved
Copyright © 2023 by REV DR MICHAEL APPIAH

No part of this book may be reproduced or transmitted, downloaded, distributed, reverse engineered, or stored in or introduced into any information storage and retrieval system, in any form or by any means, including photocopying and recording, whether electronic or mechanical, now known or hereinafter invented without permission in writing from the publisher.

Dorrance Publishing Co
585 Alpha Drive
Pittsburgh, PA 15238
Visit our website at *www.dorrancebookstore.com*

ISBN: 979-8-88729-002-7
eISBN: 979-8-88729-502-2

## TABLE OF CONTENTS

Foreword ................................................. v
Introduction ............................................ xiii
1. Introduction to entrepreneurship ......................... 1
2. Who is an entrepreneur? ................................ 19
3. Business Structure ..................................... 60
4. Initial capital saga ................................... 77
5. Discover your Strength – Potential ..................... 97
6. Temperance ............................................ 114
7. The Concept of Ants in Business ....................... 129
8. Basic Bookkeeping Skills .............................. 141
9. Taxes ................................................. 197
10. Basic Marketing [5Ps] ................................ 219
11. Separate Yourself from the business .................. 227
    a. Pay Yourself
    b. Act as an Employee + owner
12. Manage Customer with Professionalism/ Customer Relationship ...241
13. Growth ............................................... 260
    a. Invest
    b. Expansion
Bibliography ............................................ 284

Kingdom Entrepreneurship Nexus Models
Desire/Passion –> Energy –> Solving Problem -> Collective Benefit –> Serving the Community –> Fulfillment.

# FOREWORD

God raises men and women with specific assignments to carry out His purpose and to serve their generation and subsequent generations. The Bible says, "For David, after he had served his own generation by the will of God, fell asleep, was buried with his fathers, and saw corruption;" Acts 13:36 NKJV .

To fulfill His purpose here on earth and in His servants, God in His sovereign power gives unique revelation to some selected few to expound on a subject that takes them into the throne room of God to hear His mind for His people.

Rev. Dr. Michael O. Appiah has been raised by God to teach this generation and the next about the mind of God regarding kingdom entrepreneurship. "*Entrepreneurship Made Easy*" is a must-read, and I believe millions of believers will be enlightened and immensely blessed through this project. In this book, Dr. Appiah carefully and meticulously reveals to us the mind of God on how to go about a business start-up, what structures to put in place and how to do business from a Christian perspective etc.

This book intends to raise kingdom entrepreneurs who will become financial pillars in the local and global church. It is important for followers of Christ to know the principles of God regarding the market place. Jesus compared this generation of Christians to children in the market place. "But to what shall I liken this generation? It is like children sitting in the marketplaces and calling to their companions and saying: 'We played the flute for you, And you did not dance; We mourned to you, And you did not lament." Matthew 11:16-17 NKJV. This is a sad picture of the church, but it is the reality of the modern-day Christian. The market place is where business transactions are made, and millions of dollars are being moved. However, during that environment, the church is playing the flute and calling their colleagues to come and dance.

A lot of us have been raised up with a mindset that all our problems are demon problems, but *"Entrepreneurship Made Easy"* draws our attention to the fact that most of our problems are wisdom problems, and not otherwise.

God says "My people are destroyed for lack of knowledge. Because you have rejected knowledge, I also will reject you from being priest for Me; Because you have forgotten the law of your God, I also will forget your children." Hosea 4:6 NKJV. *"Entrepreneurship Made Easy"* will enlighten Christendom to help this generation of Christians, so we become informed, exempted from the liabilities of ignorance, and live purposeful lives that glorifies God.

If you are going to read any book this year, I will recommend *"Entrepreneurship Made Easy"* It is simply that good!

May the Lord quicken your faith in His word and supply you with the grace you need to live a victorious life. As you practice the principles in this book, new doors are divinely opening to you that will bring you new opportunities to prosper. Yes, your set time has come.

On a personal note, I would like to thank Dr. Appiah for adding value to the lives of Christians through this book and for inspiring a lot of Africans in the diaspora. I pray God's best on him, his family, and his ministry. I will see you at the top.

Sincerely,
Rev. Kingsley Ayesu

# FOREWORD

"You must be the change you wish to see."

It happens rarely in a person's lifetime that you come to discover someone whose very presence speaks for itself. That's Rev Dr. Michael O. Appiah. He is modest yet confident. He is gentle but strong spiritually and intellectually. A good family man. Life can be stressful, and every facet is different. Things don't always work out according to plan and our dreams sometimes fade away. One of the Christian virtues we need is to be victorious and achieve our God-given desires.

The solution to most of our prayers lies in our ability to understand Kingdom Entrepreneurship and Kingdom Marketing. The church must think business and operate with business man sets.

In this book, Rev Dr. Michael O. Appiah enlightens the body of Christ about Kingdom principles that will help an average believer to be an entrepreneur and succeed.

I, Archbishop Van Dyke Noah, had benefited from the writer's knowledge and understanding of Kingdom Entrepreneurship. The concept of ants in business, manage customers with professionalism how to invest and lastly serving our community.

Archbishop Van Dyke approves and recommends this timely book to the Universal church.

Work well done, Ayekoo!!!!!

Archbishop Dr. Van Dyke Noah<br>
Founder and Overseer<br>
Miracle Redemption Christian Center Int.

For almost twelve years, Rev Dr. Michael O. Appiah has worked behind the scenes at House of Glory Ministries preparing for his God driven purpose. As I came to know Rev Dr. Michael, I realized his ambitious goals to get things started and get it done. When Michael sat down with me and informed me of his calling to a new phase of his life, by coming up with a book to help churches and businesses manage their finances, I wasn't surprised. I had already seen such a calling in him. Rev Dr. Michael has been an instrument and an asset helping House of Glory Ministries and other individuals to manage their finances.

I was really amazed to hear that he wanted to extend his God's given talent to help other churches through "Kingdom Entrepreneurs Nexus", which is to be established in all churches to help and direct the business-minded individuals. Rev Dr. Michael understands the scripture quote that says, "I can do all things through Christ who strengthens me" (Philippians 4:13). I am well pleased, he has finally come up with his first book entitled, "Kingdom Entrepreneurship Nexus". This book will provide you with a daily path to keep taking one step closer to better business management.

God created you for his purpose and this book will help all readers for better business management. I am praying for you and believe you will be successful as you commit to God's divine plan for your life. I congratulate Rev Dr. Michael O. Appiah and recommend this book, *Entrepreneurship Made Easy*, to all churches and to business-minded individuals.

Rev. Ebenezer Otu<br>
Head Pastor<br>
House of Glory Ministries<br>
Minnesota, USA.

The attempt to satisfy the holistic ministry of the Church has been tackled from various angles of scholarship. The idea is to inform the congregation adequately of the incorporating concept of the social mandate of the gospel. In Rev Dr. Michael's Kingdom Entrepreneurship Nexus (KEN), he seeks to enlighten people desiring financial blessings to acclimatize principles relating to such outcomes.

Rev Dr. Michael has spent quality time in the past years to study and be equipped with the knowledge connecting to the subject of entrepreneurship. Furthermore, he has consulted credible sources in the field whose work gives massive support to his submissions and has cited enough biblical references as evidence of reality. The treatment of the concept of entrepreneurship is simplified and well explained under the title, "Who is an entrepreneur" in chapter two of the book. The list provided in the chapter is sufficient and justifies the presentation of the author. The awareness of entrepreneurship which Rev Dr. Michael presents, proposes to restore confidence in people in and around the church to crave ownership in life and to assume a proper place as instruments of blessing to others.

KEN is entrepreneurship made simple that breaks the fear of stepping out by potential business-minded people in and around the church. Conversely, whoever takes the bold step will never stand alone; you have a big shoulder on which you can stand on to view the business world around you.

Allow Rev Dr. Michael's KEN to be your handbook of reference and propel you to action, oh, business-minded people in and around the church!

Rev Dr. Louis Y. Oppong-Kyekyeku<br>
Senior Pastor<br>
Great Grace Assemble of God<br>
Minnesota, USA

There are many Christian books on finances and stewardship, but I think Rev Dr. Michael O. Appiah's book on "Kingdom Entrepreneurship Nexus" is one of the finest and insightful books on stewardship because of his professional background as an accountant. I believe *Entrepreneurship Made Easy: Kingdom Entrepreneurship Nexus* is a breakthrough and a profound book for Christian entrepreneurs, religious organizations, nonprofit organizations, and businesses. Dr. Appiah's new way of applying biblical entrepreneurship to practical ministry and his step-by-step overview on basic bookkeeping skills, taxes, business structures, and understanding of finances for entrepreneurs, pastors, church administrators, managers, and leaders on how to become effective stewards in managing God's resources are impeccable.

*Entrepreneurship Made Easy* offers entrepreneurs, pastors, and Christian leaders new ways to approach entrepreneurship by inspiring and encouraging business owners and church leaders to intentionally separate themselves from their business entity and ministry. The book also suggests the importance of how businesses and churches should manage their customer care with professionalism and customer relationship. I believe this cutting-edge book will revolutionize today's business culture, church culture, and customer relationship as entrepreneurs and church leaders learn how to focus on customer satisfaction as a priority for growth and expansion.

Finally, one of the topics Jesus taught his followers to avoid waste was stewardship. "And if you are untrustworthy about worldly wealth, who will trust you with the true riches of heaven? And if you are not faithful with other people's things, why should you be trusted with things of your own?" (Luke 16:11 NLT). As Christians, if we show accountability in our finances, God will endow us with spiritual things to His glory.

Rev Dr. George K. Ata-Baah<br>
(General Overseer, Glory House).<br>
Chairman, Ghanaians Ministers Association of Minnesota

# INTRODUCTION

The underlying motive of every entrepreneur is to establish a successful business and make profit that will sustain the business. Thus, profitability and sustainability are two key elements of a successful business. In this book, *Entrepreneurship Made Easy*, Dr. Michael Appiah has clearly delineated the path to establishing a successful business and the methods of sustaining it. However, the competitive edge of this book resides in its conceptualization of Kingdom Entrepreneurship. A Kingdom entrepreneur is someone who conducts business on the principles of the Bible. S/he is diligent, hardworking, honest, a faithful tither, divinely wise, obedient and prayerful. S/he draws on divine wisdom to run his/her business and attributes the success and growth of his/her business to the direction of God. Even though the Kingdom entrepreneur owns his/her business, s/he transfers such ownership to God for His grace and divine direction. The concept of Kingdom entrepreneur does not preclude a knowledge of the business environment in which one operates, in favor of blind faith; it merely asserts that such a knowledge of the establishment of business, tax systems, production and pricing of goods and services, employee relationship and growth of business must be larded by divine principles. Thus, the Kingdom entrepreneur brings trust and honesty into business operations.

Structurally, this book can be divided into four parts: ownership/entrepreneurship, business formation, production of goods and services, and expansion.

These four parts correspond with the four phases of a business or the life cycle of a business. The first phase raises fundamental questions about entrepreneurship. Who is an entrepreneur? What does it take to become one? What streaks of character should an entrepreneur possess? *Entrepreneurship Made Easy* clearly spells out those attributes for the layman to understand. By examining the characteristics of good and successful entrepreneurs, Dr. Appiah underscores the point that there is a commonality of character traits among great and successful entrepreneurs. They are usually great visionaries who are endued with tenacity, patience, and focus. They are risk-takers who have a clear picture of the bigger goal ahead and the realistic steps to achieving it. They might not have the resources to kick-start or grow the business, but they know how to access available resources to make their dreams come true. They are fearless to dream big and big-hearted enough to conquer their dreams. They are human beings who are courageous enough to try, and fail, and try again.

Following the conceptualization stage of a business is the formation of that business. Establishing a business requires a lot of thoughtful considerations such as the kind of business structure—that is, Sole Proprietorship, General Partnership, Limited Partnership, C-corporation, S-corporation, and Limited Liability Company—the location of the business, the goods and services that will be offered, etc. These business structures have tax implications as well. Dr. Appiah has provided relevant information about the United States of America's business environment to enable readers of this book to know how to register the different kinds of business options, the pros and cons of the various business registrations, the tax forms used in filing tax returns and the different lending options available in banks and other institutions. To a large extent, the location of a business—that is, whether virtual or actual or both—influences its registration, tax filing system, and marketing strategies. Knowing about such complex issues will certainly guide a conscientious entrepreneur into making informed decisions about the kind of business option to adopt.

Decisions about the kinds of goods and services to offer our clients should not be taken for granted. In fact, it is our goods and services that define our businesses;

they demarcate our lines of businesses. And the concept of business lines further introduces the notion of competition in the market. If we are in the line of business of selling cars, for example, we must be aware of the fact that there are other car dealers out there who are offering similar products. Thus, our decisions about the goods and services we offer should take into consideration our competitive edge in the market. That is, what new things are we bringing in our chosen lines of businesses that would attract customers to us. It is our competitive edges that will make us survive the competition inherent in the market place. To do business is to assert that one has something new and better to offer to customers; otherwise, their loyalties, habits, and tastes will remain with old business providers. Certainly, our decisions about goods and services must come with a knowledge of customer psychology and behavior.

Whether we decide to operate on the same scale after launching our businesses or grow our businesses to a much larger scale should definitely be dependent on a lot of factors. Scaling up our businesses, on the one hand, implies an expected growth in our profit margins; on the other hand, it calls for an increase of our operational cost. It might involve the hiring of more staff and the bloating of our wage bills, buying more vehicles and other logistical items to facilitate operations, building more market outlets to increase sales, etc. And there are times when such cash-intensive plough-backs into our businesses do not yield the expected profit margins we envisaged, and our businesses run the risk of plummeting into disaster. This book has provided information on the different types of business expansions and the various caveats to guide our decisions.

Wealth creation through business investment is a risky endeavor. Thus, to minimize the risk, one must go in with information and knowledge about how the business world works. While business success is often pictured in the luxury cars, fancy vacations, and five-star hotel conviviality of business tycoons, it takes a lot of hard work, stress, frustration, trials and errors to get there. *Entrepreneurship Made Easy* has provided the information that every entrepreneur needs to navigate the business world safely. The book is reader-friendly, and its contents of business terminologies are quite accessible to even a layman who is intending to start a business for the first time. The language of the book is mostly conversational, providing a step-by-step approach to an understanding of complex business concepts. Anyone who is thinking seriously about going into business must read this book.

Dr. Samuel Kamara
Associate Graduate Faculty
English Department
Minnesota State University, Mankato
United States of America.

# CHAPTER 1

# INTRODUCTION TO ENTREPRENEURSHIP

Entrepreneurship is simply the activity of setting up a business and taking financial risks in the hope of making a good profit. The capacity and willingness to develop, organize and manage a business venture, along with any of its risks, is to make good profit. Entrepreneurs most at times come out with new ideas or business models that help solve economic or social problems and always start new business ventures. The objective of this book is to make the concept of entrepreneurship easy and simple for those who have the passion and the ideas to help solve the problems of the community, more especially in the kingdom work. There are lots of Christians with good ideas and passion and, with a little help or push and with God's principles guiding them, they can make a great difference in the community. They can support the church financially, create employment for the church members, thereby reducing the rate of unemployment in the church.

This objective has brought about this project: Kingdom Entrepreneurs Nexus (KEN), which is to be established in all churches to help and direct the business-minded people in and around the church. KEN will corroborate with the experts in the church and help them to inculcate these new ideas and turn them into businesses until they become successful. KEN is a non-profitable organization that aims to identify, mentor, monitor, and coach kingdom entrepreneurs with the principles of God, knowing that it is God who gives us the power (ability, ideas, passion, capacity, and intuition) to make wealth (see Duet 8:17-18, NKJV). Through KEN, the entrepreneur gets to understand the importance and the blessings of putting God first as a shareholder in the business by paying tithe on the profit of the business and the owner also paying tithe from his/her income. Furthermore, the owner encourages his/her employees to pay tithes from their incomes.

With this concept of raising entrepreneurs in the church, they become the financial pillars of the church as well as kingdom investors. This is what happens when you put God first and invest in the kingdom, so shall God also increase and expand your business and drive the devourer from your business (see Malachi 3:11, NKJV). As an entrepreneur, your business becomes the apple of God's eye and God will fight anyone who steals from it and plans to collapse the business because of the covenant the business has with God. Because we are serving a creator God, He will teach us how to start our businesses from very small capital. God Himself illustrated this creative energy when He was creating this earth:

> In the beginning, God created the heavens and the earth. And the earth was without form, and void; and darkness was over the face of the deep. And the Spirit of God was hovering over the face of the waters. Then God said, 'Let there be light', and there was light. (Genesis 1:1-3 (NKJV)

The first thing God reveals about Himself in the Scripture above is not that He is loving, holy, omnipotent, gracious, or just, but that He is creative. In Genesis, He created something out of nothing. He imposed order to the chaos of earth. And He created for the good of others. The fundamental principles of entrepreneurship—building from zero, service to others, and profitability—can be found in this Genesis story. In short, God is the first entrepreneur. God can give life back to the dead, as in the case of Lazarus in the Bible. He revives and restores. Therefore, as an entrepreneur who has a covenant with God, you automatically have the ability (wisdom) to revive your collapsing business, and this is why as a Christian, you must always make God the first shareholder in your business.

The word *entrepreneur* is thrown around so much today that it has become very difficult to define. I would submit that an entrepreneur is an individual who creates something new, more especially a business, bears most of the risks and enjoys most of the rewards. He/she also creates employment for others to have better lives. The process involved in doing all of this is known as entrepreneurship. As an entrepreneur, you are seen as a source of new ideas and an innovator; you are the business and you are as well the process to the success of the business because you are the main idea behind the business. Entrepreneurship, according to Professor Nathanael Left quoted by Fajardo (2007), is the capacity for innovation, investment and expansion in new markets, products, and techniques. Entrepreneurs create jobs.

Using this definition, the Creator of the universe certainly qualifies as The First Entrepreneur. In Genesis, He clearly created something new. Before creation, the earth was formless and empty until The First Entrepreneur spoke. Then, in six days, His voice brought forth the heavens, the earth, light, evening, morning, sky, land, sea, vegetation, sun, moon, stars, animals, and man.

Not only did God create something original, but He also created it for the good of others. God certainly didn't need to create the world and humankind. So why did He? Before creation, the Father, Spirit, and Son had been enjoying a perfect community, serving, and loving each other for all eternity. If the Trinity reveals the divine bliss and perfection of the Godhead, it stands to reason that one of the reason why God created the earth was to share with us the perfect love the Trinity has been experiencing throughout eternity.

So, when the earth was created for the good of others, did the omnipotent, omniscient God really take a risk in creating it? Certainly, He didn't take a risk in the way you and I do when we launch a new business, compose a new song, or write a new book. But He took a risk in a different, far more profound way. As Pastor Timothy Keller explains, "God made the world filled with human beings made in His image, human beings with freewill. So, God made the world knowing what it was going to cost Him. Knowing what we were going to do. Knowing that [His] Son was going to have to come into the world and [die for us]." God's risk, one can argue, is a calculated risk. He knew beforehand what the outcome of creating the earth would be, but He also knew that His death for mankind was going to give them everlasting life. However, His gracious death on the cross was only for those who believe in him. Therefore, the risk of His death consists in the number of people that will be saved by His divine act. Would His death be only for a few believers? As The First Entrepreneur, God has adequately revealed His character as creator and entrepreneur in Genesis. The Godhead continues to reveal these characteristics throughout Scripture through the Spirit and the Son.

## THE SPIRIT

In the creative business of God, the Spirit is that part of the Godhead that is endowed with, and endows, wisdom. This is exemplified in the Scripture when God spoke to Moses saying:

> See, I have called by name Bezalel son of Uri, the son of Hur, of the tribe of Judah. And I have filled him with the Spirit of God, in wisdom, in understanding, in knowledge and in all manner of workmanship, to design artistic works, to work in gold, in silver, in bronze, in cutting jewels for setting, in carving wood, and to work in all manner of workmanship. (Exodus 31:1-5 (NKJV)

It is God, through the Holy Spirit, who gives us the skills and the ability to do all that we do in order to bring glory to His name. As we read in Exodus 31:1-5 (NKJV), God gave special abilities to Bezalel and Oholiab in artistic craftsmanship to help build His Tabernacle. In the same way, God has given each and every one of us a special ability to do great things in life and to help others as well, and He does that through the Holy Spirit. We must, therefore, as children of God, take notice of the abilities God has gifted us with and make sure we do not diminish our skills because we are to use them to His glory.

The call of Bezalel was an incredible one and a great responsibility because the Tabernacle was meant to be the physical place in which God met with His people as well as home to the Ark of the Covenant and the beautiful, gold-covered chest containing the stone tablets in which God had inscribed the Ten Commandments.

God chose Bezalel to do the hard, God-like work of creating the Tabernacle. But before Bezalel got "to design artistic works, to work in gold, in silver, in bronze, in cutting jewels for setting, in carving wood, and to work in all manner of workmanship," we are told that God had to first "fill [Bezalel] with the Spirit of God" (Exodus 31: 1-5, NKJV). Fascinating! Why would Bezalel need God's Spirit in order to create? Because God is the first entrepreneur, the source of all creativity, and the originator of our ability to make something of value out of the raw materials of this world. In order for Bezalel to fulfill his call to create, he needed more of God's likeness. Now, because God is the source of all power and abilities, we need His strength in doing everything because, according to John 15, we are nothing and can do nothing without Him.

It is interesting to note that the Tabernacle was meant to be a physical representation of the way the world ought to be, with God at the center of it. The design of the interior of the Tabernacle pointed worshippers to the Holy of Holies, an interior room in which the Israelites believed God physically existed. The Tabernacle was essentially its own world, with everything pointing towards God. So, when God called Bezalel to create the Tabernacle, He was inviting him to mimic His creation of earth, thus bringing glory to Him by emulating his creative Spirit.

When you and I create, when we launch a new business, write new books, compose new songs, build new things, create new art, we are not doing something "secular." We are imitating (albeit in a quite imperfect way) the work of The First Entrepreneur. Creativity is not a fringe thing. It is central to who God is, and who we are as His image-bearers.

### THE CARPENTER

Jesus, the Son of God, also exemplified the creativity of the Godhead. He learnt carpentry from Joseph, His earthly father, and He was referred to as the carpenter. When Jesus came to Nazareth and started teaching in the synagogue, His audience was amazed at the wisdom of His teaching and asked,

"Isn't this the carpenter? The son of Mary, and brother of James, Joseph, Judas, and Simon? And are not His sisters here with us? So they were offended at him" (Mark 6:3, NKJV). As a carpenter, Jesus created wooden products that were utilized by other members of the community. Like Jesus, mankind has been endowed with creative abilities. When man was created and placed in the Garden of Eden, God told him to:

> Be fruitful and multiply; fill the earth and subdue it; have dominion over the fish of the sea, over the birds of the air, and over every living thing that moves on the earth. And God said, see, I have given you every herb that yields seed which is on the face of all the earth, and every tree whose fruit yields seed; to you it shall be for food. Also to every beast of the earth, to every bird of the air, and to everything that creeps on the earth, in which there is, I have given every green herb for food. And it was so. Then God saw everything that He had made, and indeed it was very good. So the evening and the morning were the sixth day. (Genesis 1:28-31 (NKJV)

The Bible gives us very little detail of Jesus' life between the ages of twelve and thirty, when He began his public ministry. One of the things Scripture notes about this significant chunk of time is that Jesus was known in His community for His work as a carpenter. This is remarkable! The only thing the Bible tells us about what Jesus was doing for half of His life was doing the work of a creator and entrepreneur, revealing to us this important characteristic of the Trinity.

Given Jesus' ultimate purpose for coming to earth, you might have expected God to choose for the Messiah to grow up in the home of a priest, like the prophets Samuel and John the Baptist, or maybe in a pharisaical household like the Apostle Paul. Instead, God placed Jesus in the home of a carpenter, where for eighty-five percent of His working life, He would reveal God's character as a creator and an entrepreneur, creating new things for the good of others.

In just three years of public ministry, Jesus revealed countless characteristics about His Father. To the five thousand, Jesus showed us that God is our provider. To Lazarus, Jesus showed us that God is the giver of life. And on the cross, Jesus showed us that "God so loved the world" that He would sacrifice His only Son in order to spend eternity with us. If Jesus was able to reveal so much of God's character in such a relatively short period of time, precisely in twenty years, our own life-long efforts in revealing God's creative and entrepreneurial spirit in us should not stop us in our tracks.

## QUALITIES OF A GOOD ENTREPRENEUR

There are several positive characteristics that an entrepreneur must have in order to succeed. According to Fajardo (2007), entrepreneurs should have self-confidence, good leadership skills, and must be very creative. Entrepreneurs have many favorable interdependent characteristics which make them successful and extra-ordinary persons. Usually, goals are achievable if they are based on the abilities, interests, and resources of the individuals. The most important entrepreneurial characteristics that Kingdom entrepreneurs should have and develop are trust in God, reasonable risk-taking, hardworking, innovative, leadership, positive thinking, and decision making. Let us briefly review them.

## TRUST IN GOD

Trusting in God is a fundamental characteristic of Kingdom entrepreneurship. In Hebrews 13:5, 6 (NKJV) we are reminded thus: "Let your conduct be without covetousness; be content with such things as you have. For He Himself has said, 'I will never leave you nor forsake you.' So, we may boldly say 'The Lord is my helper; I will not fear. What can man do to me?" A deeper understanding of Hebrews 13:5-6 (NKJV), as children of God and Christians for that matter, leads us to become content when we realize God's sufficiency for our needs. Christians who become materialistic are saying by their actions that God cannot take care of them or at least that He would not take care of them the way they want. We must note that it is insecurity that leads to the love of money, whether we are rich or poor. Our only antidote is to trust God to meet all our needs.

## SELF-CONFIDENCE

Self-confidence is one of the greatest ways of developing our entrepreneurial skills. Fajardo (2007) states that entrepreneurs have strong faith in their abilities. They believe they can be the best in their field. They do not accept things as they are because they believe they can do things better. We succeed when we think success. Litton et al (1987) define self-confidence as an attitude that allows individuals to have positive yet realistic views of themselves and their situations. Self-confident people trust their own abilities, have a general sense of control in their lives, and believe that, within reason, they will be able to do what they wish, plan, and expect, all with the help of God through the Holy Spirit.

It is true that for an entrepreneur to succeed, he should have self-confidence, but Kingdom entrepreneurs should emphasize trust in God as the source of proper self-confidence. A Kingdom entrepreneur should have confidence in God because He is the source of all knowledge, wisdom, power, and blessings. The Bible tells the story of Goliath who was a giant Philistine and a champion warrior, and who had great self-confidence in his skills for battle; but he was defeated by David who was just a young boy because David had confidence in the Almighty God (1 Samuel 17). The story of Solomon's confidence in God (1 Kings Chapters 3 – 10, NKJV) is also an example.

## RISK-TAKING

A risk-taker is an investor or entrepreneur who is intrigued from the market volatility—that is, an ability to change rapidly and unpredictably, especially for the worse—viewing it as an opportunity to realize a higher return on their investment. Kingdom entrepreneurs should mentor members to be Kingdom entrepreneurs' risk-takers. The idea is that, as Christians, whatever business we may set up should not be for personal aggrandizement and pride, but to honor God and serve others. Ultimately, our plans and actions should be based on Biblical values and allow us to be faithful witnesses to God.

Risk-taking in Kingdom entrepreneurship service consists of serving God despite the danger of suffering loss. Many young people and adults today think that the purpose of life is to have a good time. For the sake of a good time, they are willing to take enormous risks. Why? Because they value the fleeting pleasures of life more than life itself. That is one of the reasons why teenagers are easily drawn into dangerous sports, reckless driving, drugs, promiscuous sex, and violence. Many of these vices persist into adulthood. Although many people take risks to please themselves, few are interested in taking risks to please and honor God. Certainly, there are risks in Kingdom service. And although this kind of risk may yield no immediate pleasure, God will still bless us.

There are many advantages of becoming an entrepreneur. According to Orcullo (2004), when you are an entrepreneur, you have an opportunity to gain control over your own destiny, to reach your full potential, to benefit financially, and to contribute to society and be recognized for one's effort. What stops us from taking risks as an entrepreneur? One might suggest fear, but fear in itself is not bad unless it keeps us from doing right. Among the people who will be excluded from the New Jerusalem are the "cowardly" (Rev. 21:8, NKJV) —that is, those who let fear drive them away from believing in Christ. For a Kingdom entrepreneur also, fear is dangerous. Any fear that keeps us from doing the will of God puts us out of fellowship with him and we forfeit his blessing. What empowers us to overcome fear? Faith. How important is faith? The Bible says, "But without faith it is impossible to please [God], for he who comes to God must believe that He is, and that He is a rewarder of those who diligently seek him" (Heb. 11:6, NKJV).

God asks us to trust His integrity, His character, His compassion, love, wisdom, and righteousness on our behalf. He says, "I have loved you with an everlasting love; therefore with loving kindness I have drawn you" (Jer. 31:3, NKJV). The Psalmist further says, "Trust in him at all times, pour out your hearts before Him; God is a refuge for us" (Psalm 62:8).

With such a trust in God, our risk-taking in business becomes covered by His Grace.

## HARDWORKING

When we say a hardworking person or a hard worker, we refer to someone who is diligent in laboring and who puts efforts in doing and completing tasks. Proverbs 14:23 (NKJV) points out that, "In all labor there is profit, but idle chatter leads only to poverty." The Bible further says, "He who has slack hands becomes poor, but the hand of the diligent makes rich" (Prov. 10:4, NKJV). Let's go down a bit; Proverbs 10:4, 5 (NKJV) makes it clear to us that every day has 24 hours filled with opportunities to grow, serve, and be productive. Yet, it is so easy to waste time, letting life slip from our grasp. Desist from being a lazy person because there are so many opportunities around you. Let us avoid too much sleeping or frittering away the hours meant for productive work. KEN is encouraging us to see time as God's gift and seize our opportunities and live diligently for Him.

As Kingdom entrepreneurs we believe that we should work but not destroy our body by hard work, but we should also have enough rest. We are God's temple and God's Spirit lives in us and if anyone destroys God's temple, God will destroy him (1 Corinthians 3:16-17, NKJV).

## INNOVATIVE

If you love to experiment and find new ways to do things, you are an innovative person. Entrepreneurs are said to be innovative, creative, inventive, novel, modern, unprecedented, and unfamiliar if they do things in new and different ways. For example, they create new products or services, new methods of production, new markets, and new sources of raw materials. They love to explore the unknown and to blaze new paths of progress.

1 Kings 6 tells us how Solomon built the temple with very special innovation. One of the qualities ascribed to Solomon is his wisdom. The Scripture says, "Now all the earth sought the presence of Solomon to hear the wisdom, which God had put in his heart" (1 Kings 10:24, NKJV). Clearly, Solomon was an innovator and God was the source of his innovation (see 1 Kings 3). Innovation is the ability to see situations from a different perspective, to discover new ways of satisfying a human need, and to find a new solution to an old problem. God can help us to be innovative

when we trust in Him and seek to help others. John 14:13-14 (NKJV) says "And whatever you ask in My name, that I will do, that the Father may be glorified in the Son. If you ask anything in My name, I will do it."

## LEADERSHIP

According to Fajardo (2007), entrepreneurs are leaders by the very nature of their functions. They are task-oriented, effective planners, organizers, and implementers, and they are achievers. Among their essential characteristics are selfless dedication, purpose and vision, courage, enthusiasm, integrity, tact, and hard work.

Kingdom Entrepreneurs Nexus (KEN) will provide mentors who will counsel and guide all those who sign up to be members of this Nexus. Above all, members will be taught Kingdom values by precept and example, which will make them true leaders. These values are found in the teachings and examples of Jesus, who summed them up in Matthew 22:37-39 (NKJV), "Love the Lord your God with all your heart and with all your soul and with all your mind. This is the first and greatest commandment. And the second is like it: Love thy neighbor as yourself." A leader first of all must allow love to lead him/her just as Christ Jesus lead us with love. A leader who lacks love for his/her followers cannot be called a leader. As a leader, you must be able to put yourself in others situation and see how best to solve them. Every entrepreneur must have a very good leadership skills in order to excel in all that you do. KEN is here to guide the Kingdom Entrepreneur to grow spiritually in the Lord and in business for others to benefit from them.

## VALUES & ATTITUDES OF KINGDOM ENTREPRENEURS

These principles for living that are emphasized most strongly in the Bible will distinguish kingdom entrepreneurs to stand out and bring glory to God. These principles include: (a) worship only God, (b) respect all people, (c) be humble, (d) be honest, (e) live a moral life, (f) be generous with time and money, (g) practice what you preach/don't be a hypocrite, (h) don't hold a grudge, (i) don't be self-righteous, (j) forgive others, (k) think positively, and (l) make sound decisions. The KEN calls these principles, "The Simple Steps for a Successful Living". These should be a strong guide for the Kingdom Entrepreneur.

## WORSHIP ONLY GOD

One day, a religious leader asked Jesus which of the commandments was most important. "The first of all the commandments," answered Jesus, "is: 'Hear, O Israel, the Lord our God, the Lord is one. And you shall Love the Lord your God with all your heart, with all your soul, with all your mind, and with all your strength" (Mark 12:28-30, NKJV). The Hebrews of Old Testament times tended to lapse into worship of pagan deities and statues of animals or other objects, but anything that takes the place of our devotion to God becomes an idol or false god, and that is forbidden by the first of the Ten Commandments (see Exodus 20:1-6, NKJV). Jesus particularly singled out love of wealth as a false god (Matthew 6:24, NKJV; Luke 16:13, NKJV), and other Bible passages mention greed, covetousness, arrogance, gluttony, and pride as being equivalent to idolatry.

In today's world, many things compete against God for our devotion. These are some of the things that can become modern-day idolatry if we let them become too important to us: first, excessive attention to material things such as houses, cars, clothes, jewelry, physical appearance, entertainment, etc.; second, pursuit of wealth, power, fame, pleasure, or status; third, excessive devotion to self, job, hobbies, country, ideologies, heroes, leaders, even family. Making God a partner in your business helps not to depend on the success of your company or business but rather depend on God and understand that it is the Lord who gave you the ability, the strength, the idea, and the life to make wealth (Deut. 8:17-18, NKJV).

## RESPECT ALL PEOPLE

A good leader respects all people. After saying that "To love the Lord our God" is the most important of the commandments, Jesus continued stating that we should "Love our neighbor as ourselves." According to Him there is no commandment greater than these (Mark 12:31, NKJV). The English word "love" has many different meanings, but the Greek word *agape*, used in the New Testament, is commonly known as "Kingdom love." It means respect, affection, benevolence, good-will and concern for the welfare of the one loved.

In the Parable of the Good Samaritan, Jesus made the point that we should extend our Kingdom love to all people of the world, regardless of race, religion, nationality, or any other artificial distinction. We must practice the Kingdom love even towards our enemies! (Matthew 5:43-48, NKJV). Jesus' Golden Rule is, "And just as you want men to do to you, you also do to them likewise" (Luke 6:31, NKJV). We should not say or do anything unless we can answer "Yes" to the question, "Would I want that said or done to me?" Neither should we fail to do the good things we would expect of others.

### BE HUMBLE

As Kingdom entrepreneur you should be humble. Humility is a quality of being courteously respectful of others. It is the opposite of aggressiveness, arrogance, boastfulness, and vanity. Acting with humility does not in any way deny our own self-worth. Rather, it affirms the inherent worth of all persons. Humility is exactly what is needed to live in peace and harmony with all persons. It dissipates anger and heals old wounds. It allows us to see the dignity and worth of all God's people. Humility distinguishes the wise leader from the arrogant power-seeker (see Proverbs 17:7, NKJV; Matthew 20:20-28, NKJV).

### BE HONEST

A Kingdom entrepreneur as a leader should be honest. Honesty and integrity are very important values throughout the Bible, and any deception to gain an advantage or harm another is prohibited by the Ten Commandments (see Exodus 20:16, NKJV) and other Bible passages. Deception may be by false statements, half-truths, innuendo, or failing to tell the whole truth. It is all too common in advertising, business dealings, politics, and everyday life. We must strongly resist the temptation to engage in any form of theft, cheating, deception, innuendo, slander, or gossip. Rationalization is a form of self-deception by which we convince ourselves that sinful actions are justified to achieve a good result, but this is just another form of dishonesty (see Galatians 6:7-8, NKJV; James 1:26, NKJV; 1 John 1:8, NKJV). Holiness is in living by the commandments, not in achieving a result (Matthew 4:8-10, 16:26, NKJV). In biblical teaching, the ends do not justify the means.

### LIVE A MORAL LIFE.

The Scripture calls on all Christians to live a holy life because our bodies do not belong to us. The Bible says, "Do you not know that your body is a temple of the Holy Spirit, who is in you, whom you have from God, and you are not your own? For you were bought at a price; therefore, glorify God in your body and in your spirit, which are God's" (1 Corinthians 6:19-20, NKJV).

Jesus gave a list of actions that constitute immoral uses of the body: evil thoughts, murder, adultery, sexual immorality, theft, false testimony, slander, greed, malice, deceit, lewdness, envy, arrogance, and foolishness. The Apostle Paul gave similar lists. We often think of immorality in terms of sexual sins, but according to Jesus, sins such as slander, greed, deceit, and arrogance are equally immoral. Kingdom entrepreneurs are leaders; therefore, they should live a moral life; by living a moral life, we will be more successful in our businesses.

### BE GENEROUS WITH TIME AND MONEY

The Bible tells us to share generously with those in need, and good things will come to us in turn. Each of us has something to offer to someone in need. We can give our money and our time to charity, be a friend to someone who is sick or lonely, do volunteer work or choose a service-oriented occupation. We may give unselfishly of our time to our spouse, children, or parents. Let us not forget therefore that, 'people's destiny lies on people's shoulders.' You need someone and someone needs you.

### PRACTICE WHAT YOU PREACH; DON'T BE A HYPOCRITE.

If there were any group of people that Jesus couldn't stand, it was hypocrites! The Pharisees of Jesus' time were a religious and political party that insisted on very strict observance of biblical laws on tithing, ritual purity, and other matters. At the same time, many of them forgot the true spirit and intent of the law and became self-indulgent, self-righteous, snobbish, and greedy. That led Jesus to make remarks such as: "Woe to you, scribes and Pharisees, hypocrites! For you are like whitewashed tombs which indeed appear beautiful outwardly, but inside are full of dead men's bones and uncleanness. Even so you also outwardly appear righteous to men, but inside you are full of hypocrisy and lawlessness" (Matthew 23:27-28, NKJV).

It is not the things we say that really matter; it is the things that we do (see Matthew 7:15-20, NKJV). If we claim to be Christians but do not let Jesus' teachings guide our lives, we are nothing but hypocrites. Again, Matthew 7:21 (NKJV) makes it clear that, "Not everyone who says to me 'Lord, Lord,' shall enter the kingdom of heaven, but he who does the will of my Father in Heaven." Kingdom Entrepreneurs must live a truthful and a just live to attract the Lord's favor in all we do.

## DON'T BE SELF-RIGHTEOUS

Kingdom entrepreneurs have self-confidence, but that does not mean that they should feel self-righteous. No one is perfect; we are all sinners in one way or another (see Romans 3:23, NKJV). Living a moral life means taking responsibility for controlling our own behavior. If we say or even think we are better than people we consider to be "sinners," we are guilty of the sin of self-righteousness. It is not our right to look down on, criticize, judge, condemn, or try to control other people. Judgment is to be left to God, Jesus said.

## DON'T HOLD A GRUDGE

A Kingdom entrepreneur is a leader; as such, he or she should not hold a grudge but learn to forgive and forget. Jesus said there is no place for hatred, holding grudge, revenge, retaliation or getting even in the life of a Christian: "You have heard that it was said, 'An eye for eye, and a tooth for tooth.' But I tell you not to resist an evil person. But whoever slaps you on the right cheek, turn the other to him also. If anyone wants to sue you and take away your tunic, let him have your cloak also" (Matthew 5:38-40, NKJV). Jesus further says:

> You have heard that it was said, 'You shall love your neighbor and hate your enemy.' But I say to you: Love your enemies, bless those who curse you, do good to those who hate you, and pray for those who spitefully use you and persecute you, that you may be sons of your Father in heaven; for He makes his sun rise on the evil and the good, and sends rain on the just and the unjust. (Matthew 5:43-45, NKJV)

Bearing a grudge and seeking revenge are never appropriate responses to a perceived wrong. A grudge destroys the grudge-holder with bitterness, and revenge only escalates hostilities. Jesus told us we must reconcile with our adversaries, forgive their transgressions, and let go of the anger that may tempt us to commit an act of revenge.

**FORGIVE OTHERS.**
The Bible says, "For if you forgive men their trespasses, your heavenly Father will also forgive you. But if you do not forgive men their trespasses, neither will your Father forgive your trespasses" (Matthew 6:14-15, NKJV). God is merciful and forgives our sins and failings. In the same way, we must be merciful and forgive other people who sin against us or do us harm. A Kingdom entrepreneur who embraces the values and embodies the characteristics listed above will be able to create and inspire vision by empowering and energizing people and build teamwork.

One of the most outstanding examples of leadership in the Bible is Moses. He was a great spiritual leader who embodied the great leadership characteristics listed in the Bible, and the Bible doesn't describe only Moses but every other great leader who followed God, including David, Nehemiah, and the Apostle Paul, to name just a few. Apart from those stated in the Bible, there is also Mahatma Gandhi who was described by historians as a visionary and ethical leader. He succeeded because of his peaceful approach to complex social, economic, and political problems.

## KINGDOM POSITIVE THINKING

Positive thinking can be defined as adopting an attitude of faith. It is a realistic belief in the possibility of things. It is the ability to see success where others see failure. While such optimism is good, an unrealistic optimism can lead to disaster. Gillespie (2000) warns against such overzealousness when he states that;

> While many of those who teach 'Christian' positive thinking are T.V. personalities with worldwide Nexuss, they incorporate modem humanistic psychology and stress unbiblical 'powers of the mind.' By these teachers, faith is conceived as a force that can be used to change health, people, circumstances, status, finances, etc., as well as, bring self-esteem to the one exercising it. But this so-called Kingdom Positive Thinking is dangerous because it teaches an unscriptural view of faith and substitutes a humanistic faith (p. 7).

True Kingdom positive thinking is based on biblical principles of self-worth and self esteem. These principles derive from the fundamental teaching that God created humans in His image and that Christ died to rescue humans from their sins. God has given each of us unique abilities to develop and use to serve others. In its essence, Kingdom positive thinking is faith in God and His promises. There are a lot of promises in the Bible about how God will prosper those who believe in Him.

Kingdom positive thinking is the ability to stand on those promises in faith. For example, Malachi 3:10 (NKJV) says, "Bring all the tithes into the storehouse, that there may be food in My house, and try me now in this … if I will not open for you the windows of heaven and pour out for you such blessing that there will not be room enough to receive it." The promise here is clear. Therefore, a Kingdom positive thinker will pay tithes and claim the blessings inherent in God's promise

## DECISION-MAKER

Steve Hoke (2009) states that "Kingdom decision-making involves freedom and risk" (p. 2). Scripture teaches us to confirm God's moral will (as revealed in the Bible) by following certain indicators that can be described as "wisdom signs." These signs are specific biblical ways the Holy Spirit guides us in our decision-making.

Kingdom entrepreneurs' decision-making can be divided into two categories. The first involves areas that are specifically addressed in the Bible. These are the revealed principles and commands of God, which must be obeyed. Those scriptural guidelines both exhortations and prohibitions shape the lifestyles of believers. The second category involves areas where the Bible gives no command or principle to follow. In these situations, it's the believer's responsibility to freely choose his or her own course of action within the boundaries of biblical guidelines.

# CHAPTER 2

# WHO IS AN ENTREPRENEUR?

An entrepreneur is a person or an entity that starts a business and is willing to take financial risk in exchange for profit. In 1776, Adam Smith defined an entrepreneur as "an individual, who undertakes the formation of an organization for commercial purposes by recognizing the potential demand for goods and services, and thereby acts as an economic agent and transforms demand into supply" (p 5). According to Hayes (2021) of Investopedia, the entrepreneur is commonly seen as an innovator, a source of new ideas, goods, services, and business/or procedures. The term entrepreneur has been defined differently by different authors and experts who look at it from both varying and common perspectives. We will look at a couple of them to help us appreciate the nuances of who an entrepreneur is.

**MANOUSH ZOMORODI**
Zomorodi was an author and media consultant, and he defined an entrepreneur as:

> Someone who envisions, creates, and evangelizes an idea that they are absolutely crazy about. That idea (it could be a product, book, consultancy) makes it easier for them to get up

in the morning, work at ridiculous hours, and keep their brain buzzing. The entrepreneur can work alone, within a company, or in a group, but he/she gets itchy at the thought of working a 9-5 job and following the orders of anyone who isn't efficient and imaginative (p. 7).

Manoush in his definition brings out the attitude of ownership exhibited by entrepreneurs in terms of their ideas and the effort they put into it in order to see it come into fruition. The attitude of the entrepreneur in this definition is one that differs from an employee who did not conceive the idea so may not put in as much effort to see it come to birth. An entrepreneur usually goes the extra mile to achieve his/her goals.

## MARK CUBAN

According to Cuban, owner of Dallas Mavericks, blogger and *Shark Tank* investor, an entrepreneur is "Someone who can define the business they want to create, see where it is going, and do the work to get there" (p. 1). From Cuban's definition, we see the element of vision highlighted as crucial in the role of an entrepreneur. Once the idea is coming from an individual, it is expected that he will better be able to draw the picture for others to see what the business stands for and the destination it intends to arrive, and what to do to arrive at the intended destination.

## JEET BANERJEE

Banerjee was a tech entrepreneur, founder of Statfuse.com, and blogger. He opines: "To me, an entrepreneur is someone who mixes passion, innovation, and drive to turn a vision into a working business" (p. 1). Banerjee's view on who an entrepreneur is also introduces another important element needed in what makes an individual an entrepreneur. He focuses on the ability to mix passion with innovation in making someone an entrepreneur. Passion is the fuel that keeps something going even in the face of difficulties. An innovative person is also able to find alternative ways of doing things if the existing formula doesn't work. It therefore behooves on entrepreneurs to keep moving even if the initial plan doesn't work.

## MATT MICKIEWICZ

Mickiewicz is owner of 99Designs.com, Flippa.com, and Sitepoint.com, and he defines an entrepreneur as follows: "An entrepreneur is someone who has a bias towards action. Someone who views the world through a different lens. Someone who takes "no" for a challenge, and not an answer" (p. 1). Mickiewicz helps us to appreciate the quality of singleness of purpose as an important ingredient in the role of an entrepreneur. For the entrepreneur, it is all about the opportunity he/she sees and not what others fail to see. Everything he/she does is geared towards that thing he wants to build. Challenges are a stepping-stone for an entrepreneur and not a hindrance.

## ROB IRIZARRY

Irizarry is a tech entrepreneur, investor, consultant, owner of StartupBozeman.com, and he has this to say about who an entrepreneur is: "What differentiates entrepreneurs from everybody else is a vision of something that doesn't exist (either at all or in the form they envision) and the willingness to do what other people are unwilling to do to make that vision a reality" (p. 1). Irizarry brings out the power to dream as a key element in what defines an entrepreneur. For him, an entrepreneur sees what others are unable to see and does what others are unwilling to do.

## JAMIE TARDY

Tardy is an entrepreneur, public speaker, and blogger at Eventual Millionaire.com, and he defines entrepreneur as "someone that goes out and does the work to create something that didn't exist before" (p. 1). From his definition, we see entrepreneurs as creators and doers. They create and act on it.

## MICHAEL FITZGERALD

Fitzgerald is the founder of Submittable.com, and his definition of an entrepreneur is "Someone who makes something useful or pleasurable out of nothing" (p 1). He also sees an entrepreneur as an innovator.

## MATTHEW TORREN

Torren is co-founder of Young Entrepreneur.com, Blogtrepreneur. com, iSell.com, and Kidpreneurs.org, mentor & investor, award-winning author of *Potential Business BIG Vision*, and he says, "An entrepreneur is someone who conceives an idea, creates a path to success, does whatever it takes to succeed and tries to dominate their market" (p. 1).

## BRAD FELD

Feld is the founder of TechStars. He is also an investor, and author of *Startup Communities*. He defines an entrepreneur as "someone who creates a new company from scratch" (p. 1). Brad Feld sees an entrepreneur as a starter who builds from foundation to the top.

## JARED TANNER

Tanner is owner of the e-commerce store Uplanders.com, and his definition describes an entrepreneur as "A person who has so much passion for an idea that they're willing to risk almost everything to make their dream a reality" (p. 1). Tanner in his definition brings out the element of risk-taking as part of the characteristics of an entrepreneur. An entrepreneur knows there could be a loss but will still attempt it to see the outcome

## LUKE KUPERSMITH

Kupersmith is owner of Source Consulting, and Kupersmith's understanding of an entrepreneur is: "a person that orchestrates through their own personal gumption, initiative, and resources with a degree of insanity, collectively towards an effort to turn a business concept into a business reality" (p. 1). Kupersmith's definition recognizes various attributes which have been highlighted in earlier definitions such as a creator, innovator, risk-taker, and action oriented.

## BARBARA CORCORAN

Corcoran is a real estate developer, business consultant, and *Shark Tank* investor. His take on the definition of an entrepreneur is that "the single most defining characteristic of an entrepreneur is passion. It helps to be pushy – pushy people deliver. It helps to have a gimmick – a unique gimmick will give you a great leap over your competitors. It helps to be willing to fail – all my best business successes came on the heels of what first appeared to be a big flop. But great passion is what it really takes to build a successful business" (p 1).

## BILLY COX

Cox is a keynote speaker, author, and sales trainer. He is also the author of *Get in the Game* and *All-Star Sales Book*. He says, "Entrepreneurs are business minded individuals who can see what others can't. They are willing to go after their vision until they hit it and expand it once they get it" (p. 1). Cox's definition of the entrepreneur as a visionary and someone who turns dreams into reality is similar to other definitions above.

## ANDREW SCHRAGE

Schrage is a blogger and owner of MoneyCrashers.com. He says, "An entrepreneur is an innovative, risk-taking individual who identifies a need in a market and finds a way to fill it, whether by using his or her own expertise and passion, the knowledge of others, or a combination of the three. More simply stated, an entrepreneur is someone who sees an opportunity and invests in it to turn a profit or provide a solution to some larger issue in the world" (p. 1). In this view, an entrepreneur is a problem-solver for profit-making.

## CALEB WOJCIK

Wojcik is a blogger with ThinkTraffic.net and Pocketchanged.com. He says, "An entrepreneur is a starter, not just a dreamer. Anybody can think up an idea for a business, but not everyone can put rubber to the road and grow something that both matters and earns money. Taking action is the difference between entrepreneurs and non-entrepreneurs" (p. 1). An entrepreneur, according to this view, is an action-oriented person.

## JARED JOYCE

Joyce is an inventor and entrepreneur. He is also a *Shark Tank* contestant. He says an entrepreneur is "A person who solves problems for people at a profit"

(p. 1). We see here the element of problem-solving as a key ingredient in an entrepreneur.

### CARRIE SMITH
Smith is the owner of Carefulcents.com. She is also a consultant and blogger. She says, "To me an entrepreneur is someone who looks at life a little differently. They don't see the normal obstacles that life puts in our way and shy away like most of us do. They think the word 'no' means 'to find a different or better way.' They're continually learning, growing, and reaching higher" (p. 1). This definition casts the entrepreneur as a stubborn, innovative person.

### PETE SVEEN
Sveen is the owner of Think Entrepreneurship.com, blogger/consultant, and owner of SignsoftheMountains.com, an e-commerce store. He defines an entrepreneur as: "Someone with the drive, persistence, and mindset to change the world by filling a need in the marketplace" (p. 1). The quality of a persistent inventor comes across in this definition.

Kingdom Entrepreneurship means biblical entrepreneurship. This involves moral obligations, economic creativity, and productive aspects as well. According to Tracy & Phillips (2007), the principle of entrepreneurship is rooted on the dominion mandate and the biblical doctrines of work, stewardship, and fruitfulness. Biblical entrepreneurship incorporates principles of biblical patriarchy with its emphasis on multi-generational faithfulness, freedom in Christ, inheritance, jurisdiction, and the household as a vibrant, economically productive, God ordained unit for cultural transformation. It is impossible to have a vision of entrepreneurship without a careful consideration for the scriptural doctrine of the family. Phillips also states that any approach to entrepreneurship which is divorced of these considerations inevitably leads to the idolatries of materialism, individualism, and the love of money.

What leads a person to strike out on his own and start a business? Sometimes it is a proactive response to a negative situation. Perhaps a person has been laid off once or more. Sometimes a person is frustrated with his or her current job and doesn't see any better career prospects on the horizon. Sometimes a person realizes that his or her job is in jeopardy. A firm may be contemplating cutbacks that could end a job or limit career or salary prospects. Perhaps a person already has been passed over for promotion. Perhaps a person sees no opportunities in existing businesses for someone with his or her interests and skills. Some people are repulsed by the idea of working for someone else. They object to a system where reward is often based on seniority rather than accomplishment, or where they must conform to a corporate culture. Other people decide to become entrepreneurs because they are disillusioned by the bureaucracy or politics involved in getting ahead in an established business or profession. Some are tired of trying to promote a product, service, or way of doing business that is outside the mainstream operations of a large company

Some people are attracted to entrepreneurship simply for the sake of the advantages of starting a business. These include:

- Entrepreneurs are their own bosses. They make the decisions. They choose whom to do business with and what work they will do. They decide what hours to work as well as what to pay themselves and others and whether to take vacations.
- Entrepreneurship offers a greater possibility of achieving significant financial rewards than working for someone else.
- It provides the ability to be involved in the total operation of the business, from concept to design and creation, from sales to business operations and customer response.
- It offers the prestige of being the person in charge.
- It gives an individual the opportunity to build equity, which can be kept, sold, or passed on to the next generation.
- Entrepreneurship creates an opportunity for a person to contribute. Most new entrepreneurs help the local economy.

Scripture contains several cases of entrepreneurship, but we must first make sure that we are using the proper definition of the word. Entrepreneurship is a creative act that brings higher levels of satisfaction to people, results in more order, and finds ways to create greater value than existed before.

## GREAT EXAMPLES OF ENTREPRENEURS IN THE BIBLE
## ABRAHAM

We know from Genesis 13 that Abram was very wealthy in livestock, gold, and silver. By the time he had to rescue Lot in Genesis 14, he had over 300 trained men, presumably trained in the use of arms. Beyond his wealth, Abram was an entrepreneur. The evidence for this is in Genesis 13, when Abram and Lot separated, and Lot chose to go to the fertile plain. This was an area favorably compared to the Garden of Eden. Presumably Abram got a less attractive, less fertile area, yet he continued to prosper. Lot's material and spiritual condition both deteriorated due to his choice. He started out as wealthy as his uncle Abram but ended up living in a cave (see Genesis 19, NKJV).

After getting the lesser land, Abram's wealth grew, as did his faith, and walk with the Lord. By Genesis 21 Abraham (as God had renamed him by this time) was making treaties with kings and generals. Abraham had a faith and God-given vision of the future, and the perseverance to leave his home, obey, and see the task through.

## LYDIA OF THYRATIRA

Lydia, a dealer of purple cloth in Thyratira, is largely an unknown figure, and we must be careful not to read more than we know into her story. What we do know is that Roman women were allowed to own property and conduct business. We also know that Thyratira was a center for dying cloth, especially purple. Thus, Lydia may not have been a pioneer or entrepreneur in her profession, but she certainly was in her personal life.

Although we only get a few verses about Lydia in Acts 16:14-15, 40 (NKJV), we do learn several things. She had a household, she may have been a widow, and her household probably included children and may have included servants. She had a house large enough to accommodate guests and was willing to take Paul and Silas in after they had been in jail. In addition, her house also seemed to serve as the center for Kingdom work in the area. Her hospitality undoubtedly carried some risk with it, and a willingness to take on risk is an entrepreneurial characteristic.

### OTHERS TO CONSIDER

The Bible is not a book about the great entrepreneurs of the past, and so the information that we must use to make assessments is somewhat limited. We can make some inferences, however.

We know that several of the apostles ran a fishing business, and Matthew's tax collecting was a private independent business in those days. In addition, the apostle Paul made tents, Luke practiced medicine, and less-discussed believers operated businesses as well.

One common biblical act was church planting, as practiced by Paul, Barnabas, Timothy, Silas, and many others. This was and still is an entrepreneurial act because it took faith, vision, perseverance, and a willingness to stand strong in the face of opposition. Church-planting does not afford material profits to measure success. However, one can gauge success in other ways to see that church-planting improves the lives of many people.

To envision a thriving, successful church preaching the word, evangelizing, and serving where there currently stands an empty lot, and a few believers is as entrepreneurial as any business start-up. Anyone who has been involved in a church planting business knows that it takes a special kind of person to lead such work.

One may argue that the people in the examples above are exceptional since God was directing and blessing them. Yet the Lord is with all believers, directing us (see Proverbs 3:5-6, NKJV) and blessing us (see Ephesians 1:3, NKJV).

While we revere the men and women of the Bible, we must also remember what James tells us about Elijah: he was a great man of faith, but he was still a man like us (see James 5:17, NKJV). What God did through the heroes and entrepreneurs of the Bible, God can do through us.

### THE WOMAN IN PROVERBS 31

The woman of virtue described in Proverbs 31 has an entrepreneurial spirit about her. She has a strong work ethic (see Proverbs 31:17, NKJV); she makes and sells her own products (see Proverbs 31:24, NKJV); she makes sound investments (see Proverbs 31:16, NKJV) and she is even able to make a profit (see Proverbs 31:18, NKJV)—all while raising a family and running a home! She's certainly an inspiration for aspiring female entrepreneurs and homepreneurs today.

## APOSTLE PAUL

We all know the apostle Paul as the person who wrote most of the New Testament. He was trained as a Jewish lawyer and later became an entrepreneur by making and selling tents (see Acts 18:3, NKJV). It's likely that Paul chose to go into business because of the flexibility it gave him to focus on his primary calling as an apostle.

## SOLOMON

Solomon was unique among Jewish kings, as he seems to be the only one to have seen and profited from the geographical advantage of his kingdom. Ancient Israel was located on two great ancient trading routes, the King's Highway and Way of the Sea (the Via Maris), in addition to several lesser routes. Solomon engaged in trade, and he appears to be the only Jewish king to fully exploit the advantages afforded by these routes (see 1 Kings 5, 9, NKJV).

The Bible tells us Solomon was extremely wealthy, but he had to create his fortune, as much of it did not exist before (see I Kings 3, 4:26, NKJV). Solomon generated wealth by bringing peace to the kingdom, which allowed him to use his resources for production, rather than protection. In addition, he encouraged trade and was the only Jewish king with a trading fleet (see 1 Kings 9, NKJV).

Conversely, Solomon's son, Rehoboam, had a chance to solidify Israel's position in the world. Instead, he chose poor advisers and made poor decisions. The kingdom essentially split over tax policy and forced labor (see I Kings 12, NKJV). A wiser, more entrepreneurial man would have reduced these burdens and advanced the kingdom through other means, such as trade.

However, Solomon was renowned as the wisest of kings. This wisdom and insight manifested itself through his recognition of opportunity, his sound judgment, his management skills, and what we would today call his venture capitalism. His history from I Kings 3 to 10 (NKJV) is a textbook example for business owners, and for national leaders. He recognized that Israel's greatest natural resource was being located on the two great trading routes, known as the King's Highway and the Way of the Sea. It also had a long coastline with natural harbors.

Solomon used those natural advantages to make his nation an economic superpower through trade. Throughout his history, we read of traders, merchants, and cooperative ventures (see I Kings 9: 26 – 28; 10: 15, 28, NKJV). He built a fleet of trading ships and had those ships out at sea in rotation (see I Kings 9: 26, 10: 22, NKJV). In his wisdom, Solomon sought peace with the nations around him, and Israel was able to turn its efforts from national defense to economic prosperity (see I Kings 4: 24, 25, NKJV). He turned former enemies into business partners, working cooperatively with King Hiram of Lebanon (see I Kings 5: 1 – 12, NKJV).

Solomon brought sound and orderly administration throughout his kingdom, with clearly defined lines of authority (see I Kings 4, NKJV). He organized large work forces (see I Kings 5: 13 – 18, NKJV). He brought in excellent talents (see I Kings 7: 13, 14, NKJV). Through these efforts, Solomon created great wealth for himself and his nation (see I Kings 4: 20 – 28; 10: 14 – 23, NKJV). He made "silver as common in Jerusalem as stones" (see I Kings 10: 27, NKJV). The foundation of it all was his commitment unto God, to seek His blessings, to ask for wisdom, and to humble himself before the Lord (see I Kings 3: 1 – 9; 8: 55 – 61, NKJV).

The deeds of Solomon make him perhaps the greatest manager and greatest entrepreneur in the Bible. From him we can take instruction to:

(i) Identify our business's natural advantages and to build on them
(ii) Be aggressive in building from strength
(iii) Avoid useless disputes that divert your attention and sap your resources
(iv) Have clear lines of authority
(v) Bring in excellent talents
(vi) Work cooperatively with other businesses.

But Solomon left us with more than an example, as the principal author of Proverbs and Ecclesiastes, Solomon wrote advice that businesses today are wise to follow:

**1. Be Diligent and Work Hard.**
He who has a slack hand becomes poor; but the hand of the diligent makes rich (see Proverbs 10: 4 (NKJV). Nothing can substitute for good work ethic. Many people see a business owner after he or she has achieved success and think that advancement in business is easy. Those in it know that creating and running a successful business requires harder work than any way to earn a living. It is no place for those without a superior commitment to work. As Solomon wrote in Proverbs 20: 4 (NKJV), "The lazy man will not plow because of winter; he will beg during harvest and have nothing."

**2. Work Wisely.**
Solomon admonishes Kingdom entrepreneurs to work wisely. He notes, "Wisdom is the principal thing; therefore, get wisdom. And in all your getting, get understanding" (Proverbs 4: 7, NKJV). It is not enough to work hard; you also must work smart. You have to capitalize your business with wisdom as well as with money because wisdom is a defense as money is a defense (see Ecclesiastes 7: 12, NKJV). The great majority of business start-ups will fail. The great majority of businesses started by Christians will fail. It will not matter if the business is founded with the best of purposes and dedicated to the glory of God. Being a successful entrepreneur requires training and skill to be able to see and seize opportunities, working with wisdom as well with diligence.

**3. Pursue Excellence.**
Excellence makes one outstanding in his/her endeavors, and its reward is always recognition and respect. The Bible says, "Do you see a man who excels in his work? He will stand before kings" (Proverbs 22: 29, NKJV). Never be satisfied with being satisfactory. You should set the bar of excellence high. Vince Lombardi, the great football coach, said in his first speech to his Green Bay Packers (who had finished in last place the prior season): "Gentlemen, we

will chase perfection, and we will chase it relentlessly, knowing all the while we can never attain it. But along the way, we shall catch excellence" (p. 1).

### 4. Work Proactively.
To be proactive is to have the ability to preempt problems and work out the solution even before they happen. The Bible says, "In all labor there is profit; but idle chatter leads only to poverty" (Proverbs 14: 23, NKJV). There is great benefit in careful planning, but in the end, you need to act. Many businesses fail to grow, or fail altogether, because of an inability or an unwillingness to act decisively. Solomon was extremely proactive, constantly building and always reaching towards the next venture (see I Kings 7, NKJV).

### 5. Be Honest—Always.
The old adage that honesty is the best policy should be iterated here. Scripture cautions that "Dishonest scales are an abomination to the Lord; but a just weight is His delight" (Proverbs 11: 1, NKJV). Character counts. Honesty in business should be given and without exception. "Bread gained by deceit is sweet to a man; but afterward his mouth will be filled with gravel" (Proverbs 20: 17, NKJV). Honesty should extend beyond individual dealings and reach to larger societal issues. "He who oppresses the poor to increase his riches… will surely come to poverty" (Proverbs 22: 16, NKJV). We read that Solomon ruled with "largeness of heart" and was generous to all (I Kings 4: 29, NKJV).

### 6. Use Debt Sparingly.
In business cash is king, or as Solomon would say it: "But money answers everything" (Ecclesiastes 7: 12, NKJV). Maintain a cash reserve. Use debt for needed capital items but avoid debt to pay operating expenses. Otherwise, you will end up working for the bank (or your private lender) and on its terms, not yours. "The rich rules over the poor, and the borrower is servant to the lender" (Proverbs 22: 7).

### 7. Work Cooperatively.
Build strategic partnerships with others in business, where you can quickly call on reliable source providers to meet the needs of your clients. The Bible states

that "As iron sharpens iron; so, a man sharpens the countenance of his friend" (Proverbs 27: 17, NKJV). Solomon built such a partnership with King Hiram of Lebanon, and it greatly benefited both nations, making Israel the economic superpower of the day and Jerusalem the showpiece of the world.

**8. Establish Relationships with Valued Professionals.**
Be smart enough to know that you don't know it all. It is especially dangerous when you don't know what you don't know. Scripture admonishes us that "Without counsel, plans go awry; but in the multitude of counselors, they are established" (Proverbs 15: 22, NKJV). Establish trusted relationships with legal, financial, IT and other professionals. Use them efficiently to get out ahead of problems.

**9. Play the Long Game – Remain Focused and Patient.**
Many businesses make the mistake of running from one plan to another, from one supposed opportunity to another and losing the focus of their core product or service. The Bible says, "The plans of the diligent lead surely to plenty; but those of everyone who is hasty, surely to poverty" (Proverbs 21: 5, NKJV). Be patient enough to let your business take root, find its customer base, and grow from there.

**10. Know that Your Work Is for God's Glory First.**
Solomon in Psalm 127 says: "Unless the Lord builds the house; they labor in vain who build it. Unless the Lord guards the city; the watchman stays awake in vain" (NKJV). In other words, an admonition to business owners is that it is vain for you to rise early, to sit up late. If you want your effort to count for something, if you want to reach significance and not just success, direct your efforts to God's glory and build your business as a testimony of excellence to His Name.

## SOME PRINCIPLES OF BIBLICAL ENTREPRENEURSHIP EVERY KINGDOM BUSINESS OWNER SHOULD KNOW

As an entrepreneur, it's easy to conform to worldly business practices, but as a Christian, it's important that you follow biblical entrepreneurship principles so you can continue to stand firm in your faith (see Romans 12:2, NKJV).

When you start a business, your goal and expectation is to make your business profitable, get lots of customers and be happy. However, things do not always go according to plan. When that happens, you start feeling some pressure and maybe some anxiety.

At this point, you may start considering some business practices that aren't biblical because you need to drum up some business. In some cases, you may start receiving advice from some well-meaning people (including Christians), to change some of your business practices or to be a little bit more flexible on your values, if you want to succeed in business.

When you build your life and business on biblical principles, you won't be tossed to and fro by every wind of doctrine (in this case business practices), instead you'll remember God's promises and choose to do the right thing (obey God's word). This is by no means an easy thing to do, but God's grace is sufficient, and his strength is made perfect in your weakness. You need the help of the Holy Spirit to stand firm when you face difficult situations in your business, so don't try to do this alone or think your willpower is sufficient.

### WHAT IS BIBLICAL ENTREPRENEUR?

Biblical entrepreneurship is basically doing business God's way and knowing what the Bible says about entrepreneurship. It's using godly principles to make business decisions and understanding that your business isn't separate from your faith.

Kingdom entrepreneurship is applying godly principles to everything that concerns your business including how you serve your customers, how you treat your employees, how you market your business, how you treat your suppliers and the kind of business ventures you enter.

If this appears clear enough, it's because it is! It is about following God's commandments and instructions for you as a believer and using them in your business. You don't have to jump through hoops or do anything different from what you should already be doing as a Christian.

### 3 WAYS KINGDOM ENTREPRENEURSHIP IS DIFFERENT

Kingdom business seeks to honor and glorify God. That's the first and most important objective for a Kingdom entrepreneur. One of the principles of biblical entrepreneurship is to put God first in your business and follow your convictions no matter what other people think.

A Kingdom entrepreneur uses business to further the gospel and the kingdom of God. She uses her business as a platform to bear witness to the truth of God's word and to be a light to everyone she comes across.

A Kingdom entrepreneur is not greedy for gain. The Bible says that a laborer is worthy of his wages so there's nothing wrong with making money in your business. However, the Kingdom entrepreneur doesn't focus on getting rich through shady or unethical practices.

You don't toil ceaselessly because you are desperate to get rich. Also, a godly business doesn't exploit its customers, employees, or business partners to make more money. There are more ways biblical entrepreneurship is different, but these are three of the most important ways and what separates Kingdom business owners from non-Christians.

### PRINCIPLES OF BIBLICAL BUSINESS OWNERSHIP

**1. God Owns It All**

As a business owner, it's easy to think you are the boss and everything you own belongs to you. In a sense, you're correct, but for us Christians, we understand that we are merely stewards, and God owns it all. We are reminded of this principle in Psalm 50:10 (NKJV) "For every beast of the forest is mine, and the cattle upon a thousand hills." Everything you own belongs to God, just as you belong to him. So that's the mindset with which you approach and run your business. When you accept that God owns it all, it becomes easy to be guided by biblical principles.

Knowing God owns it all, you'll strive to do everything for His glory and shun business practices and ethics that are not pleasing to God. This is one of the fundamental principles of biblical entrepreneurship, and you must keep it front and center of your mind if you want to be a faithful servant who honors his master.

## 2. Do unto Others as You Want Them to Do to You

This is known as The Golden Rule and this principle can be found in Matthew 7:12 (NKJV). The premise of this Bible verse is to treat others the way you'd like to be treated. For example, don't disrespect others if you don't like being disrespected. Don't cheat others or lie to them if you wouldn't like the same thing to be done to you.

This is a very helpful principle that reminds us to be kind and to treat others fairly. It's basically a reminder to do no harm. So how does the Golden Rule work in business?

Some examples of how this principle works in business include:

- Providing a helpful and good quality product or service at a fair price
- Treating your customers or clients politely and kindly
- Addressing customer complaints in a fair, honest and timely manner
- Paying your employees or contractors a fair wage and treating them with respect
- Advertising and marketing in truth
- Paying your bills and credit notes (if you have them) when due
- Keeping your promises
- Using every opportunity and every interaction with others to honor God and further the gospel with your words and actions

As you can see, there are lots of ways to apply this principle to your business and personal life, so there's really no excuse for not doing it.

3. **Act and Work Hard**

The Bible says, "So also, faith by itself, if it does not have works, is dead" (James 2:17, NKJV). As a Kingdom entrepreneur, faith doesn't replace the setting of goals, creating an action plan, then acting. To run a business successfully, you must invest a lot of time and money. You're not going to get the results you desire if you don't put in the effort.

Sadly, I see a lot of Kingdom business owners who fail to follow this principle because they think that prayer, faith and confessions can bridge the gap, but remember, you reap what you sow. For example, if you spend all your time listening to one sermon after the other or reading the Bible, you're going to become more knowledgeable about the word of God, but that wouldn't do much for your business if you don't do the work.

A lot of the principles of biblical entrepreneurship are simple and common-sense principles, but many fail in their applications. So, if you have been running away from taking action, it's time to check yourself and commit to putting in the time that's required to grow your business.

4. **Be Wary of Debt**

Lack of funding is one of the reasons so many aspiring entrepreneurs can't realize their dreams. Depending on the type of business you have (or want to start), you may need a large amount of money which you probably don't have right now.

Borrowing money to fund a business is a common business practice, but as a Kingdom entrepreneur, you want to tread carefully because the borrower is the servant to the lender, and we are told to owe no man anything.

However, I recognize that many businesses couldn't operate without some debt and the Bible doesn't forbid borrowing. With that said, don't go around borrowing money because you have access to loans.

Large debts can crumble your business even with a little change in your financial circumstances. Don't overleverage your business when times are good because you don't know the future. Too much debt will eat into your profits and can make it difficult to fulfill other financial obligations like payroll etc.

For a lot of businesses, debt leads to more debt, so if you must borrow to fund your business, only borrow what you need. Then, focus on growing your business with profits so you can repay all the money you borrowed.

## 5. Plan and Strategize

Planning and strategizing your business is the foundation of success. The Bible says, "For which of you, desiring to build a tower, does not first sit down and count the cost, whether he has enough to complete it?" (Luke 14:28, NKJV). Let me show you the process many small business owners use to start and run their business.

First, they come up with a business idea, build a website, create or buy their products and voila! They are in business. If you're wondering how I know this, it's because this is the same process I failed to follow many years ago and no wonder I failed spectacularly. You can't start or run a business without a plan. Also, you won't get very far without a business strategy or strategies.

Like the Bible says in Luke 14:28 (NKJV), how do you start a business without first sitting down and figuring out the cost to run your business, how your business is going to make money and how you are going to get customers? No, this doesn't mean you should have every single detail mapped out, but you should have a general idea and a plan which you can tweak as you go along.

You should also have some basic strategies outlined: like your marketing and sales strategy and your financial strategy. If you started your business without a plan, it's not too late to create one. It's never too late to start planning or strategizing. So, if you are feeling stuck or unsure about what to do next, take some time to create a business plan and figure out some strategies to help you move ahead in your business.

You want a simple, easy-to-use weekly planner to help you stay on top of your business; that is a good idea. The Bible is replete with wisdom we can implement in our businesses, if only we took the time to study God's word and apply them faithfully. I have shared what biblical entrepreneurship is and some principles you can follow. What you do with this information is up to you, but hopefully, you'll be challenged to build a solid foundation for your business and honor God in whatever you do. Are you struggling with any of these principles of biblical entrepreneurship? Then contact KEN or 3mb Management Consultants (www.3mbconsult.com).

## HABITS OF KINGDOM ENTREPRENEURS

### 1. They Are Diligent

A kingdom entrepreneur is diligent in her work. According to Merriam-Webster, diligence means "steady, earnest, and energetic effort." As a business owner, you must be earnest and energetic. It's imperative you understand that building a successful business requires focus, hard work and dedication. In today's world, we spend so much time looking for hacks, tips and tricks to make our work and lives faster and easier. While there's nothing wrong with learning how to work smarter and faster, there is a tendency for us to ignore the value of working hard, which in turn creates an unrealistic expectation of success while doing the barest minimum.

But diligent entrepreneurs aren't looking for shortcuts or a fast lane to business success. They understand the importance of hard work and perseverance. They see work as a good thing and are thankful for the privilege. The Bible has a lot to say about diligence and I encourage you to pay attention to these words because they are important if you want to keep your Kingdom testimony and be a light in the marketplace.

Some of my favorite Bible verses about diligence are:

Proverbs 13:4 (NKJV): "The soul of the sluggard craves and gets nothing, while the soul of the diligent is richly supplied."

Ecclesiastes 9:10 (NKJV): "Whatever your hand finds to do, do it with might…"

Proverbs 14:23 (NKJV): "In all toil there is profit, but mere talk tends only to poverty." As Kingdom entrepreneurs, there's a tendency for us to spiritualize everything. While prayer and faith should play a big role in your life, they can't replace diligence or working on your business.

So many times, I must remind myself of this truth because it's easy to hide under prayer and faith when I should be working. There was a time in my life when I had to read Proverbs 14:23 every day to remind myself that work comes before profit and merely believing wasn't going to make a difference in my life, business, or finances.

So let me encourage you to be diligent and steadfast in your business. Work hard to grow your business. Invest the time and resources you need into your business and in time, you will see the reward. Diligence is the first habit every kingdom entrepreneur needs to succeed.

### 2. They Have Self-Discipline & Self-Control

As Christians, we are commanded to exercise self-control. This admonition is even more important to a business owner. So, what does it mean to have self-discipline and self-control? When you own a business (especially if you're a small business owner), you're responsible for the success or failure of your business. You are responsible for making decisions for your business and growing it. Unfortunately, many Kingdom entrepreneurs lack self-control and discipline that's why they struggle so much to grow their business. Self-discipline means you show up to work because you know it won't get done otherwise. When you're self-disciplined, you're not ruled by your feelings or emotions. Now let me explain what I mean. When you run a business, you're going to have good days and bad days, it's just the way things are. A disciplined entrepreneur knows she must work through the bad days. You don't allow hiccups and challenges to derail you or stop you from moving forward.

You don't sit around looking for any excuse to justify your laziness. Disciplined entrepreneurs are critical thinkers, and they make decisions thoughtfully and are willing to endure discomforts to achieve their goal. When you have self-control, it's easier to make the right choices for yourself and your business so you can achieve your goals.

A Kingdom entrepreneur should exercise self-control to avoid making bad choices or decisions that could land you in trouble. So, what other ways can you display self-control and discipline in your business?

Managing your time well so you can achieve your goals, making wise financial decisions for your business (like borrowing money, where and what to invest in, business practices to adopt etc.). These are some ways you can exercise self-control and self-discipline.

When you have self-control, you don't chase after everything or jump from one idea to the other because it looks or feels good. You are wary of debt because you understand borrowing too much money could hurt you in the long run. Self-control means you don't embrace everything that comes your way no matter how appealing it looks or sounds. It means you're not motivated by greed or other vain pursuits, but everything you do should be to honor and glorify God.

In my experience, I have discovered that, more than any other quality, self-discipline is what decides whether you'll be successful in your business (and life in general) or not. This also applies to your Kingdom walk. Many Christians struggle because they lack self-discipline and self-control. If you carry these habits into your business, you're going to have a hard time growing your business.

If you struggle in this area, please know it's possible to develop these habits if you're willing to change. Yes, it requires some practice, but it's something anyone can develop. Check out the Bible verses below to see how important self-discipline and self-control are to your faith and business life. See 1 Timothy 4:6-10 (NKJV), Galatians 5:23 (NKJV).

### 3. Kingdom Entrepreneurs Are Honest and Trustworthy

We live in a world where people believe that the end justifies the means. A world where anything goes if it increases your bottom line. But as Kingdom entrepreneurs, we are called to a higher standard. We are answerable to God, and we must be always mindful of that. Scripture says, "Moreover, it is required in stewards that one be found faithful" (1 Corinthians 4:2, NKJV). God is the real owner of our business, so we must always act according to his word.

An Kingdom entrepreneur is honest and trustworthy even if it means making less profit. Being honest means, you treat your customers, creditors, employees, and everyone you do business with fairly. You don't cheat or undercut people because you want to get rich quick. When you give your word or make a promise, you are careful to fulfill it. A kingdom entrepreneur runs her business by the book. She/he practices good business ethics even if people think she's being foolish.

As a kingdom entrepreneur, you should foster trust and loyalty in your business. Your employees, customers, creditors, vendors, and competitors should know they can trust you. People should feel confident doing business with you because they know you always deliver on your promise and sometimes you go over and beyond. If people are wary of doing business with you, or if your customers or clients can't trust you because of the quality of your products or services, then you need to ask yourself if you're operating with honesty and trust.

While we all want to make money and profit from our business, it shouldn't come from cheating people, undercutting your competitors, stealing ideas, or acting unethically. Remember, God is the owner of your business, and He is able to supply all your needs according to his riches in glory, so you don't need underhanded practices to succeed. We must remember what the Bible says in 1 Corinthians 4:2 (NKJV) and always keep it front and center of our mind. Put your trust in the Lord, be faithful, do your part and God will bless your effort.

### 4. Kingdom Entrepreneur Are Good Stewards

In John 3: 25-27 (NKJV), there was a discussion between some of John's disciples and a Jew and they came to John to report that his convert was baptizing people and they were flocking to him. In verse 27, John answered, "A person cannot receive even one thing unless it is given him from heaven." So, my question to you is, who really owns your business? Do you run your business like it belongs to God and you're his steward or do you run your business like you are accountable to no one?

If you truly believe that it is God who gives us the power to get wealth, and that the earth is the Lord's and the fullness thereof, you must start by acknowledging that your business belongs to God and you're merely a steward.

And as a steward you're accountable to God, which means you should run your business like someone who knows they have an overseer to report to. It's easy to forget this important fact because many Christians treat their businesses or work as something separate from their faith. But you can't separate them. Your faith in God should permeate every area of your life because you're a Kingdom child first and an entrepreneur second. You don't drop your Kingdom hat when you are at work, you keep it on no matter the activity you're engaged in.

Being a good steward means you manage the resources that have been entrusted to you by God and use them for his glory. While you may no longer have an earthly boss you answer to, you still have someone you're accountable to. So as a good steward you must be faithful, diligent, make smart decisions for your business, be resourceful, avoid waste and use the resources and gifts God has given to you to make the world a better place. That's one of your responsibilities as a kingdom entrepreneur.

### 5. Contentment Is the Mark of Kingdom Entrepreneur

What does the Bible say about contentment? How do we accomplish contentment in our business while being diligent and not lazy? As a business owner, it's quite easy to fall into the trap of pursuing too many worldly goals which can sometimes lead to discontentment when you fall short. Now don't get me wrong. You need goals for your business and also a plan for achieving those goals. Without goals, you can easily go off track and lose focus because you don't have a target you're trying to reach. So having goals is a good thing. The problem is when you start chasing after big and better goals just for the pleasure of it or because you want to conform to the standard of this world.

For example, it's okay to want to make money in your business, but it becomes a problem when you start desiring to make as much money as someone else does or wanting all the things your competitors or other people have. The constant need for more is what causes discontentment and we must be mindful of that. As Christians, our identity is in Christ and not in our possessions or bank balances. Desiring more and more money or possessions isn't going to make you happy, so focus on serving God and seeking His blessing instead of chasing after stuff. So again, it's okay to make money. It's okay to grow your business and desire nice things if your desire for things isn't what drives you. I used to struggle with this issue a lot because I was a victim of the comparison trap. I was always looking over the fence at what others are doing, monitoring their progress, and wondering why I wasn't making as much progress as them.

Here is the thing. If you fix your gaze on others and keep comparing yourself to them, you're going to keep being frustrated, and discontentment usually stems from frustration. It is fine to be inspired by other business owners, but you must draw the line at comparing yourself with them or wanting the same things they must feel happy about. A Kingdom entrepreneur lives a life of contentment because she knows who she is and she has learned to be content whatever the circumstances. So, remember as a Christian, our only desire is for the glory of God. We mustn't lose sight of that.

**KINGDOM ENTREPRENEUR—FINAL THOUGHTS**

It's possible to be a Kingdom entrepreneur if you remember you can't separate your Kingdom witness from your work. We are called to be the light of the world and we can use our businesses as our platforms to live out our faith and share our testimony.

Being an entrepreneur usually means starting and building your own successful business, although people with entrepreneurial skills can thrive within larger organizations, too. Entrepreneurs generally take a creative, innovative approach, and they may take risks that others would avoid.

Regardless of how you define the term, becoming a successful entrepreneur isn't easy; so be prepared to do the "hard yards," even after you've learned the skills we describe below. Many researchers have studied the subject, but there are no definitive answers. What we do know is that successful entrepreneurs tend to have certain traits and skills in common:

- Personal characteristics.
- Interpersonal skills.
- Critical and creative thinking skills.
- Practical skills and knowledge.

The following sections examine each area in more detail and look at some of the questions you will need to ask yourself if you want to become a successful entrepreneur.

## THE PERSONAL CHARACTERISTICS OF AN ENTREPRENEUR

First, examine your personal characteristics, values, and beliefs. Do you have the mindset to be a successful entrepreneur? Ask yourself these questions:

1. **Optimism:** Are you optimistic in your business? Optimism is an asset, and it will help you through the tough times that many entrepreneurs experience as they find a business model that works for them.
2. **Vision:** Can you easily spot areas for improvement? Can you quickly grasp the "big picture," and explain it to others? And can you create a compelling vision of the future, and then inspire other people to engage with that vision?
3. **Initiative:** Do you have initiative, and instinctively start problem-solving or business improvement projects?
4. **Desire to lead:** Do you enjoy being in charge and making decisions? Are you motivated to lead others?
5. **Drive and persistence:** Are you self-motivated and energetic? And are you prepared to work hard, for a very long time, to realize your goals?
6. **Risk tolerance:** Are you able to take risks, and make decisions when facts are uncertain?
7. **Resilience:** Are you resilient, so that you can pick yourself up when things don't go as planned? And do you learn and grow from your mistakes and failures?

## INTERPERSONAL SKILLS AND ENTREPRENEURSHIP

As an entrepreneur, you'll likely have to work closely with others. So it's essential that you are able to build good relationships with your team, customers, suppliers, shareholders, investors, and other stakeholders.

Some people are more gifted in this area than others, but you can learn and improve these skills. The types of interpersonal skills you'll need include:

1. **Leadership and motivation:** Can you lead and motivate others to follow you and deliver your vision? And are you able to delegate work to other people? As an entrepreneur, you'll have to depend on others to get beyond the early stages of your business if there's just too much to do by yourself!
2. **Communication skills:** Are you skilled in all types of communication you need to be able to communicate well to sell your vision of the future to a wide variety of audiences, including investors, potential clients, and team members.
3. **Listening:** Do you hear what others are telling you? Your ability to listen and absorb information and opinions can make or break you as an entrepreneur. Make sure that you're skilled at active listening and empathic listening.
4. **Personal relationships:** Do you have good "people skills"? Are you self-aware, able to regulate your emotions, and respond positively to feedback or criticism?
5. **Negotiation:** Are you a good negotiator? Not only do you need to negotiate favorable prices, but you will also need to resolve differences between people in a positive, mutually beneficial way.
6. **Ethics:** Do you deal with people based on respect, integrity, fairness, and trust? Can you lead ethically?

## CRITICAL AND CREATIVE THINKING SKILLS FOR ENTREPRENEURS

As an entrepreneur, you need to come up with fresh ideas, and make good decisions about opportunities and potential projects. Many people think that you're either born creative or you're not. But creativity is a skill that you can develop, and there are many tools available to inspire you.

1. **Creative thinking:** Are you able to see situations from a variety of perspectives to generate original ideas? Tools like the Reframing Matrix can help you do this.
2. **Problem solving:** You'll need sound strategies for solving business problems that will inevitably arise. Tools such as Cause & Effect

Analysis, the 5 Whys technique, and CATWOE are a good place to start.
3. **Recognizing opportunities:** Do you recognize opportunities when they present themselves? Are you able to create a workable plan to take advantage of the opportunities you identify?

## PRACTICAL ENTREPRENEURIAL SKILLS AND KNOWLEDGE

Entrepreneurs also need practical skills and knowledge to produce goods or services effectively, and to run a company.

- **Goal setting:** Setting SMART goals that are Specific, Measurable, Achievable, Relevant, and Time-Bound will focus your efforts and allow you to use your time and resources more effectively.
- **Planning and organizing:** Do you have the talents, skills, and abilities necessary to achieve your goals? Can you coordinate people to achieve these efficiently and effectively? Effective project management skills are important, as are basic organization skills. And you'll need a coherent, well thought-out business plan, and the appropriate financial forecasts.
- **Decision making:** Your business decisions should be based on good information, evidence, and weighing up the potential consequences. Core decision-making tools include Decision Tree Analysis, Grid Analysis, and Six Thinking Hats.

They include:

- **Business knowledge:** Ensure that you have a working knowledge of the main functional areas of a business: sales, marketing, finance, and operations. If you can't fulfill all these functions yourself, you'll need to hire others to work with you, and manage them competently.
- **Entrepreneurial knowledge:** How will you fund your business and how much capital do you need to raise? Finding a business model that works for you can require a long period of experimentation and hard work.

- **Opportunity-Specific Knowledge:** Do you understand the market you're attempting to enter, and do you know what you need to do to bring your product or service to market?
- **Venture-Specific Knowledge:** Do you know what it takes to make this type of business successful? And do you understand the specifics of the business that you want to start?

You can also learn from others who have worked on projects similar to the ones that you're contemplating or find a mentor.

## TIP 1:
As an entrepreneur, you must also learn the rules and regulations that apply in the territory or territories that you're operating in. These websites may be useful:

- Australia – Business.gov.au
- Canada – Canada Business Nexus
- India – Business.gov.in
- United Kingdom – GOV.UK
- United States – U.S. Small Business Administration

## TIP 2:
Working in a business like the one you want to launch is a great way to learn the ropes. But be aware of non-compete clauses in your employment contract. In some jurisdictions, these clauses can be very restrictive. You don't want to risk your future projects by violating the rights of another entrepreneur or organization.

## IS ENTREPRENEURSHIP RIGHT FOR YOU?
Before you proceed with your plan to become an entrepreneur, assess your skills against all of the questions and considerations above. Use a Personal SWOT Analysis to examine your Strengths and Weakness, your Opportunities, and the Threats that you may face.

Be honest with yourself about your motivations and the level of commitment you are prepared to give to your project—this could prevent you from making a costly mistake. As you work through your analysis, you may feel that you're ready to plunge into your exciting new venture. Alternatively, you may decide to wait and further develop your skills. You may even decide that entrepreneurship isn't for you after all. Being an entrepreneur can take a huge amount of time and dedication, so make sure that it feels right.

**KEY POINTS**

While there is no single set of characteristics for being a successful entrepreneur, there are many skills that you can learn to help you succeed.

These can be divided into four broad categories:

- Personal characteristics.
- Interpersonal skills.
- Critical and creative thinking skills.
- Practical skills and knowledge.

Examine your own personal strengths and weaknesses in these areas and assess the time and commitment you'll need to "up to speed."

Becoming an entrepreneur is a career decision like any other. So, avoid the temptation to act impulsively. Do your homework. Reflect on your needs, your objectives, and your financial and personal circumstances, and take time to decide whether this is the right path for you.

**WAYS TO BECOME A MORE SUCCESSFUL KINGDOM ENTREPRENEUR**

Whether you're just starting out or are an old pro, who doesn't want to be a more successful entrepreneur? Owning a business gives you a sense of freedom and empowerment. You can build things and watch them grow. Entrepreneurs make decisions for themselves, realize their creative visions, and develop lasting relationships with other entrepreneurs, customers, and vendors. It's a great way to live.

1. **Get Gritty**

Grit is perseverance. Grit is the go-get-em attitude that we expect of entrepreneurs. Grit is the ability to keep working when everyone tells you that you should give up. If you want to be a successful entrepreneur, you must be gritty. Honestly, without hard work and perseverance, you're not going anywhere in the entrepreneurial world.

2. **To Become a Successful Entrepreneur, You Must Challenge Yourself**

If you want to be a successful entrepreneur, you must challenge yourself. No one else is going to push you; so it's up to you to do it. Challenges keep entrepreneurs nimble and on their toes. If you're constantly looking for the next challenge, you'll always be prepared for what comes your way. Challenging yourself with new and difficult tasks will make your other tasks seem even simpler. As an entrepreneur, you always must be looking for the next big challenge.

3. **Successful Entrepreneurs Are Passionate about Their Work**

If you don't love what you do, don't do it. I truly believe it's as simple as that. As an entrepreneur, you're going to have to put in long hours and make sacrifices for your business. When you're passionate about what you do, putting in the long hours won't feel like a sacrifice anymore. If you're not passionate about what you do, you're not going to have the motivation to keep going when you're stressed and tired. Have you ever noticed those entrepreneurs who never seem to get tired? Those entrepreneurs who get that gleam in their eyes when they talk about what they do? That's passion.

4. **To Become a Successful Entrepreneur, You Must Take Risks**

Humans are generally risk-averse, but part of being an entrepreneur is recognizing the risks that you should take. Successful entrepreneurs take risks. It's part of the job. Successful entrepreneurs also know which risks to take and which they shouldn't. Learn to recognize the risks that will benefit your business and take them. Taking risks has a dangerous side, but the opportunities they present often far outweigh the potential dangers. Learn how to identify which risks are worth taking and you'll likely become a more successful entrepreneur.

5. **Trust Yourself**

If you don't believe in yourself, who will? Being a successful entrepreneur means that you've learned to listen to your intuition and rely on your wisdom when making decisions. Your ability to trust and believe in yourself will show your confidence. People are more likely to follow and trust confident leaders. Trusting in your own skills will also take some of the pain of uncertainty out of being an entrepreneur. When you feel uncertain, remember how much experience and knowledge you have. Most entrepreneurs start their businesses after years of experience working for someone else. There's nothing wrong with asking for help when you need it or turning to a mentor for advice, but you also must learn to trust yourself and your own judgment without input from others. Learn to trust yourself and you're already starting down the path of entrepreneurial success.

6. **Reduce Fear**

Fear stops action. Entrepreneurs must be able to pivot and quickly take action when they see an opportunity or recognize a mistake. With fear riding on your shoulder, you won't be a successful entrepreneur. As an entrepreneur, if you let fear be your guide, you won't be able to listen to your intuition, you'll be afraid to take the necessary risks, and your judgment will be clouded by emotion. If you can find ways to reduce and manage your fear and you'll be a much more successful entrepreneur. Keep in mind that fear blurs your perspective.

For example, studies have shown that the truer crime you consume, the more scared you are of crime. My favorite tip for managing fear as an entrepreneur is to do confidence-building exercises. For me, I like to take a few moments at night to think of the decisions I made that day that had a successful outcome. Thinking each day about the decisions that you made that benefited you, others, or your business will help you to quickly build your confidence and reduce fear.

7. **Successful Entrepreneurs Visualize Their Goals**

This tip is less abstract than you might think, so bear with me. When I recommend that entrepreneurs visualize their goals, I don't intend for them to close their eyes and see the goal in front of them. What I want you to do to visualize your goal is to define it so clearly that it's real and tangible. For example, which of these is a more accomplishable:

1. I want to become a successful entrepreneur.
2. I will become a successful entrepreneur by starting a business that solves a problem for this specific niche of my audience.
3. The second one, right?

When you can clearly articulate and visualize your goal, it becomes more achievable. There are many ways to visualize your goal if you aren't sure how to start. You can write it down or draw it out. You can tell someone, such as a friend or business partner, or take photographs that represent your goal. Go with your strengths. When you ask a successful entrepreneur what their goal is, they can tell you in great detail what it is that they're working to achieve.

## 8. Hire Great Partners to Help You Become a Successful Entrepreneur

I'll admit that this one might be a little bit obvious. Successful entrepreneurs aren't successful within a vacuum. We all have a great team and support Nexus behind us. When I recommend hiring great partners, I don't just mean someone who can do the job you're hiring them for. You should seek partners who have great character and who you like and respect. You and your partners will be working long hours together and making stressful decisions. If you don't respect your partner(s), your team won't last long. Fill your team with people who have great character and you're well on your way to success. When choosing your partners and team members, always remember that you can teach skills, but you can't teach character.

## 9. To Become a Successful Entrepreneur, You Must Act Fast

Talk only delays action. Successful entrepreneurs act. It's easy to get wrapped up in planning, considering potential failures, discussing funding, and talking in meetings with board members. If all you do is talk, you'll get nothing done. At some point, you must halt the talking and make something happen.

## 10. Successful Entrepreneurs Spend Time on Important Tasks and Are Patient to See Results

Do you think that there's such a thing as an overnight success? I recommend that you take a closer look. Upon examination, the people and businesses that became "overnight sensations and successes" worked hard and long for their achievements. When you think you've found an overnight success, check again, and examine closely the hours, days, and years that went into their success. Look at their life, the things they learned, and how many times they failed.

Successful entrepreneurs take the time that's required to reach success. And many of them have failures along the way. If you think it's taking too long to find success, give yourself a break. Keep plugging along, putting in the hours, and before long, you'll be a successful entrepreneur. Just imagine looking back at all the hard work and knowing it paid off. Keep that image in your head to motivate you forward through the long, slogging hours.

## 11. Plan Your Finances

Startups and entrepreneurial businesses need money. It's just a part of the lifestyle. Many entrepreneurs spend too much time looking for money and not enough acting, but that doesn't mean that you can leap into the abyss without a plan.

There are a few ways you can fund your business.

- Self-funding
- Investors
- Startup Loans

Decide which is best for you and plan out your finances in the beginning. Try to stick to your budget, but know that the plan will have to be adapted along the way.

## 12. Who's Your Customer? Successful Entrepreneurs Know the Answer

One of the most common reasons that entrepreneurial businesses fail is that there isn't a customer. If you start a business or make a product but don't know who will buy it, that person might not actually exist. Before you make a financial plan, raise capital, or even choose a name, make sure that there's a customer who would buy your product or use your services. Without a customer, you don't have a business. Successful entrepreneurs know who their customers and target market are.

## 13. Successful Entrepreneurs Listen to Complaints

This is one of the tips that I think is the most important for entrepreneurs to learn. Your customers' complaints are how you identify your business's weaknesses. Similarly, to the last tip, without customers, you can't have a successful business. There's another possible scenario, though. You might have customers who are interested in your product or service, but if you don't listen to their complaints, you soon will have no customers. Take your customers seriously, treat their complaints with respect, and listen. You might think you're giving them value, but they may not agree. Your customers know what they want, and they're going to tell you what they think. A smart and successful entrepreneur listens to those complaints and uses that information to fix the business's weaknesses.

## 14. Exceed Everyone's Expectations

If you deliver more than you promised, you're sure to have satisfied customers, investors, and business partners. Making promises and not delivering is a quick way to lose your business. In contrast, successful entrepreneurs exceed expectations.

## 15. Manage Risks to Become a Successful Entrepreneur

Remember when I said that you should take risks? You should, though you shouldn't take every risk that presents itself. Instead, manage your risks. As a successful entrepreneur, you need to learn how to identify which risk is worth taking but also when to take these risks. Be sure to recognize where you are in the entrepreneurial cycle when calculating which risk is worth taking.

## 16. Read Case Studies

As an entrepreneur, you'll be inundated with your business, needing to take care of it all the time. When you get home and have some leisure time, you might be tempted to read fiction or books for entertainment. Instead, I encourage you to read case studies. Read biographies of successful entrepreneurs. Read everything you can get your hands on about those who have already been successful. There's always something to learn from those who have already done it.

I especially think it's important to learn from the mistakes of others. If you learn from their mistakes, you won't have to make those mistakes yourself. And if you do make mistakes yourself, learn from those. The more you learn from their mistakes and successes, the faster you can grow your business and become a successful entrepreneur.

### 17. Successful Entrepreneurs Self-Promote

Many people don't want to self-promote or talk about their business too much for fear of sounding like an egomaniac, but if you don't promote your business, who will? Egotistical self-promotion and self-promotion can be differentiated. Know your business, know some key stats, and have your 15-second elevator pitch polished and ready to go. Then, when someone asks you about your business, you can promote it factually and quickly. Another way to self-promote without sounding cocky is to know what your customers say about your business. When someone asks how your business is going, you can tell them your customers' feedbacks. Don't forget to provide some of the bad as well as the good.

### 18. Successful Entrepreneurs Set and Oversee a Positive Company Culture

There may have been a time when company culture wasn't important, but with social media and the 24-hour news cycle, your company and employees are always under scrutiny. Set a positive company culture from day one and you'll be more likely to work with people you enjoy and who inspire you as well as attract great customers. Many entrepreneurs are working with family, from home, and even across borders. It's important to set and know what you want your company culture to look like.

### 19. Nexus, Nexus, Nexus

There is no such thing as too much Nexusing (well unless it's getting in the way of building your business, of course). What I mean to say is that you shouldn't ever stop Nexusing because you never know where your next lead will come from. Chances are, if you Nexus with enough people, you'll bump into another entrepreneur who might have the ideas and connections you need. You might find a new connection while grabbing a beer at the airport bar, you might meet your next business partner in an elevator on your way to a meeting, and you just never know who's sitting next to you on the bus. Meet everyone you encounter and have a short chat. You never know who you're sitting next to and what connections or resources they might be able to offer you.

## 20. Learn and Create

The successful entrepreneur's mindset is that of learning and creation. As an entrepreneur, you always want to be taking in new information and creating. This type of mindset can be draining and tiring, but without it, you're not going anywhere. To stay in the learner and creator mindset, stay away from TV, social media, and movies. These types of entertainment cause us to be passive and just take in information.

Pursue everything in moderation, but in general, these activities are time-wasters for entrepreneurs. Limiting your entertainment time is a sacrifice that must be made to become a successful entrepreneur. Instead of watching TV and movies, read case studies and meditate. Take care of your mind and body in constructive, healing ways. It may "feel good" to watch TV, but it's not actually a rejuvenating way to relax. To be a successful entrepreneur, find relaxing activities that help to restore your learner and creator mindset.

## 21. Successful Entrepreneurs Deliver, Not Sell

Honestly, no one likes to be sold to. I mean seriously, who enjoys going to the car lot and buying a new car? We all know what we're getting ourselves into and dread it. Instead of selling to your potential customers, deliver. Offer them a free trial and deliver a great product. When your company delivers a great product or service, you'll build customer loyalty faster than you can say, "successful entrepreneur."

## 22. Take Baby Steps to Become a Successful Entrepreneur

Building a successful entrepreneurial business can seem daunting, and that's okay. Building a business from the ground up is a massive undertaking. Luckily,

I have a foolproof tactic: break it down. Any problem that seems insurmountable, break it down into baby steps. Once you've broken it down into baby steps, take them one at a time. Before you know it, just by placing one foot in front of the other, you'll be halfway up the mountain. With grit and perseverance, baby steps will get you far toward becoming a successful entrepreneur.

**23. Put Everything on Your Calendar**
You think I'm kidding, but I'm not. Put everything on your calendar. Think something doesn't need to be on your calendar? It does. Put your meetings, quiet work periods, time with friends, happy-hour business meetings, kids' soccer games, workouts, meal times, and anything else that you do on your calendar. Once something is on your calendar, then everyone who needs to meet with you knows that time isn't available. An additional benefit is that once everything is on your calendar, there aren't excuses for not getting things done.

I want to also draw your attention to one of the items I included: quiet work time. That is time when you can work, solve problems, or think creatively without being interrupted. Everyone needs these periods of time. To be a successful entrepreneur, guard your quiet work times with your life. The success of your business may depend upon them.

**24. Exercise to Become a More Successful Entrepreneur**
Did you know that sitting down all day long is bad for your health? It is. Being a successful entrepreneur doesn't just mean running a profitable business. Run yourself to ragged managing that business and you might not be around to enjoy its success. You must take care of yourself as well as your business. One of the many self-care tasks that I recommend is exercise.

Make sure to book time in your calendar to get in some exercise and get out of your chair. Maybe you go to yoga, walking meetings, climb the stairs instead of the elevator, or simply go to the gym. Build time into your calendar every week (dare I hope for every day?) to be physically active and take care of your body as well as your business. A sick or unhealthy entrepreneur isn't a successful entrepreneur.

## 25. Successful Entrepreneurs Stay Focused

The life of a successful entrepreneur can feel scattered and disjointed, but it's important to limit your time spent multitasking. Research has shown time and time again that multitasking doesn't work. Humans aren't capable of it. And yes, multitasking includes being distracted by your phone and email tabs. Close them and put them away.

Learn to focus and take time to do just one task. Giving one task your full attention will mean that you're more likely to get it done and do it well. It's also important to know that too many tasks on your to-do list can make you ineffective and distracted. Learn to focus your to-do list on the tasks that you're capable of finishing in the amount of time you've allotted for them. For example, each night, set the three tasks that you'll complete the following day. Each month, set the overarching goal for your company that you want to achieve in the next 30 days. These techniques can help you to learn how to focus and more effectively manage your business.

## 26. Take Time Off

We finally made it to the tip that I think is the toughest for successful entrepreneurs to put into practice. I really mean that you need to take time off. Americans don't do it enough. You might not need time off every day or every week, but you do need to take time off. If all you do is work, you'll burn out. Fast. I think this is the most challenging for entrepreneurs because they often see themselves as invincible or believe that they must be invincible. This just isn't true; we're all humans and we need time off.

Time off allows your brain to roam, to rest, and to think. Ever wonder why you think of so many ideas in the shower? It's because your brain has free range to just think and roam. Even the most successful entrepreneurs don't work all the time. Everyone needs time off, so don't shame yourself for being human and normal. When you do take time off, notify your staff ahead of time and let them know why it's important to you. Teaching your staff the importance of time off will help them respect your time away and to recognize when they need time off. By the way, you should allow your staff time off too. They also are human and will occasionally break. Take time off before you need it and recognize that it's important for healing, creating, and becoming a more successful entrepreneur.

### 27. Successful Entrepreneurs Ask Questions

You don't know everything. No one does. You should ask for help, advice, mentors, and everything else you need as you get your business set up and running. Asking questions is a valuable skill to have as an entrepreneur. The more information you have, the more you will know and be able to take that into consideration. Asking questions also helps you to remain in a learner mindset, ready to accept advice and information. Learners and those who ask questions are more likely to become successful entrepreneurs.

### 28. Learn from Your Failures

A failure is an option. Better to accept it now than later. You will fail at some point. It's how you adjust to these failures that will make or break your business. Failure is an aspect of becoming a successful entrepreneur, so you'd better get used to it now. If your first business does fail, keep in mind that you can create another with the lessons you learned from your first.

### 29. Get Inspired

Being an entrepreneur is a creative pursuit. As an entrepreneur, you have to make connections, solve problems, and create new things that no one has thought of before. Creators and creatives need to be inspired. Successful entrepreneurs take time for the things that inspire them. Maybe your inspiration comes from being in an art museum, maybe it's reading books, maybe it's doodling, whatever it is that inspires you, do it. It's good for your business. Successful entrepreneurs are inspired. Don't let that magic slip for too long. Whenever you can, and when you're feeling burned out, get out there and get inspired. Inspiration is the spark for ideas. Ideas make successful entrepreneurs.

### 30. Successful Entrepreneurs Lend a Helping Hand

Entrepreneurs are busy, so this tip sometimes trips them up. It's easy to think, "I don't have time to help anyone else! I'm so busy already!" However, helping others can be inspiring and massively beneficial. It makes you feel good. Furthermore, as an entrepreneur, you have a Nexus with whom you can share your expertise and jobs you can hire people for. Why wouldn't you help when you can? When you help someone, they will likely find a way to help you. It might not be today or tomorrow, but somewhere in the future, they will be there to help you when you need it. Helping others is also a great way to build a loyal and supportive Nexus around you.

# CHAPTER 3

# BUSINESS STRUCTURE

**BUSINESS ENTITY FOR TAX PURPOSES**

In simplest terms, a business entity is an organization created by an individual or individuals to conduct business, engage in a trade, or partake in similar activities. There are various types of business entities: sole proprietorship, partnership, LLC, corporation, etc. and a business's entity type dictates both the structure of that organization and how that company is taxed.

When starting a business, one of the first things you want to do is choose the structure of your company in other words, choose a business entity type. This decision will have important legal and financial implications for your business. The amount of taxes you must pay depends on your business entity choice, as does the ease with which you can get a potential business loan or raise money from investors. Plus, if someone sues your business, your business entity structure determines your risk exposure.

State governments in the U.S. recognize more than a dozen different types of business entities, but the average potential business owner chooses between these six: sole proprietorship, general partnership, limited partnership (LP), limited liability company (LLC), C-corporation, and S-corporation. Which business entity is right for you? This guide is here to help you make that decision. We will explain the types of business entities and the pros and cons of each so that you have all the information you need to determine what is best for your company.

## TYPES OF BUSINESS ENTITIES: AN OVERVIEW

As we mentioned above, at a considerably basic level, a business entity simply means an organization that has been formed to conduct business. However, the type of entity you choose for your business determines how your company is structured and taxed. For example, by definition, a sole proprietorship must be owned and operated by a single owner. If your business entity type is a partnership, on the other hand, this means there are two or more owners.

Similarly, if you establish a business as a sole proprietorship, this means for tax purposes, you are a pass-through entity (the taxes are passed onto the business owner). Conversely, if you establish your business as a corporation, this means the business exists separately from its owners, and therefore, pays separate taxes.

Generally, to establish your business's entity structure, you will register in the state where your business is located. Most business owners will choose from the six most common options: sole proprietorship, general partnership, limited partnership, LLC, C-corporation, or S-corporation. Below, we have explained each of these popular business entity types, as well as the pros and cons of choosing each structure for your company.

## SOLE PROPRIETORSHIP

If you're operating an unincorporated business and are the only owner, then you're automatically a sole proprietor. This is the most common business entity with over 23 million sole proprietorships in the United States. It's the easiest to set up and manage, but also one of the riskiest since you personally assume all financial and legal obligations. Sole proprietorship taxes are straightforward since you can report business income and losses on your personal tax return (Form 1040), using Schedule C. Your company profits are added to other income (interest, dividends, etc.) on your personal tax return.

With the new tax law, sole proprietors can take advantage of the 20% tax deduction, which allows them to deduct 20% of the business's net income from their taxable income, which reduces their tax liability. A sole proprietorship is the simplest business entity, with one person (or a married couple) as the sole owner and operator of the business. If you launch a new business and are the only owner, you are automatically a sole proprietorship under the law. There is no need to register a sole proprietorship with the state, though you might need local business licenses or permits depending on your industry.

Freelancers, consultants, and other service professionals commonly work as sole proprietors, but it is also a viable option for more established businesses, such as retail stores, with one person at the helm.

## Pros of sole proprietorship

- Easy to start, it cost nothing to set up—unless you register a fictitious name, and then it's about $155 in MN and renewal fee of $55 every year.
- You have complete autonomy in the business operation and decision.
- You are not required to keep a balanced set of books—but you should do it anyway.
- You are not required to have a separate bank account—but for prudent business management you should.
- No corporate formalities or paperwork requirements, such as meeting minutes, bylaws, etc.
- You can deduct most business losses on your personal tax return.
- Tax filing is easy; simply fill out and attach Schedule C-Profit or Loss from business to your personal income tax return.

## Cons of sole proprietorship

- As the only owner, you are personally responsible for all the business's debts and liabilities someone who wins a lawsuit against your business can take your personal assets (your car, personal bank accounts, even your home in some situations).
- Your profits are subject to self-employment taxes.

- There is no real separation between you and the business, so it is more difficult to get a business loan and raise money (lenders and investors prefer LLCs or corporations).
- It is harder to build business credit without a registered business entity.
- There is no continuity of life for the business; when you die, the business too dies.
- Your business gets no tax benefit for medical expenses and insurance, without the complication and expense of a special plan.

Sole proprietorships are by far the most popular type of business structure in the U.S. because of how easy they are to set up. There is a lot of overlap between your personal and business finances, which makes it easy to launch and file taxes. The problem is that this same lack of separation can also land you in legal trouble. If a customer, employee, or another third party successfully sues your business, they can take your personal assets. Due to this risk, most sole proprietors eventually convert their business to an LLC or corporation.

## GENERAL PARTNERSHIP (GP)

Partnerships share many similarities with sole proprietorships, but the key difference is that the business has two or more owners. There are two kinds of partnerships: general partnerships (GPs) and limited partnerships (LPs). In a general partnership, all partners actively manage the business and share in the profits and losses.

Like a sole proprietorship, a general partnership is the default mode of ownership for multiple-owned businesses there is no need to register a general partnership with the state.

### Pros of general partnership

- Easy to start and inexpensive to set up. You may even write your own agreement. That is not a great idea, but it is a good starting point from which your attorney or consultant may prepare the partnership

agreement. Even if there is no agreement, if two or more people are together you are automatically in partnership in the eye of the IRS.
- No corporate formalities or paperwork requirements, such as meeting minutes, bylaws, etc.
- General partnership (entity) pays no taxes.
- Losses are fully deductible on personal returns, unless they are real estate losses, those face passive loss limits.
- You do not need to absorb all the business losses on your own because the partners divide the profits and losses according to their share (%).
- vPartnership profits may qualify for the new Section 199A 20 percent qualified business income deduction.
- Owners can deduct most business losses on their personal tax returns.
- Certain partnerships can get out of filling a tax return altogether. The partnership may file an election which is a formal announcement to the IRS that the partners chose to report the transactions on their personal tax returns. You may do this with investment clubs, certain real estate rentals, or groups of people simply sharing expenses but not in business together.

## Cons of general partnership

- Each owner is personally liable for the business's debts and other liabilities.
- All the partners must be consulted in decision making.
- In some states, each partner may be personally liable for another partner's negligent actions or behavior.
- Profits are generally subject to self-employment taxes.
- Disputes among partners can unravel the business (though drafting a solid partnership agreement can help you avoid this).
- It is more difficult to get a business loan, land a big client, and build business credit without a registered business entity.
- There can be continuity issues if a partner dies, an heir (spouse or child) who's in the position to make business decision may create confusion

if the heir don't understand the business operations. Avoid this by using the key person insurance policies.

Most people form partnerships to lower the risk of starting a business. Instead of going all-in on your own, having multiple people sharing the struggles and successes can be extremely helpful, especially in the early years.

If you do go this route, it's very important to choose the right partner or partners. Disputes can seriously limit a business's growth, and many state laws hold each partner fully responsible for the actions of the others. For example, if one partner enters a contract and then violates one of the terms, the third party can personally sue any or all the partners.

## LIMITED PARTNERSHIP (LP)

Unlike a general partnership, a limited partnership (LP) is a registered business entity. To form a limited partnership, therefore, you must file paperwork with the state. In an LP, there are two kinds of partners: those who own, operate, and assume liability for the business (general partners), and those who act only as investors (limited partners, sometimes called "silent partners").

Limited partners do not have control over business operations and have fewer liabilities. They typically act as investors in the business and pay fewer taxes in some cases because they have a more tangential role in the company.

### Pros of limited partnership

- An LP is a good option for raising money because investors can serve as limited partners without personal liability.
- LPs do not pay federal taxes.
- General partners get the money they need to operate but maintain authority over business operations.
- Partnership profits may qualify for the new Section 199A 20 percent qualified business deduction.
- They provide complete liability protection for all limited partners

- Limited partners can leave anytime without dissolving the business partnership.
- Profits and losses may be split by formula instead of only by ownership percentage just like general partnership.
- Limited partners' earnings are not subject to self-employment taxes.
- Although there must be a general partner, the general partner can be an LLC or other limited liability entity.

**Cons of limited partnership**

- General partners are personally responsible for the business's debts and liabilities.
- More expensive to create than a general partnership and requires a state filing.
- A limited partner may also face personal liability if they inadvertently take too active a role in the business.
- Limited partners have no control over decisions. They could lose their investment if the general partner is crooked.
- Some states charge minimum annual taxes.
- General partners are fully liable if the company is sued.
- Limited partners' income or losses are considered passive; loss deductions are limited to passive income from other sources.

Multi-owner businesses that want to raise money from investors often do well as LPs because investors can avoid liability.

You might come across, yet another business entity structure called a limited liability partnership (LLP). In an LLP, none of the partners have personal liability for the business, but most states only allow law firms, accounting firms, doctors' offices, and other professional service firms to organize as LLPs. These types of businesses can organize as an LLP to avoid each partner being liable for the other's actions. For example, if one doctor in a medical practice commits malpractice, having an LLP lets the other doctors avoid liability.

## C-CORPORATION

Traditional corporations are C corporations (C corps). The organizational structure of a C corps consists of shareholders, a board of governors, officers, directors, and employees. Although Fortune 500 firms are the most well-known C corps, it's still a viable option to structure your potential business this way. It provides legitimacy to investors and clients, allowing you to raise funds faster and land larger contracts. If you anticipate quickly transitioning from a startup to a more established company, then the C corporation structure may be right for you.

C corps are the only type of businesses discussed here that must pay taxes on the company level. The current corporate income tax rate for C corps is a flat 21%. Additionally, in contrast to S corps that lets shareholders report profit and losses on their personal tax returns, shareholders receive dividends (i.e., a share of company profits). Shareholders must pay personal taxes on those dividends.

The taxation structure on both the company and shareholder levels is referred to as double taxation. This turns off many potential business owners. When starting out, LLCs tend to be a more popular option than C corps for various reasons.

A C-corporation is an independent legal entity that exists separately from the company's owners. Shareholders (the owners), a board of directors, and officers have control over the corporation, although one person in a C-Corp can fulfill all these roles, so it is possible to create a corporation where you're in charge of everything.

With this type of business entity, there are many more regulations and tax laws that the company must comply with. Methods for incorporating, fees, and required forms vary by state.

### Pros of C-corporation

- Owners (shareholders) do not have personal liability for the business's debts and liabilities.
- The business may have unlimited shareholders.
- No general partner, with liability exposure is needed.

- All shareholders, including officers have liability protection from corporate debt.
- Corporate dividends to shareholders have a preferred tax rate of 0 to 20 percent if the stock is held long enough.
- C-corporations are eligible for more tax deductions than any other type of business.
- C-corporation owners pay lower self-employment taxes.
- Corporations receiving dividends to shareholders have a preferred tax rate of 0 to 20 percent if the stock is held long enough.
- You can offer stock options, which can help you raise money in the future.

**Cons of C-corporation**

- More expensive to create than sole proprietorships and partnerships (the filing fees required to incorporate a business range from $100 to $500 based on which state you are in).
- IRS may impose taxes for constructive dividends if you draw too much money.
- The IRS may decide your wages are too high or too low and penalize you accordingly.
- C-corporations face double taxation: The company pays taxes on the corporate tax return, and then shareholders pay taxes on dividends on their personal tax returns.
- Owners cannot deduct business losses on their personal tax returns.
- The corporation may be subject to an accumulated earnings tax if you draw too little money.
- There are a lot of formalities that corporations must meet, such as holding board and shareholder meetings, keeping meeting minutes, and creating bylaws.
- Undistributed income of personal holding companies may get hit with personal holding taxes.
- C-corporation profits do not get the benefit of the Section 199A 20 percent qualified potential business income deduction.

Most potential businesses pass over C-corps when deciding how to structure their business, but they can be a good choice as your business grows and you find yourself needing more legal protections. The biggest benefit of a C-Corp is limited liability. If someone sues the business, they are limited to taking business assets to cover the judgment they cannot come after your home, car, or other personal assets.

Corporations are a mixed bag. From a tax perspective, there are more tax deductions and fewer self-employment taxes, but there is the possibility of double taxation if you plan to offer dividends. Owners who invest profits back into the business as opposed to taking dividends are more likely to benefit under a corporate structure. Corporation formation and maintenance can be complicated, but you can trust 3mb Management Consultants (www.3mbconsult.com) to provide professional consulting services to you.

## S-CORPORATION

S corporations may pass income directly to shareholders to avoid double taxation. Double taxation means that a firm's profit is taxed on a business tax return, and any after-tax profits distributed to owners is taxed again as personal income. But this won't happen if your company is set up as an S corporation.

S corporations must have no more than 100 shareholders, all shareholders must be U.S. residents, and each member is only allowed to own one class of stock. Shareholders report business income, expenses, losses, and deductions on their personal tax returns. S corps are also eligible for the 20% tax deduction, but shareholders pay taxes on business profits at their personal income tax rate. It's one of the most common types of legal structures for potential business owners because they have the same advantages as traditional corporations but with more tax flexibilities.

An S-corporation preserves the limited liability that comes with a C-corporation but is a pass-through entity for tax purposes. This means that, like a sole prop or partnership, an S-corps' profits and losses pass through to the owners' personal tax returns. There is no corporate-level taxation for an S-corp.

## Pros of S-corporation

- Owners (shareholders) do not have personal liability for the business's debts and liabilities.
- All shareholders, including officers have liability protection from corporate debts.
- No general partner with liability exposure is needed.
- S-corporate do not need to keep detailed minute books like a C-corporate; though it would be wise to do so.
- When a member dies, the company continues. Remember to set up buy-sell agreement and key-person insurance policies in case of death or disagreement.
- No corporate taxation and no double taxation: an S-Corp is a pass-through entity, so the government taxes it much like a sole proprietorship or partnership.
- S-corporation profits do not get the benefit of the Section 199A 20 percent qualified potential business income deduction.
- You may choose to switch to a C-corporation format or back, once every five years if you file Form 2553 by the fifteenth day of the third month of your fiscal year. But don't make a habit of switching, you pick up extra taxes and lose certain benefits in the process each time.

## Cons of S-corporation

- Like C-corporations, S-corporations are more expensive to create than both sole proprietorships and partnerships (requires registration with the state).
- S-corporation stock is not eligible for the qualified potential business stock benefits (QSBS).
- You may have no more than 100 shareholders.
- Nonresident aliens may not own S-corporation stock.
- When shareholders are added, all shareholders should sign the S-corporate election Form 2553 all over again. Companies often overlook this.

- There are more limits on issuing stock with S-corps vs. C-corps.
- There are restrictions on the employee benefits of shareholders who own more than 2 percent of the business.
- You still need to comply with corporate formalities, like creating by-laws and holding board and shareholder meetings.

To organize as an S-corporation or convert your business to an S-corporation, you have to file IRS form 2553. S-corporations can be a good choice for businesses that want a corporate structure but like the tax flexibility of a sole proprietorship or partnership.

## LIMITED LIABILITY COMPANY (LLC)

Many potential businesses tend to form as an LLC. LLC members have two important tax advantages: no double taxation and deductible business losses.

Unlike C corporations, where business income is taxed twice at the corporate level and at the individual level, LLCs are only taxed once at the individual level. This means that members pay taxes on business income on their personal tax returns in the same way a sole-proprietorship or an S corps does. This treatment is referred to as a "pass-through" tax treatment.

Another advantage of owning an LLC is that you can have an unlimited number of members (i.e., potential shareholders) in your LLC, which makes it easier to raise capital and expand your business. If you have multiple members in your LLC, you must determine the ownership percentages for each member.

With multiple-member LLCs, you can choose to be taxed as a partnership or as a C corporation. If you choose to be taxed as a partnership, then you'll report your share of the business income on your personal income tax returns. If you choose to be taxed as a C corporation, you will be subject to double taxation.

Single-member LLCs, on the other hand, are automatically taxed as a sole-proprietorship.

You may pay upfront costs to set up and maintain your LLC with your state. To operate an LLC in California, for instance, potential business owners pay $800 in state taxes annually regardless of how much money the LLC is making or losing.

If you're in a state where you must pay annual taxes to operate an LLC, then your job is to grow the business enough to offset that cost. Every state has different annual taxes to operate an LLC, and some may not have any annual state taxes, so it's important to check before you establish your business.

But the tax advantages, pass-through profits, and management flexibilities still make LLCs a popular option. Your tax situation depends on doing your research to determine which legal entity best suits your needs.

A limited liability company takes positive features from each of the other business entity types. Like corporations, LLCs offer limited liability protections. But LLCs also have less paperwork and ongoing requirements, and in that sense, they are more like sole proprietorships and partnerships.

Another big benefit is that you can choose how you want the IRS to tax your LLC. You can elect to have the IRS treat it as a corporation or as a pass-through entity on your taxes.

**Pros of LLC**

- Owners do not have personal liability for the business's debts or liabilities.
- You can choose whether you want your LLC to be taxed as a partnership or as a corporation.
- Not as many corporate formalities compared to an S-Corp or C-corp.
- One-person LLCs may report either as an S or C corporations or on a personal Schedule C.
- LLCs may have multiple classes of ownership; this allows companies to give nonvoting shares to consultants and employees. Those members can share in profits but not decisions. Sharing profits with employees is a good way to attract workers without losing voting control.
- LLCs are permitted to issue shares that may not be sold. Again, this is perfect for consultants and employees. If they leave, you may buy them out at a prearranged price or formula, whether they like it or not.
- LLCs filling as a partnership do not pay federal taxes

- They provide complete liability protection for all members from the LLC's debts.
- No general partner, with liability exposure, is needed
- There is no requirement for keeping minutes, thus reducing paperwork. But only a fool does not maintain detailed records of all key business decisions, compensation changes, reimbursement policies, and employee or member benefits.
- Profits may be split by formula, time devoted to the company, or other criteria, instead of only by ownership percentage just like general partnership.
- Even if a member dies, the company continues. Remember to set up buy-sell agreements and key person insurance policies in case of death or disagreement.
- If the LLC is established as a pass-through entity for tax purposes, profits may qualify for the new Section 199A percent qualified business income deduction.

### Cons of LLC
- It is more expensive to create an LLC than a sole proprietorship or partnership (requires registration with the state).
- Rules are different in each state.
- Profits are subject to self-employment taxes if the LLC files a Schedule C or a partnership return.
- Some state charge minimum annual taxes.

LLCs are popular among potential business owners, including freelancers, because they combine the best of many worlds: the ease of a sole proprietorship or partnership with the legal protections of a corporation.

### HOW TO CHOOSE THE BEST BUSINESS ENTITY TYPE.
With a better understanding of how the common business entity types work and their respective pros and cons, you can now determine which type works best for your potential business. The best course of action, if you can afford it, is to consult a business consultant and tax professional (www.3mbconsult.com) on

which structure is optimal for you, given where your business is currently and where you hope to take it.

As a starting point, however, there are three general factors to consider when choosing among business entity types: legal protection, tax treatment, and paperwork requirements. In the section below, you can see how the entities stack up about each of these factors.

## BUSINESS ENTITY SUMMARY

### Sole proprietorship
Limited Liability Protections? No Tax Treatment: Taxed at personal tax rate Level of Government Requirements: Low

### General partnership
Limited Liability Protections? No Tax Treatment: Taxed at personal tax rate Level of Government Requirements: Low

### Limited partnership
Limited Liability Protections? For limited partners only Tax Treatment: general partners taxed at personal tax rate Level of Government Requirements: Medium

### S-Corporation
Limited Liability Protections? Yes, Tax Treatment: taxed at personal tax rate Level of Government Requirements: High

### C-Corporation
Limited Liability Protections? Yes, Tax Treatment: must pay corporate taxes (but beware of double taxation on dividends) Level of Government Requirements: High

### Limited Liability Company (LLC)
Limited Liability Protections? Yes, Tax Treatment: can choose how you want to be taxed Level of Government Requirements: Medium

As you can see, sole props and GPs are light on liability protections, so they expose you to greater legal risk if someone sues your business. But taxation is simple when you have a sole prop or GP, and you do not have nearly as many government regulations to comply with. That means more time to do what you love, running your business.

The simplicity of a sole prop or a partnership makes either of these business entity structures a good starting point for freelancers and consultants, particularly if the industry they are in brings little legal risk with it.

Along these lines, fashion and beauty influencer Joanna Faith Williams said: "Being a sole proprietor now seems most appropriate as there is not much that I am liable for at this time. I keep well-written contracts to protect myself, but as I begin to dive more into creating content such as eBooks… or things that my audience will have to pay for, I will definitely consider registering as an LLC" (p. 951).

If your business is in a more litigious industry, on the other hand, such as food service, child care, or professional services, that is a strong reason to create an LLC or corporation right off the bat. And regardless of industry, as your business grows, and more dollars are at stake that can be the ideal time to "graduate" to an LLC or corporation. What works for a freelancer or hobbyist likely will not work for someone who is trying to hire employees, bring on additional owners, or expand.

Brett Helling, owner of ridesharing blog Ridester.com, found this to be true. "Initially, I started this blog as a part-time thing. However, once the site began to experience growth at a very rapid pace and began making money, I realized it was turning into an actual business. I quickly realized that I should register an LLC… to shield myself from liability in case something went wrong," he explains (p. 1).

Although it is certainly possible to change business structures at any point in your business's journey, some changes are easier to make than others. For instance, it is relatively simple to convert from a sole prop or partnership to an LLC by filing the right paperwork with your state.

Converting to a corporation, however, is more difficult, particularly if you plan to issue stock. Additionally, converting from a C-Corp to an S-Corp can bring unexpected taxes. Therefore, before changing your business structure, you will want to think through the possible advantages and potential problems associated with doing so and consult a business attorney for professional advice.

Moreover, you will want to keep in mind that the IRS places certain limits and deadlines on how often you can change your business's entity type. Plus, it's also worth remembering that different government tax plans (like the Trump Tax Plan, for example) can change how business entity types are taxed, and this may contribute to how taxes factor into your ultimate decision.

**THE BOTTOM LINE**

At the end of the day, your choice of business entity is an especially important one. The entity you choose can affect how people perceive your business, and more importantly, it has a big impact on your legal exposure and finances.

All in all, you will want to keep the following in mind when deciding among the different types of business entities:

- Sole proprietorships and general partnerships are good "starter" entities.
- As your business grows and generates more income, you might consider registering as an LLC or corporation.
- Think through the pros and cons of each business entity type in terms of legal protection, tax treatment, and government requirements.
- Work with a business lawyer and accountant to get specific help for your business.

Ultimately, although there is not a single best business entity choice for all potential businesses, by referring to this guide and consulting legal or financial professionals, you'll be able to determine which type is right for your business.

# CHAPTER 4

# INITIAL CAPITAL SAGA

We asked several prominent entrepreneurs what their biggest business challenge is. Most agree that finding business financing is a big problem. Starting a business comes with a lot of obstacles, but for entrepreneurs who have been through it, one challenge stands out in their mind: financing.

Cash is essential to keep your business afloat but paying the bare minimum to cover basic operating expenses only gets you so far. To grow your business, you also need a healthy amount of capital to invest in bigger projects. More working capital can free you up to focus on long-term growth efforts, like hiring, relocating, or purchasing a second business.

In terms of small business challenges, Guidant Financial ranks high in providing support to business entities which lack capital or lack of cash flow. That's partly because acquiring funding can be difficult. According to Biz2Credit's May 2018 Small Business Lending Index, big banks only grant about one in four small business loan applications. Though the approval rating has gone up slowly since the recession, it still hovers around 25 percent.

The major limiting factor in approval seems to be tied to business credit. According to Nav's Small Business American Dream Gap Report from 2015, one in five business owners who applied for funding in the last five years were denied, and 82 percent of all the business owners surveyed didn't know how to interpret their credit scores. The research also showed that individuals who have a better understanding of their business's credit score are 41 percent more likely to be approved for a loan.

That's why it's critical to lay out a plan for identifying and improving your business credit score. Then, before you move forward with financing, get clear on how you would use any extra capital and check out your options to see what makes the most sense to help you grow your business.

Many businesses and startups failed because of lack of funding, but is it really money that the world lacks? With more than 13 million investors in the US alone in 2020, perhaps money is not the problem. These great numbers of investors leave founders and entrepreneurs in a big and highly competitive environment where hearing back from an investor can be a big achievement in and of itself. With that in mind, it can be stressful to raise the money you need and get your business going, the question is:

## HOW CAN ENTREPRENEURS OVERCOME CAPITAL CHALLENGES?

- **Having a Scalable Business Model**

Investors are always looking for remuneration. So preparing a business plan with a realistic scalability report for your startup would increase your chances of getting an investor's attention. It should demonstrate that your business will be able to generate the highest possible revenues with the least expenditure rate within a specific period of time.

- **Determining the Uniqueness of Your Idea**

When you are trying to come up with a model that would prove successful, the idea of copying already successful models will sound very alluring. However, relying on the same model your competitors have—if we can name them "competitors" at this early stage—has been proved to be a failing way to initiate your business.

Remember that your idea must be unique and authentic; so if you have an idea that solves the same problem in the same industry that another business already solves, just make sure not to copy the same model already in the market. Instead, you should think out of the box and be innovative. Your business plan should show how creative your idea is and how it does have improvements that could serve the market. We will also help in matching you with investors and in raising the capital needed!

- **Having a Realistic Time Frame**

Most entrepreneurs underestimate the time they will need to raise capital, hoping that the less time raising capital takes up, the quicker the process moves forward.

Give yourself the time you need and if you are putting in the right amount of effort, your journey will lead you either to raising the capital required for your business or to gaining experience and valuable feedback to start again.

- **Not Giving Up**

No matter how many times you got rejected, do not quit! Remember, winners don't quit, and quitters don't win. Keep doing what you are doing and improving your process and the results will come sooner or later. Sometimes you approach investors who initially show interest in your startup and when you try to call them again you enter the maze of the uncertain "yes" and the horrible "no". It can be frustrating, but you just need to go on with your quest and the awaited "yes" will come at the right time. Time and experience will make your business model more mature and ready for the future growth and scaling phase.

- **Business Nexusing**

Try to increase the number and the quality of your connections as much as you can, as the more intricate your Nexus is the more you can learn and the more alternatives you have. Of course, it might take some time, but it is definitely worth being executed.

- **Prioritizing Opportunities**

Finding the right investor should happen after making sure that you're well prepared for the challenge. You need to make sure that you are backed up with the essential required equipment, an interesting innovative idea, a good business plan, and a reliable co-founder who can support you and give you extra knowledge and extra opportunities to secure the funds that you need. Try to show up in as much business Nexusing websites as possible to increase your chances of meeting investors and industry leaders.

- **Checking Global and Local Banks and Special Credit Cards Opportunities**

Some banks offer special credit cards for entrepreneurs and small business owners. But you shouldn't miss the point that this is the most expensive option, and because most of the credit cards are personal, then you will be personally liable for any debt.

- **Approaching Venture Capitals**

Surely, this is not a usual option for startups in the early stages, as venture capitalists usually tend to invest large amounts of money, so trying to find venture capitals interested in your ideas would probably be in vain. Before approaching any venture capital and losing the chance altogether, you have to be really prepared by having the right approach and enough understanding about the industry and the competitors out there.

- **Starting a Crowdfunding Campaign on Crowdfunding Platforms**

These platforms are considered the perfect places and hubs for entrepreneurs and investors worldwide, but as the name suggests, they are usually crowded, and you usually need to have access to a wide and well-established Nexus of friends and contacts of professional people for support to succeed in your campaign which needs to be unique and properly executed and planned for. After the long journey of raising capital, it might not be surprising if you have forgotten why you raised capital in the first place! The sure thing is that you have refined your business plan and gained a lot of insights because of all the meetings and conversations you have had with different experts and investors AND that you finally have the money to get your business running.

## FINANCIAL CHALLENGES THAT KINGDOM ENTREPRENEURS FACE

Starting up a new business is always challenging, no matter how old you are. Entrepreneurs of all ages must face down the negativity of well-meaning friends and family members who think that they'll end up bankrupt if they follow their business dream. There's also the added burden of self-doubt and fear that the naysayers will be right. Following your dream of starting your own business requires a lot of strength and determination. Along with all of this, there are some specific financial challenges that kingdom entrepreneurs must contend with which don't affect older businessmen as frequently. Here are six challenges facing kingdom entrepreneurs that you might not have considered.

### Lack of Personal Capital

Every new business idea, no matter whether it's for products or services, requires one vital thing: money. It can take years before a new business is making a profit, but that doesn't mean it won't succeed. Every entrepreneur needs to begin with a certain amount of seed capital to pay for the cost of hiring staff, renting premises, buying, or leasing equipment, marketing, etc.

Entrepreneurs who are middle-aged or older have often built up some savings that they can draw on in the very early stages. In contrast, young entrepreneurs are just at the beginning of their earning days. Not only do they not have any savings, but they are also frequently still paying off their student loans. They don't have any nest egg to use as emergency funding.

### Fewer Nexusing Contacts

When you start a business while still in your twenties or thirties, most of your schoolmates and college friends are still just starting out too. You don't yet have a web of connections in high places or contacts with successful jobs who would be willing to invest in your business idea just because they believe in you.

When you're searching for funding options you also lack those well-placed connections who could suggest your nascent business to a venture capitalist they know, or who would serve as a valuable reference in your hunt for funding.

With fewer established connections in the business world, young entrepreneurs also lack a natural way to promote their products or services. It can take longer for your business to become known without the support of any well-respected businessmen, which means it can also take longer to turn a profit.

## Poor Credit History

In general, the older you are, the better your credit history is. Older entrepreneurs have generally had time to build a solid and high credit rating. Their youthful mistakes disappeared off of their credit reports long ago. But young entrepreneurs aren't in the same situation. All their foolish financial mistakes are still very prominent on their credit reports, making credit card companies and loan companies alike turn them down for financing or offer only very high rates.

Sometimes, young entrepreneurs only have a poor credit history because they are still young. If you only got your own credit card for the first time a few years ago, you might not yet have built up enough credit history to show a good credit score. Notice that there are credit cards for borrowers with fair credit that might be useful for young entrepreneurs.

## Age Discrimination

Youth might have the energy, but as you get older, you tend to be viewed as wiser and more responsible. This is an advantage when you need to convince investors that you're a reasonable financial risk. Young entrepreneurs can find that some bank managers and investors are very reluctant to trust them with a loan or venture funding simply because they think that they are too young.

## Fearing Debt

No one likes the feeling of owing money, but as you get older you realize that some debt can be positive, depending on the loan and its purpose. A short-term business loan that's taken out with careful planning of repayment schedules and with the right APR rates can be an excellent way to deal with startup capital or early cash flow issues.

However, young entrepreneurs often still feel nervous or even scared about getting into debt. For many younger entrepreneurs it's not even an issue of fearing debt but of fearing piling it too high. Many people who start a business in their twenties and thirties are still paying off student loan debt and have a mortgage and/or auto loan to pay off, as well. Adding a business loan to that might just be too daunting.

**No Safety Net**
Older entrepreneurs also often already have retirement fund and pension that they can fall back on if their business fails. Young entrepreneurs can be struggling to raise money for their startup at the same time as wanting to settle down in a relationship and perhaps start a family. The lack of a financial safety-net can be very worrying to young entrepreneurs. Although young entrepreneurs must deal with unique challenges that don't affect older entrepreneurs, they also have energy and a fresh perspective that bring unique advantages so that they can still succeed.

## WHY IS IT SO HARD FOR ENTREPRENEURS TO GET FUNDING?

Traditional bank loans for small businesses have historically been tough to obtain, but recent market trends are making it even more difficult for new startups to get the funding they deserve. According to Ewing Marion Kauffman Foundation, there are three primary barriers entrepreneurs face in accessing capital:

1. **The disappearance of community banks.** Small community banks are often more willing to take a chance on budding business owners, but their numbers have been steadily declining since the Great Recession of 2008. Large banks have become larger by swallowing up their smaller competitors and are often unwilling to make loans under $100,000 because they're simply not profitable. This hurts the average startup founder, who only needs about $30,000 on average.

2. **The rise of service-based businesses with no collateral.** Most modern startups are service-based businesses with a cash flow business model. Traditional bank loans are typically made against a business's assets, but without significant collateral, these new service firms don't meet the underwriting criteria for many big banks.

3. **Venture capital's focus on 'high growth potential.'** Stories of wildly successful investor-backed startups and aspirational shows like *Shark Tank* have fueled dreams of venture capital (VC) for new entrepreneurs. While it's true that VC firms have helped founders achieve astounding growth, it's an incredibly small percentage of them. Kauffman Foundation found that just 0.6% of businesses raise VC due to the industry's focus on companies with the potential for "high growth."

Among the startups that received VC in 2016, more than three quarters of them were in California, Massachusetts, or New York. Moreover, almost all of them were white, male founders: Women and founders of color received less than 2% each of VC that year. The rise of alternative lenders issuing faster, smaller loans with less restrictive criteria is a beacon of hope for current and aspiring founders. However, there's still a long way to go before access to funding is truly equitable for all entrepreneurs.

## STARTUP FUNDING CHALLENGES AND HOW TO OVERCOME THEM

Innovative products and business models are the foundations of a promising startup. However, you'll also need a steady flow of funds, especially in the early stages, to turn those ideas into reality. Funding is crucial for improving technology, hiring the right people, and launching a comprehensive marketing strategy to get a foothold in the market. However, sourcing enough money to start your new venture can be difficult. As an entrepreneur, you will face several challenges while seeking the funds, in part because you'll have to convince others that your idea is a solid investment.

1. **Creating a Scalable Business Model**
Whether you are hoping to expand a small business with a loan or going for a round of venture capital, you will need a scalable business model. Investors in particular want to fund only scalable or ready to scale businesses. Your business model must show the potential to increase the revenue with minimal expenditure in the coming months or years.

This means being able to increase profits without increasing costs at an equal (or higher) rate. Sure, it should be unique. But without scalability, it is less likely to be investable. Usually, scalable business models have higher profit margin and lower infrastructure and marketing investment. While expanding, your business model needs to remain aligned with the company's core offerings. In other words, if your business model is likely to result in the overextension of time, money, and resources, investors will be hesitant to welcome you with open arms.

2. **Determining How Much Money to Ask For**
Whether you are asking angel investors to fund your expansion or seeking a bank loan, you must know how much money you need. Most people would say you should raise as much money as you can. However, in many cases, more isn't always better.

   a. **Write a business plan.**
   It is not possible to chalk out how you are going to spend the money without having a business plan. In fact, most investors (and zero banks) will fund your venture without a complete business plan. Your business plan also needs to have a realistic financial forecast. You should forecast the expected cost the investment or loan will cover, and the returns it will generate in future. The projected statistics, facts, and figures must have a justification.

   b. **Be specific and concrete.**
   When investors pay you, they expect to see how you plan to spend their money. They will expect you to spend the funds to grow your business to its next milestone. In other words, they wouldn't be impressed if you intend to invest in fancy furniture or unnecessary automation. Milestones need to be measurable achievements such as launching a new product or reaching a specific market share. Every business will have a few rollercoaster moments. However, your business should be able to show consistent achievements.

- c. **Demonstrate that your company has positive cash flow**

    Showing that you are cash flow positive is key, especially for small startups and small businesses looking for expansion. There is no single approach here. Usually, better cash flow increases the chances of receiving desired funding. Calculate how much money you will need to for the necessary production, training, hiring, marketing, and automation to create a viable financial model. Figure out where your cash flow bottoms out and add appropriate buffer accordingly. Make sure your funding request is in-line with your financial projections.

- d. **More investment isn't always better**

    More funding can equate to increased pressure to scale up your business quickly. Although it can be helpful for healthy growth, sometimes it can prove detrimental. Companies that have received huge amounts of investment fail every day because they couldn't manage the rapid expansion. The bottom line is to ask for money your business needs and can handle.

3. **Finding the right funding option**

As mentioned in the beginning, many new startup funding options are available today. To increase your chances of getting the funds, you need to choose the most suitable funding alternative. Sometimes, you may also need to use more than one option to fund your startup.

- a. Bootstrapping or self-funding

    The best (and the cheapest) option for funding your business is using your own savings or borrow from your family and friends. Flexible investment terms and quick availability make it an attractive funding source.

- b. Your own savings and income

    Tapping into your 401(k) or personal savings may seem tempting. However, if things don't pan out, you lose your business and your nest egg. Many entrepreneurs choose to both run their startup and work a day job until their startup is profitable.

c. **Family and friends**

Asking your family and friends to invest in your startup also comes with considerable risks. You are not only risking their financial future but also potentially jeopardizing personal relationships. You can, however, readily overcome these risks by writing a formal business plan just like the one you would use to attract professional investors. Then, handle the loan with professionalism. Document the terms (particularly what will happen if you can't pay back the money) and stick to your agreement.

d. **Credit cards**

Your bank may offer special credit cards for individual entrepreneurs and small business owners. If you have good credit, it can be a simple option. It is also the most expensive option, as credit card debt comes with high-interest rates. Most credit cards are also personal, meaning that if your business goes bankrupt, you are still personally liable for any debt. Plus, your credit score will take a hit the moment you miss a payment—this can affect your ability to secure funding in the future.

e. **Bank loans**

A bank loan is also a reliable funding option for a small business or startup. You may also be able to apply for government-subsidized bank loans or soft loans. Small Business Administration (SBA) loans can be a good option. The SBA doesn't administer loans, but when you apply for an SBA backed loan from your bank, the SBA promises to pay back a portion of the loan to the lender if you default. Basically, this makes it possible for banks to take a risk on granting a loan to a small business that might not otherwise qualify. Most traditional bank loans require at least two years of tax returns showing gross and net profits. In other words, you need a good credit history. Banks will also ask for collateral such as equipment or real estate. They will always ask you for your full, traditional business plan. Make sure it includes financial statements or projections, personal and business credit reports, tax returns, bank statements, and growth projections.

f. **Angel investors**

Angel investors may offer more flexible investment terms compared to the venture capital firms. They tend to invest large sums of money (but no more than $1 million) in exchange for equity in the startup. Angel investment may not be the right option for a small shop owner, but small plant owners, tech startups, or firms can take advantage of this source. The significant disadvantage of using angel investors is losing the ownership of a part of your company in exchange for the money. They will also have a say in how the business is run, and they'll be highly interested in your exit strategy, as they will make most of their money when your business is sold.

g. **Venture capital**

Venture capitalists are like angel investors. However, they tend to invest upwards of $2 million. Being professional investors, they can provide guidance in growing your business; they'll also probably be interested in having a say in how your business operates. Most VC firms will rarely invest in small businesses such as coffee shops, bars, and proprietary stores because they're not built on business models that are designed for rapid growth and huge expansion. But, if your coffee brand is trying to expand into a super chain like Starbucks, for example, they might be keenly interested in investing.

Keep in mind that venture capital firms will invest at a point when injecting more capital into your business will result in further growth and more profit.

h. **Crowdfunding**

Crowdfunding can help you to reach a broad group of potential investors and possibly generate publicity for your startup. However, crowdfunding campaigns require a significant amount of time and planning, and your ability to achieve funding often rests on whether you already have a wide Nexus that you can access to ask for support. Plus, some platforms mandate that if your campaign fails to raise the target amount, you don't receive any funding at all. To succeed, you must make your campaign visible, measurable, and understandable. Having a well-established Nexus of friends and professional contacts can increase the chances of a successful campaign. Each option comes with a distinct set of advantages and disadvantages. You will have to make your decision based on your situation and you might seek several different types of funding.

4. **Spending wisely once you're funded**

   a. **Stick to your plan**
   If you took investment, you're accountable to your investors to do what you said you would do with their funds and to be transparent if you're thinking of changing course. Avoid going on a spending spree. Don't spend the money on overly expensive furniture, workspace, infrastructure, equipment, business trips, and lunches. Save the splurge for when you're bringing in more revenue.

   b. **Spend wisely on tech**
   If you haven't assessed your technology needs already, you need to do it before spending the funds. Find out what type of software and hardware upgrades are available for your business and choose the most affordable yet feature-rich options. Technology spending should always focus on future marketing and branding successes.

   c. **Keep your investors in the loop**
   Chances are you decided to seek outside investment, your contract requires you to give investors their proper return in due time. However, showing them that their money is being put to good use will help forge a bond of trust.

# THE TOP 10 CHALLENGES FACED BY KINGDOM ENTREPRENEURS TODAY

Entrepreneurs face many challenges in today's ultra-competitive business world. Fortunately, entrepreneurs also have more resources than ever before to tackle those problems. The following 10 challenges are faced by many entrepreneurs today. Perhaps you've run up against some of them already. Read on to learn why each challenge exists and to get solutions and workarounds so you can operate your business efficiently and successfully.

## 1. Cash Flow Management

**The challenge:** cash flow is essential to small business survival, yet many entrepreneurs struggle to pay the bills (let alone themselves) while they're waiting for checks to arrive. Part of the problem stems from delayed invoicing, which is common in the entrepreneurial world. You perform a job, send an invoice, then get paid (hopefully) 30 days later. In the meantime, you must pay everything from your employees or contractors to your mortgage, to your grocery bill. Waiting to get paid can make it difficult to get by, and when a customer doesn't pay, you can risk losing everything.

**The solution:** proper budgeting and planning are critical to maintaining cash flow, but even these won't always save you from stressing over bills. One way to improve cash flow is to require a down payment for your products and services. Your down payment should cover all expenses associated with a given project or sale as well as some profit for you. By requiring a down payment, you can at least rest assured you won't be left paying others' bills. By padding the down payment with some profit, you can pay your own.

Another strategy for improving cash flow is to require faster invoice payments. Invoice clients within 15 days, which is half the typical invoice period. This means if a customer is late with a payment, you have two weeks to address it and get paid before the next month's bills are due. In addition, more and more companies are requiring immediate payment upon project completion and in our digital age when customers can pay invoices right from their mobile phones, it's not a stretch to request immediate payment.

You can also address cash flow management from the other side of the equation by asking your own vendors to invoice you at 45, 60 or even 90 days to allow ample time for your payments to arrive and checks to clear. If you can establish a good relationship with vendors and are a good customer, they may be willing to work with you once you explain your strategy.

## 2. Hiring Employees

**The challenge:** do you know who dreads job interviews the most? It's not prospective candidates, it's entrepreneurs. The hiring process can take several days of your time: reviewing resumes, sitting through interviews, sifting through unqualified candidates. Then, you only hope you can offer an attractive package to get the best people on board and retain them.

**The solution:** be exclusive. Far too many helps wanted ads are incredibly vague in terms of what qualifications candidates must have, what the job duties are, what days and hours will be worked, and what wages and benefits will be paid. You can save yourself a ton of time by pre-qualifying candidates through exclusive help wanted ads that are ultra-specific in what it takes to be hired at your firm, as well as what the day-to-day work entails. Approach your employee hunt the same way you would approach a customer-centric marketing campaign through excellent targeting.

Once you have a pool of prospects, arrange for a "walking interview" in which you take candidates on a tour of their working environments. Ask questions relevant to the job and to candidates' experiences, expectations, dedication, and long-term goals. Don't act like an overlord determining which minion gets to live another day; rather, behave as though you're seeking a partner to help you operate and grow your business.

Take the time to seek real references, not the neighbor lady your candidates grew up with, but people who can honestly attest to their work ethic and potential. Once you've picked a candidate and before you've made a job offer, ask them specifically what it will take to keep them employed with you for the long haul. Tell them to be honest with their expectations. Provided they do a good job for you, you'll know what kind of rewards they're seeking, and you can adjust accordingly. Find out: do they want more vacation? The opportunity for advancement? More pay? Freedom from micromanagement?

This isn't to say you must bend backward for your employees; however, it stands to reason that if you make expectations clear for both parties you can lay the foundation for a long-term, mutually rewarding client-boss relationship.

### 3. Time Management

**The challenge:** time management might be the biggest problem faced by entrepreneurs, who wear many (and sometimes all) hats. If you only had more time, you could accomplish so much more!

**The solution:** make time. Like money, it doesn't grow on trees, so you have to be smart about how you spend it. Here are some tips:

- Create goal lists: you should have a list of lifetime goals, broken down into annual goals, broken down into monthly goals, then broken down into weekly goals. Your weekly goals then will be broken down into specific tasks by day. In this manner, what is on your task list in any given day is all you need to do to stay on track with your lifetime goals.
- If any tasks do not mesh with your goals, eliminate them.
- If any tasks do not absolutely have to be completed by you, delegate them.
- Consistently ask yourself: "Is what I'm doing right now the absolute best use of my time?"

### 4. Delegating Tasks

**The challenge:** you know you need to delegate or outsource tasks, but it seems every time you do, something gets messed up, and you have to redo it anyway.

**The solution:** find good employees (see above) and good outsourced contract help, for a start. You might have to pay a little more for it, but the savings in time (and the resulting earning potential) more than make up for it.

Next, be specific as to what you want done. It will take a little more time at first but write down detailed steps listing exactly what you want your help to do. Don't make assumptions, and don't assume your help will be able to think for themselves right off the bat. So, don't say, "List stats in a spreadsheet," when it's more effective to instruct them to "Alphabetically list XYZ in the first spreadsheet column, then list statistic A in the next column," and so on. It might seem like overkill, but take the time to be specific once, and your help will get it right every time thereafter.

5.  **Choosing What to Sell**

**The challenge:** you know you could make a mint if you just knew what products and services to sell. You're just unsure how to pick a niche.

**The solution:** admit that you're weak in identifying prosperous niches, and delegate the task to someone who is strong in this area. You don't have to hire a huge, expensive marketing firm; rather, recruit a freelance researcher who has experience in whatever type of field you're considering entering (retail e-commerce, service industry, publishing, etc.). Have them conduct market research and create a report with suggested niches, backed by potential profit margins and a complete SWOT analysis: Strengths, Weaknesses, Opportunities and Threats.

This isn't to say you should have someone else decide for you; however, if you're not good at identifying niches, it makes sense to receive suggestions from someone who is. You can then analyze the suggestions for yourself to determine if you agree. Taking this step now can save you a lot of time, money, and hassles later not to mention your entire business and livelihood.

6. **Marketing Strategy**

**The challenge:** you don't know the best way to market your products and services: print, online, mobile, advertising, etc. You want to maximize your return on investment with efficient, targeted marketing that gets results.

**The solution:** again, if you're not adept at creating marketing plans and placing ads, it's a good idea to outsource your marketing strategy to someone who is. At this point, all you need is a core marketing plan: who is your audience, and what marketing activities will you undertake to motivate purchases? Give your planner a budget and tell them to craft a plan that efficiently uses that budget to produce profits.

This is not the time for experimentation. You can do that later, after you've established a baseline that works.

7. **Capital**

**The challenge:** you want to start or grow your business, but you have little capital to do it.

**The solution:** there are many ways to earn funding, from traditional bank loans to Kickstarter campaigns and self-fueled growth models.

Instead of trying to launch a multimillion-dollar corporation overnight, focus on your initial core customers. Continually work to find new customers, of course, but consistently strive to be remarkable to those customers you already serve. Word-of-mouth will spread, and more customers will come looking for you. As they do, develop systems and business processes that allow you to delegate tasks without sacrificing quality. Your business will grow slow and steady, and you'll be able to solve problems while they're small.

Think about where you want to be five years from now. Can you get there without help, even if you must delay growth a bit while you're doing it? If you do feel you need funding, however, be sure to consult an attorney to make sure you're not giving up too much of your business to get it.

8. **Strapped Budget**
**The challenge:** even though cash flow is fine, it seems you never have enough in your budget to market your company to its full potential.

**The solution:** nearly every entrepreneur struggles with their budget at one point or another. The key is to prioritize your marketing efforts. With efficiency in mind, spend your money where it works and reserve the rest for operating expenses and experimenting with other marketing methods.

Keep a close eye on your money too: there may be areas you can skim to free up more funds. Unless an expense is critical to your business and/or represents an investment with an expected return, cut it. In fact, do this exercise: see how lean you can run your business. You don't have to do it but cut everything you can and see if you still feel you can run your business (save for what you have to delegate and market with). Somewhere in between your leanest figure and your current budget is a sweet spot that will allow you to be just as effective and leave funds leftover to fuel growth.

9. **Business Growth**
**The challenge:** you've come to the point at which you can't take on any more work in your current structure.

**The solution:** create new processes that focus on task delegation. Many entrepreneurs, used to wearing all the hats, find themselves in this position once they've achieved a modicum of success. Because you're doing everything, your growth halts to a stop when it hits a self-imposed ceiling. The only way to break through is to delegate tasks to others to take yourself out of the production end and segue into management and, finally, pure ownership.

10. **Self-Doubt**
**The challenge:** an entrepreneur's life is not enviable, at least in the beginning. It's extremely easy to get discouraged when something goes wrong or when

you're not growing as fast as you'd like. Self-doubt creeps in, and you may feel like giving up.

**The solution:** being able to overcome self-doubt is a necessary trait for entrepreneurs. Having a good support system will help family and friends who know your goals and support your plight, as well as an advisory board of other entrepreneurs who can objectively opine as to the direction of your business.

One of the best ways to deal with self-doubt is to work on your goals and tasks lists. When you're down and lack motivation, look at your lists and know that the tasks you do today are contributing to your lifetime goals. By doing them, you're one step closer, and you can rest assured that you are, indeed, on the path to business success.

Entrepreneurs face many challenges, and volumes have been written about how to overcome them. Perseverance and intelligence are your allies; use them to your advantage to keep working toward your goals. Understand that you're not the first to struggle. Because of that, there are many resources available to help you get through your darkest days as an entrepreneur, so you can reap the immeasurable rewards that come with building your own successful business.

# CHAPTER 5

# DISCOVER YOUR STRENGTH – POTENTIAL

How do you discover entrepreneur potentials in you? How do you improve on your overall personality so that those hidden natural gifts could be discovered? We all have some traits of potential greatness in ourselves. But the daunting task lies in discovering ourselves. Entrepreneurship is an inbuilt attribute we all seem to possess. However, the problem is how to discover and apply all these great attributes. Each of us has those attributes that many successful entrepreneurs possess, but our problem is discovering and working on it. But how to discover our entrepreneur potentials is the only problem with most of us. Nowadays, it's even much easier to discover your potential. All you must do is to look inward, and you will see that there are several real-life challenges that can wake up your entrepreneurship brain.

## CAN YOU DESCRIBE YOURSELF?

I was recently asked the above question by a friend at a seminar for aspiring young CEOs and it took me longer than usual to answer the question. It's not because I don't know what to say but it's just that I didn't expect such a question to come up at such gathering. After all, it's not as if it's a blind date gathering or an online matchmaking website where you will be expected to describe yourself in one or two sentences. So, after the seminar and exchange of pleasantries with other participants, I had a second thought of the question—"Can you describe yourself?"

Now, I am writing about it because not many of us young people can describe ourselves and our potentials. This is because most young people don't even know who they are in the first place. Also, most young people have no idea of who and what they can aspire to become.

## DISCOVERING ENTREPRENEUR POTENTIALS IN YOU

Entrepreneurship inspiration can come from anywhere; it can come from watching a movie, listening to inspiring podcasts, or attending a seminar. Also, you can get motivation from reading inspiring books, novels, or magazines. Some people are 'accidental entrepreneurs'—something just happened, and they are motivated to cash in on the situation.

So, what kind of an entrepreneur are you? Have you been able to discover who you really are? Take note of the fact that you will never be able to describe yourself if you have not yet discovered who you truly are. Discover yourself and what you want to achieve in life is the first major step you need to take. This is the only belonging you will be taking along with you anywhere you go.

The important thing to remember is that most of the young CEOs of today started at the average age of 17. So, as at the age of 20, if you still have not discovered yourself, then you will have to sit tight and have a serious thought about your future.

## ATTRIBUTES OF ENTREPRENEUR POTENTIALS

Young people of today are more enterprising than before most especially because they are being inspired by other successful entrepreneurs, and the inspiration helps them to discover their potentials.

**1. Always Want to Improve Everything**
If you are that type of person that is always interested in improving everything you lay your hands upon, then there is something in you that can potentially

make a name for you as an entrepreneur. Some people always seem to know how they could do things better; they are constructive critics and highly opinionated. So, if you are one of them, you must sit tight and think about how you can better present your ideas.

2. **Be Creative**

Some people have been fired from their jobs not because they're not good but because they are deemed too good. Some people are so creative that their manager feels threatened that they might end up taking their position. So, rather than tapping into their creative skills, the manager will get them sacked out of jealousy and fear for their jobs. Being creative could be a good sign for you to start your own business and become your boss. If you think you are too creative when it comes to working for others, then you really need to explore the possibility of you doing it your way. Remember someone once said that necessity is the mother of invention; it is true, but invention's father is creativity, and knowledge is the midwife.

3. **Be Persistent**

You can discover the entrepreneur's potentials in yourself if you are persistent and wouldn't let something you started to go until you are a hundred percent sure that it's completely done to your taste. At times, your being obsessive is not a disease or deficiency and doesn't necessarily mean that you have a problem. It could mean you wouldn't give up until you get a result and that the result is satisfactory. This is a common attribute amongst all of the great entrepreneurs that helped them achieve lots of things.

## HOW TO DISCOVER AND UNLEASH YOUR STRENGTHS AS AN ENTREPRENEUR

If you want to become a successful entrepreneur, you need to discover your strengths and give yourself every possible opportunity to leverage them each day. You need to be good at what you do. Taking the time to discover your strengths and focus on perfecting the skills that'll help you become the best in your industry becomes a very crucial decision point in every entrepreneur's journey. Especially on the road to validating a business idea, getting the early traction and acquiring your first paying customers is crucial.

Through my interviews and experiences working with successful entrepreneurs, I've come to notice many remarkable similarities they tend to share. They're often ruthless when it comes to both opportunity management and time management, which very quickly become defining traits as an entrepreneur. They know the importance of optimizing their lifestyle and doing their most challenging work at the time of day that best suits them. They never give up and actively refuse to take no for an answer.

However, what I've found interesting is that while every entrepreneur I've had the opportunity to meet shares a common resilience and drive for success, they also have just as many glaring differences between each other.

Their approach to achieving success, and the tools they employ in doing so vary greatly. Often, their most noticeable differences lie in the core strengths they possess. On the other hand, their similarities emanate from how well they've identified and improved their strengths over time to compensate for what they lacked in other skills, talents, and character traits.

## THE IMPORTANCE OF DISCOVERING YOUR STRENGTHS AND LEVERAGING THEM

Here's a real-life example.

Early tech rivals Bill Gates (of Microsoft) and Steve Jobs (of Apple) both introduced radical innovations in the world of computing that have had a far-reaching impact on the lives of nearly everyone on the planet. But they could not have been more different when it comes to their entrepreneurial strengths.

While Gates himself was a highly skilled software engineer who personally wrote code for Microsoft products as late as 1989, Jobs was an unmatched design thinker who attended calligraphy classes as an informal student and never wrote a single line of code for Apple.

These two entrepreneurs made lasting impacts with very similar product offerings, in the same industry, during the same period, with a completely different set of strengths and skills. It was their shared ability to identify and lean on their most useful strengths and skills that allowed them to achieve such greatness.

Some entrepreneurs, like Richard Branson and Mark Cuban, thrive on interpersonal skills, leveraging their people Nexuses to grow their businesses over time. Others get their start by leveraging their well-trained technical skills, like Elon Musk and Mark Zuckerberg.

Yet still, others are driven by creativity, like Leo Burnett and Walt Disney, which enables them to inspire large numbers of people with their creations. Or on the other hand, my own mastery of useful blogging skills has been immensely helpful in skyrocketing my business... which has led to new opportunities talking about subjects like podcast hosting, the best blog hosting, and much more over time.

There are a nearly unlimited number of character traits such as leadership ability, being a good negotiator, and having a laser-like focus, that can contribute to your success as an entrepreneur.

The deciding factor in how successful you'll become in the world of business is really how quickly and effectively you can find your strengths, build them into valuable assets for your cause, and focus relentlessly on only doing activities and getting into business ideas that engage your strengths.

In 2014, Gallup revealed the findings of a mind-blowing study about entrepreneurship, which involved years of research and collaboration with 2,500 entrepreneurs towards building a better understanding of business creation and growth. Among other things, the study uncovered two very interesting findings.

While other business icons and researchers may disagree on what the ten talents are that drive entrepreneurial success, there's undoubtedly an overwhelming consensus that success is most often achieved by focusing on utilizing your core strengths and talents.

This could not be truer for me, and in everything I do with my business.

I'm a huge advocate of never starting a business in an industry I haven't operated in, and never serving customers I'm not already very familiar with. It's part of my system for launching a successful business. Thus, nurturing my core strengths and focusing on doing only what I do best (for the people I can best serve) has become crucial to my success.

### SHOULD YOU IMPROVE UPON YOUR WEAKNESSES?

I feel very strongly that unless your weaknesses will truly cripple your business goals, you should do everything in your power to avoid business opportunities and roles where you'd be forced to use them at all. Sometimes it's inevitable that you'll need to do things you're not good at, and that's fine. However, you should strive to limit that exposure whenever possible.

When new opportunities come my way as a freelance content marketer, if they require doing activities that aren't within my core strengths if they're not around building and executing on a content marketing strategy, I've found it best to either actively turn down that work or outsource those weaknesses to others who can help compliment me.

Here's my reasoning. Time is infinitely more valuable than money to me. Would you rather spend your time driving business growth by using the strengths you're already skilled at, or should you spend your limited personal time learning a new skill that's currently outside of your wheelhouse? There are times when taking a pit stop to pick up a new skill, like learning how to code, can be very worthwhile (or essential), but only if your goal is to develop that skill into a core strength for the years to come.

### 8 STEPS TO DISCOVER YOUR STRENGTHS AS AN ENTREPRENEUR

Some people are good with numbers. Some are skilled at coding. Others (like me) are great at telling stories and simplifying complex ideas.

How about you? What are you good at?

We've established that knowing your strengths and actively playing to them is key to succeeding in any business you start. Your strengths (talents, skills, passions, character traits) may have been the spark that drove you to want to start a business in the first place. That's why you need to focus on building the best strengths for entrepreneurs.

Before moving on, it's important to first make a clear distinction between soft skills and hard skills, as they'll combine to make up your entrepreneurial strengths. Soft skills are personal attributes that enable you to interact effectively and harmoniously with other people. Hard skills are specific, teachable abilities that can be defined and measured.

1. **Determining Your Soft Skills**

As we mentioned above, soft skills are the attributes that enable you to interact effectively and harmoniously with other people.

In short, these are the skills you possess that you can't necessarily quantify. This is your EI (Emotional Intelligence), not your IQ (Intelligent Quotient). Here are some examples of soft skills:

- Having a strong sense of self-awareness
- Being optimistic
- Being resilient
- Having patience
- Being a good listener

Some people pretty much only possessed soft skills. What I lacked in hard skills like coding talent, marketing chops, and writing abilities at the time, I significantly made up for in determination, optimism, and people skills that would help me build the meaningful connections I'd need, to get my business off the ground without doing everything myself. Later, I trained myself to become proficient with the hard skills my business (and future companies) would need.

In our comparison between Bill Gates and Steve Jobs from above, Jobs possessed and leaned on his strongest soft skills, to champion Apple through to success. In many ways, Jobs was a phenomenal example of the best skills for entrepreneurs to possess in terms of dedication to creating for the customer. Gates, on the other hand, in the beginning, took the opposite approach and utilized his hard skills within Microsoft.

## 2. Breaking down Your Biggest Wins

During the week I launched my very first online course on winning freelance clients, I slept an average of 4-5 hours each night and still made it into work at my day job.

Yet still, I felt energized every single day of that week. I was emailing back and forth with people who were considering buying my course, answering tons of questions, and giving away some of the content for free to the motivated people that simply couldn't afford to buy it at the time. I built so many great relationships that continue to flourish. I loved it, even though it was an incredibly difficult week. This was a huge win for me.

From the events that transpired that week, I learned so much about myself in terms of which soft skills of mine continued to bubble up to the surface and help me become successful. To name just a few, I learned that I very naturally fall into the role of becoming a personal mentor to people, I learned that I was even more open to critical feedback than I previously believed, and I got to see a direct, positive impact on how my sense of humor helped me drive clear business results. This launch experience taught me a lot about which soft skills I'd need to continue leveraging within my business.

Now, it's your turn. Think of a time you did a challenging work project, or a time you felt particularly accomplished with something you worked on. Ask yourself what exactly you were doing at the time, and which soft skills you employed to help you achieve your result.

## 3. Figuring Out What Comes Naturally to You

Part of determining what your strengths are as an entrepreneur is taking an inward look back into the past and figuring out what you've always been natural at.

What have your friends, coaches, teachers, managers, or even your parents always told you you're a natural at? This can fall into many different categories, so don't get hung up on thinking of this as a strictly "on the court" or "in the classroom" type of strength. Start by asking yourself these questions:

- Did you always find yourself being the mediator between your group of friends?

- Was it always easier for you to pick up complex physics theories in class?
- Were you often the one making plans and figuring out the logistics of getting from point A to point B?
- Are you a naturally talented athlete?
- Do you make others smile and laugh?

Focus on coming up with at least five things you're natural at, and then break down which soft skills of yours have helped you be so natural. These are most likely the strongest soft skills you've possessed since very early on in your life.

### 4. Asking Others What Your Strengths Are

Once you've done some introspection and come up with a handful of strengths that you believe to be your strongest assets, it's time to turn to the people you know and trust, to get an outside opinion. Left completely to my own devices a few years ago, I would've thought that one of my most valuable strengths at the time was my ability to build my WordPress website without needing outside development or design assistance to create my dream blog layout.

And you know what? That is still a strength in my book. However, in the grand scheme of things, working on website features isn't the best utilization of my time and it's not what I'm best at. I decided that to be as successful as possible with my business, I need to be only doing what I'm best at and leveraging my strongest skills in the process.

It was my close group of friends and business mentors that helped guide me to a place where I could identify the fact that I'm much better suited at spending my time writing (one of my greatest strengths) and connecting directly with the people in my community, as opposed to getting deep in the woods of working on website features. Without that clarity, I would've been wasting some of my talents.

You're going to ask them to share with you what they believe to be three of your biggest strengths, and if they can include any examples of when you demonstrated those abilities, that's a major plus. Your goal is to get a consensus back from those who know you best, about what they perceive to be your strengths. The responses could completely surprise you or help validate your business idea and confirm what you already believe to be true about yourself.

## 5. Run through a Hypothetical Scenario

Imagine your boss, coach, or teacher gives you a group project that needs to be completed by the end of the week. Your success at your job, on the court, or in the classroom depends solely upon completing this activity well, and it's a great opportunity to show what you're made of. Seriously, think of an example in your head. Create a hypothetical situation that's relevant to your life and where you're at right now, in which you have three team members joining you on this project. Now, ask yourself which role you naturally assume within your group. Do you become the organizer, leader, creator, moderator, take a back seat, or something else entirely?

- Is there a specific part of the project you're more naturally inclined to take on?
- Do you like the overall planning phase (like creating a blog business plan), or do you prefer getting straight down to business and doing the actual legwork during the project?
- Do you take the initiative to assign responsibilities, or do you prefer to be given your role within the group?
- Do you interject if someone else starts to take over the role you want within the group?

Answering all these questions for yourself will tell you a great deal about how you work in teams, and which strengths you'll naturally play to. From there, you can take a look back at which soft skills help you through the process of working on a group project.

## 6. What Are Some of Your Hard Skills?

Hard skills are your well-defined, easily measured strengths and abilities. These are what most people think of when it comes to "skills," but they aren't, in my opinion, what is most important when it comes to becoming a successful entrepreneur. They can always be learned over time, whereas a soft skill, like being a strong leader, isn't acquired by attending an online business course on nights and weekends.

Nevertheless, acknowledging, understanding, and focusing on using your hard skills is essential to maximizing your success potential. Here are a few examples of common hard skills that entrepreneurs possess:

- Coding: Writing HTML, CSS, Ruby, JavaScript, etc.
- Design: Proficiency with Adobe Photoshop, Illustrator, InDesign, etc.
- Writing: Being able to take complex ideas, break them down into digestible bits and craft them into compelling stories
- Analysis: Advanced financial modeling abilities in Microsoft Excel, complex statistical analysis, data mining, advising on taxes for bloggers
- Marketing: Search Engine Optimization, SEM, proficiency with social media platforms, being adept at promoting a blog

For me, my most prominent hard skills are my writing ability, advanced working knowledge of the Adobe Creative Suite, and a deep understanding of SEO. The combination of these three hard skills is what helped me start a blog, come up with smart blog post ideas that can become high-quality content, develop visually appealing content for my online blogging courses and execute on my plans to make money blogging.

On top of that, I've been able to grow in my ability to teach others how to write a blog post, how to write a headline that converts, best practices for outlining a blog post, writing an eBook, identifying, and finding a target audience, what it takes to nail your blog SEO and plenty more blogging-related skills that can now be monetized in many different ways.

7. **What Do You Love to Do?**

How would you spend your time if you didn't have to go to work every day? Look first to the things you already do in your limited free hours around work and spending time with friends and family. Do you like helping your friends talk through difficult situations at work or in their personal lives? Do you spend your free time writing about life lessons you've learned through your travels? Do you go on outdoor adventures every weekend?

If you're anything like me, then you love to do the things you're already good at. It's human nature. Trying new things and risking failure can be uncomfortable at first. At this point in my life, I have a true love for sharing my experiences in business through my writing and pushing myself to my limits with long-distance running. If I could do any two of those things completely full-time, I would (and that's the plan). By my measure, I'm already good at both writing and running.

However, when I think back to how painful it was, as I was just beginning to sharpen my abilities at both, there were many times I contemplated giving up. Once I got my first handful of breakthroughs, I had the momentum and confidence to keep pushing, and slowly I began to love them both. Looking at the things you truly love doing and identifying which soft skills you employ most when doing these activities will help you further narrow down your core strengths as an entrepreneur.

## 8. Deciding What Comes Next

Once you've gone through the process of identifying all your core soft and hard skills, the real question is, what will you do with this knowledge? What you decide to do with this knowledge is completely up to you. The easiest thing to do is to stay contented with what you're doing at your day job, even if your work is meaningless.

I challenge you to start looking for more meaningful remote jobs (or for that matter, freelance jobs, work from home jobs, or blogging jobs that might be a good fit) where you can focus on building your core skills, engaging your strengths, and continue discovering what you're truly passionate about in life.

I've found that starting a side project can often be one of the most rewarding experiences you'll ever have. Mine (this website) has been an instrument by which I've gotten to have a connection, however small, with hundreds of thousands of people over the past couple of years. Now that's more motivating than any motivational quote I've seen.

## TIPS TO MAXIMIZE YOUR POTENTIAL AS AN ENTREPRENEUR

Any good entrepreneur will tell you the key to success is hard work. In a way, they're right, but they're also missing out a lot of other factors that will lead to true success. In the run-up to our Potential Workshop, we're sharing the essential factors that will improve your business and chances of success greatly.

### 1. Agility

For a business, agility refers to the ability to rapidly respond to change and adapt accordingly. Agility within yourself is also key—you'll need to recognize changes, build flexibility into your plans, and learn to adapt without causing yourself the stress. If you find it hard to be as agile as your business may need you to be, we recommend coming along to one of our workshops.

### 2. Awareness of Opportunities

Some people may list "luck" as a factor for success, but we interpret this as awareness of opportunities. By psychologically training yourself to be aware and appreciate incoming opportunities, you'll be far more likely to stumble across some golden opportunities.

### 3. Confidence

By stepping out into the business world on your own, you've already shown that first glimmer of confidence. You'll need to continue with it when growing your business. The best way to do that is to stay up to date with your industry and keep learning. Fear is a natural reaction when we feel uninformed or unsupported, so instead, breathe through that fear. Invite it in. And action is, accordingly, turning it into confidence.

### 4. Enjoyment

The key to enduring the entrepreneurial journey is finding joy along the way. Taking a moment to step back and make the most of your small wins and your growth will keep you moving forwards. Especially at this time of year, it's worth taking a moment to pause, reflect, and enjoy.

5. **Introspectiveness**

Nurturing the connection with yourself will strengthen many of the points on this list. Many business leaders meditate because introspection is so important for staying strong, open, and recognizing ways to realize your full potential. A connection is one of our key principles at Calmer.

6. **Patience**

For many entrepreneurs, waiting for success is especially tough. You may have planted the right seeds, and watered them correctly, but sometimes they take a while to bloom. Being patient is one of the hardest struggles for entrepreneurs, but there are ways to alleviate the stress it causes. Reflecting on small wins—i.e., steps towards success—is just one quick and easy way to realize how well you're doing. If waiting for success is affecting your wellbeing, we recommend following our Digital Wellbeing Training to learn how best to manage yourself and your business.

7. **Persistence**

Persistence is the sister to patience. Waiting for success to happen only works when we continue doing what we're doing. Whatever industry you're in, we bet there's no formula for success. Instead, it will take frequent and consistent hard work. And you have it in you.

8. **Self-discipline**

In our guide to successful habits of entrepreneurs, we placed routine as the #1 habit. While there's no routine to business—it comes in waves—you can take control by giving yourself a routine that suits you. That doesn't have to be the usual 9 a.m. – 5 p.m. either—only 6% of the UK workforce keeps to those hours! A good routine will foster a certain level of self-discipline, too. You'll be more focused during your designated hours and will have downtime to look forward to.

9. **Support Nexus**

We believe every entrepreneur deserves a support Nexus. Finding people who are in your position to swap stories with, learn from, and grow together is both fulfilling and will give you a sense of belonging. If you haven't already, please do join us in the Calmer Entrepreneur Facebook Group.

## 10. Willingness to Learn

A good entrepreneur never stops learning. Keeping up with your industry and growing your business knowledge is so important. And for the management of your mental health, we've got you covered.

### DISCOVERING THE ENTREPRENEURIAL POTENTIAL IN YOU

When you think of a successful entrepreneur, you immediately think of personality traits or values that define who they are. Richard Branson is associated with fun. Anita Roddick was an environmentalist. Steve Jobs lived by simplicity. Each one of these evokes an emotional connection with what they were good at (Richard still is).

So, what is an entrepreneur? What is entrepreneurship? There are many definitions, but the one that rings true to me is that of Peter Drucker: "This defines entrepreneur and entrepreneurship – the entrepreneur always searches for change, responds to it, and exploits it as an opportunity."

## 1. Have a Goal and a Plan and Work on It

Make sure that your goal is as specific as you can get it. If your goal is to increase your income, be specific about how much income you want increased. Decide your time frame—when you want your goal to be achieved. Create your plan to achieve your goal and get started. Don't procrastinate. If your plan isn't going the way you want it, don't give up. The secret is to have a plan. The content of the plan may change; you will make corrections as you go along, but if you persist regularly, you will reach your goal. It may be uncomfortable at first. You may feel that you're not making progress, but after a time, things will start happening very quickly to help you reach your goal. Persistence works.

2. **Get Over Your Limiting Beliefs**

It's more likely that the one thing that is stopping you from achieving what you want to do is YOU. Your self-belief influences your attitudes and behaviors. Stop and listen to the voice in your head. Is it a negative voice telling you you're not good enough, or that you can't afford XYZ? Where is that coming from? When you face a problem, sit down and try to write down as many reasons as you can think of (and some) on one half of a sheet of paper why you can't. Then on the other half, write down the exact opposite.

Focus on why you can. It is an excellent exercise for working out what in your past or childhood influenced your mind to believe the way it does. When you've finished—FLIP THE SWITCH. Use positive wording. When you wake up in the morning, make your first thoughts positive as they will influence your mood for the rest of the day.

3. **Your Five Best Friends**

Jim Rohn, a well-known entrepreneur and motivational speaker, said: "you are the average of the five people you spend the most time with" (p. 8). Look around, who are you spending your time with? Are these people able to motivate you to achieve your goals? Can they help you on your journey? If your friends are living a mundane existence, chances are it is comfortable for you to do the same. Snap out of it. Seek out new alliances to help you get to where you want to be.

Start with your goal and identify what skills and support you'll need. Identify five people and connect with them. One may be your mentor. One may be someone with the characteristics you wish to emulate. One may be someone with the contacts and Nexuses you need. Examine your Nexuses. Are there new Nexuses you can join that can open doors for you?

4. **Get a Mentor**

As Richard Branson said, when you think about the missing link between a promising businessperson and a successful one, mentoring comes to mind. On a lonely journey to discovery and success, a mentor provides a trusted arm and beacon along the way. You don't have to be a business owner to have a mentor.

You just need to have a goal and a strong desire to get there. A good mentor will guide you along the way.

**5. The Power of the Mastermind**

Napoleon Hill in *Think and Grow Rich* told of the power of the mastermind. Bring two or more minds together, and you create "a third invisible intangible likened to a third mind (the mastermind)" (p. 173). Bring two or more people together to work on their businesses in a mutual, trusting, tough love environment, coupled with voluntary accountability, will over-time, strengthen each business. A mastermind group that works well will achieve results through learning, sharing new ideas, and stimulating new ideas and business models.

# CHAPTER 6

# TEMPERAMENTS IN BUSINESS

A person's temperament is formed as an infant and never changes. It simply develops over time. Studies have shown that temperament remains constant and serves to help you determine how you will react to situations. It's a way to recognize consistent personality traits.

One study indicated that temperament is determined by brain-stem processes. Each person has a unique brain stem that cannot change throughout their life. More information will be provided about this as we look into the various temperaments you may hold.

**CAN YOUR TEMPERAMENT BE ALTERED?**
If you have a generally negative outlook, you have a lot of company. While your underlying temperament may be a permanent aspect of who you are, especially as you get older and continue building your experience based on how you see the world, you can certainly heal some of the ways that you feel and change your outlook on life. You're not going to be a whole other person, but you can make sure that a better tomorrow is possible with the right tools and mindset.

## THE FOUR TYPES OF TEMPERAMENT

Psychologists recognize four primary temperament types. The names of the types were originally names of humor in more distant times. It was believed that humor caused people to behave in certain ways. Although science has refuted the existence of humor in that fashion, the names of the four temperament types stuck.

It is possible, in fact likely, that someone will have both primary and secondary temperament types. A person can have any combination of temperament types to make up their overall personality. The four primary temperament types are explored below.

1. **Sanguine**

    Sanguine is the most common temperament type. It is typically either a primary type or a secondary type, although, of course, not everyone is sanguine. This temperament type is just as likely to be found in men as it is in women. Some people are considered "super sanguine" in that they are so overly talkative and active that it can be overwhelming to be around them.

    **Sanguine Orientation**

    Those with the sanguine temperament type are extremely people-oriented. They are outgoing and extroverted, and extremely talkative and social. They encourage people to work together and do good things for one another.

    **Sanguine Characteristics**

    People with the sanguine temperament type have a wide range of emotions and a wide range of behavior. They are the most versatile of all the temperaments. Depending on their secondary temperament, they might be involved in nearly any human activity. However, they enjoy occasions when they can interact with or change their environment.

    Sanguine temperament people are playful and impulsive. They are constantly active and always optimistic. They have a good sense of humor, are entertaining, and are easily amused. They are also expressive and affectionate. They build relationships easily and are trusting of others.

**Sanguine Traits**

When you first meet someone with a sanguine temperament, you're likely to feel you've known them for a long time. They are comfortable to talk to and get to know. They are extremely friendly, talkative, and social. They will frequently get caught up in conversations and lose track of time. However, if they get bored, they can lose attention quickly. Their attention span is directly related to how much they are enjoying the conversation or what they are doing.

Sanguine temperaments are also highly emotive. If they think it or feel it, they will say it. They have no filter. Their hyperactivity often leads to forgetfulness and being disorganized. This temperament type is extremely competitive. They dominate sports, politics, and the business world. They also fear making a bad impression and rejection. They want mostly to be accepted but also to be the best they can be.

2. **Phlegmatic**

Phlegmatic temperaments are also common, but they can be seen as almost the opposite of sanguine temperaments. However, it is possible to have a primary type of sanguine and a secondary type of phlegmatic, or vice versa.

**Phlegmatic Orientation**

People with the phlegmatic temperament type are service-oriented. They are introverted but will frequently work together with others to achieve a common goal. They are passive, which leads to a lack of ambition or sense of urgency, even when working with others.

**Phlegmatic Characteristics**

The passiveness of the phlegmatic temperament type leads to a distinct set of characteristics. They are easy-going, calm, and unemotional. They can be indecisive and agreeable and are usually happy to allow others to make decisions for them. Phlegmatic temperament people are slow to warm up to others but will make friends easily. They are one of the easiest temperament types to get along with because they are so agreeable and patient. However, they stick closely to their routines and resist change.

### Phlegmatic Traits

People with a phlegmatic temperament tend to live quiet lives centered around home and family. They don't get involved in the world around them or with other people. However, they are fiercely loyal to their friends and will stick to a relationship regardless of what the other person does or says. However, once a relationship does break, they are not likely to return to it.

This temperament type is content to let things happen. They are not quick to make decisions, and they are not ambitious. However, they resist change. They may need quite a bit of time and patience to adapt to change, especially if it is sudden.

3. ## Melancholy

When most people hear the word melancholy, they think of depression. However, the melancholy temperament type is not necessarily depressed so much as they are cautious. This is another common temperament type.

### Melancholy Orientation

People with the melancholy temperament type are detail and quality oriented. They are obsessed with finding what is right rather than being right all the time. They are also conscientious and work to make sure all details are as perfect as possible. They can be perfectionists in general.

### Melancholy Characteristics

The melancholy temperament is a rule follower. They can be cautious and tentative in unfamiliar environments, but they can also become aggressive when faced with an unfavorable situation. They are private and introverted.

This temperament is factual, logical, and analytical. To function without anxiety, these people need to have a solid plan of action and follow it to the letter.

### Melancholy Traits

The melancholy temperament is usually anxious. They worry about the future and what others think. They also tend to be high-guilt individuals, worrying about how things might have been done differently in the past. They rarely live in the present.

This temperament is generally well organized, even if they become cluttered. They are usually on time for appointments and expect others to be as well. Before making decisions, they will gather as much information as they can and ask specific questions to make sure they are making the right decision.

People of the melancholy temperament are also suspicious and conscientious. They are slow to trust others until they are sure of their intentions. It is difficult for them to form relationships, and they have high standards for the relationships they do form.

### 4. Choleric

The choleric temperament is the rarest of the four primary types. In particular, females with the choleric type as their primary temperament are extremely rare. It is more common for choleric to be a secondary temperament, although even this is not as common as other combinations.

**Choleric Orientation**

People with a choleric temperament are results-oriented. They make goals and stick to them. They are driven to succeed and tend to stay positive with constant forward movement. They face opposition head-on with the mindset of getting results.

**Choleric Characteristics**

Choleric temperament people are extroverted and exude self-confidence. They are independent and strong-willed. They have quick minds and are generally active and practical in their activities. Their communication style is assertive and direct, often brief almost to the point of rudeness.

This temperament type enjoys taking risks and gets bored easily. They can be domineering and opinionated. They find it easy to make decisions, not only for themselves but for others as well. They can be somewhat controlling in relationships. Choleric types also tend to require less sleep than other temperament types.

**Choleric Traits**

People with the choleric temperament are creative. They never seem to run out of ideas or plans, all of which tend to be practical. They are steadfast in their ideas, however, and will not give in to peer pressure.

While they can be compassionate and rally for social causes, in their personal life, they are slow to build relationships. They likely only have a few close friends, even though they are not afraid to meet and talk to new people. They don't tend to empathize with others. However, they are also very slow to anger, though their domineering personality and direct manner of speaking can be misconstrued as anger.

## MANAGING DIFFERENT TEMPERAMENTS

The different temperament types don't always mesh well. Two people of very different temperaments have difficulties in relationships. While temperament cannot be changed, you can learn to understand each other and learn ways to cope with each other's needs. Here are a few tips to get you started.

## UNDERSTAND HOW YOUR TEMPERAMENT AFFECTS YOUR LIFE

The way you perceive the world around you has a direct impact on how you interact with it. Armed with more knowledge about your temperament, you can cultivate more awareness around this personality and what it means for you in your daily life. Awareness is always the first step in cultivating change.

## DEVELOP A MORE POSITIVE OUTLOOK ON LIFE

If you have a temperament that tends to lean more towards the negative or prevents you from taking chances, you might want to develop a more positive outlook on life. Being more positive will give you the ability to thrive without fear holding you back from fully experiencing or enjoying the world. Just make sure you are always realistic in your positivity, or you run the risk of disappointing yourself and hindering your progress.

These four temperament types—Sanguine, Melancholic, Choleric, and Phlegmatic—play their role in how we react and interact. In a nutshell, there is this drawing by Hitchcock with one simple situation describing four reactions. On the drawing, a man accidentally sits on another man's hat, and triggers the following: the Choleric person yells on the clumsy one, the Phlegmatic doesn't care at all, the Melancholic cries with big tears, and the Sanguine laughs on the situation.

In a business environment, choleric people tend to rule and perform as decision-makers. Sanguines are good with clientele and all kinds of negotiations. Phlegmatic staff like to be ruled making the best backstage performers, and melancholics are usually successful pursuing careers where perfectionism and patience are required. Of course, there are many more features to know about these four temperament types at the workplace. Let's see how to interact with your colleagues who possess different temperaments, and what to expect from each of the types.

### 1. Choleric

Choleric seek to supervise others, being however true goal achievers. Not all choleric dream about reaching the top of the corporate ladder (only 99% do), but they tend to control any situation while interacting with colleagues. They are usually good in challenging situations and they are always ready to help their crew to perform according to their plan of action, enforcing it occasionally.

Provided a stable upbringing was the case during childhood, a choleric could make a true leader, possess a high level of responsibility for others and exude a high confidence in making decisions. Choleric short fuse adds to their ability to react quickly and be tough when it's needed. It's their pleasure to take part in any competition to prove their dominance. Their demanding nature sometimes translates into aggressive communication and a desire to argue. Therefore, it could be hard to oppose choleric, the confrontational behavior being not the style to choose.

### 2. Phlegmatic

This temperament type seems to be opposite to the choleric one. Being introverted and slow to react, phlegmatic tend to avoid potential conflicts as well as excessive communications. They eagerly let others speak and rule. However, they rarely team well with choleric (who cannot exist without domination) as it takes phlegmatic naturally long to execute an order, while choleric expect an instant performance.

Being first to please others, phlegmatic choose the path of minimal resistance. In a conflict, a choleric would prove himself right at all costs, whereas a phlegmatic strives for peace getting distressed in a confrontational situation. Therefore, they never rebel, nor compete for a position. This makes them obedient followers of managerial instructions, the type being also stable-loyal-never-job-hopping. Phlegmatic often need people around to make choices for them, and sanguine being suited perfectly well for the role.

### 3. Sanguine

Maximum extraverted, sanguine-temperament people recharge when interacting socially, as well as they truly enjoy meeting new contacts. Although charismatic, sanguine make the most approachable personalities—people around them feel like they've known their new sanguine friends for ages. Therefore, they have tons of friends, possessing developed communicative skills and a high level of emotional intelligence.

People with this temperament like to show off and require praise as a reward. They have a high level of empathy and openly express their emotions, being extremely sad one minute and becoming the happiest ever people the next moment. The other social feature of sanguines is their ability to convince and engage others. The encouraging role they are good at may go great when co-working with both choleric and melancholics. However, non-creative responsibilities that take a prolonged time to perform could be hard for that temperament, even distressing at some point.

### 4. Melancholic

Perfectionism being the defining feature of melancholics, they get upset when things are not ideal according to their high standards. Self-depression and pessimism are common among this temperament type as they live in their "imperfect" world. Sanguinis usually add some optimism when working in one team with melancholics.

Melancholics are those who complain a lot, although blaming themselves for every possible mistake. This type is the most introverted, and the modest reactions rarely show deep feelings/emotions. Their stubbornness and an urge for perfection make social interactions quite uneasy for melancholics. However, deep and serious melancholics are successful with analytical roles. No impulsive decisions make them good at planning things.

## CARD DECK

There is no pure temperament type—all four types co-exist in each of us, but in different proportions. Based on the upbringing style and social environment, our personality type interacts with our temperament mixture making sometimes quite an unexpected combination. Though, it's no surprise to meet a successful leader whose temperament is predominantly choleric and sanguine (50/50), which makes her both emotionally intelligent when negotiating and tough at making quick decisions when required.

## THE GOOD MIX

While making teambuilding decisions for an employee-employee or employer-employee combination the following should be considered:

1. Mix a choleric manager with a sanguine assistant.

This combination works best, as the two of these types of balance greatly each other's drawbacks.

2. Melancholics work well self-supervising.

They are perfectionists, but require clear goals set by the management.

3. Phlegmatic find it difficult to pair well with choleric.

The combination is distressing for both, because of the choleric's demanding nature and the expectation of quick reactions; phlegmatic are neither comfortable with them nor capable of accomplishing anything.

4. Sanguine cope greatly with any type.

Smart HR managers adore adding sanguine to any conflict team for the sake of resolving the difficult situation. Though, you don't want to overload sanguine with uncreative routine.

## HOW TEMPERAMENT IMPACTS ENTREPRENEURS

What personality types are best for business? Perhaps you've asked yourself what traits or personalities successful entrepreneurs possess. Were they merely lucky to be born with one or another personality type, or did they just make the best of what nature had given them, whatever it had been? Let's look at what pros and cons are tied to different types of temperament in business.

In the most widely used typology, whose foundation had been laid already by Hippocrates, people can be divided into four types based on their "sense of humor" in the original sense liquids that, in ancient Greece, were presumed to reside in our bodies and whose imbalance led among other things to different types of temperament in people. This theory was followed up by others and the typology, although no longer associated with the original theory, remains used even today. So, let's have a look at what (dis)advantages the four basic personality types face in entrepreneurship.

### Sanguine

Their main advantage is their composure so that others can't easily read them. They adapt well to changes and new situations. It's easy for them to act kind and friendly toward clients or competitors. They also tend to be good in PR, communication, and marketing. On the other hand, they may lack the ability to understand others deeply or empathize with other people, including clients or rivals.

### Choleric

These impulsive and active people can easily grow enthusiastic about new things. Choleric also tends to act quickly on these impulses, which is a great advantage in fields where change is daily bread and it's necessary to react quickly to it. However, they are easily thrown off balance and into fits of anger when things aren't going as they should, which can be harmful in workplace and client relationships. They can achieve extreme performance in their enthusiasm, but also perceive failures more dramatically.

### Melancholic

It may seem as though melancholics are quite unsuitable types for starting and running a business. The current commercial environment isn't very compatible with their pensiveness, disposition towards pessimism, and solitude. However, they too can be successful in entrepreneurship. Their reliability and stability as both business and relationship partners are appreciated. They are persistent and frequently achieve stable long-term success through their tenacious work.

### Phlegmatic

Their essential positive trait is calmness. What can be disadvantageous is their lower inclination to become enthusiastic about their work and keep the enthusiasm aflame despite initial setbacks. They tend to be meticulous and loyal. But their penchant for reacting to changes with a latency, if at all, can prove problematic.

The two "fast" types, sanguine and choleric, have an advantage in their faster tempos; their "calm" characters rather work well in their thoughtful approach to conflict situations. This is reflected in the initial growth of the business: it can be fast and followed by a time of uncertainty about whether the invested funds and work would ever return, and on the other hand, it can grow slowly and steadily due to hesitation, sometimes unwarranted, before each vital step.

People often think that some personality types are just unsuitable for entrepreneurship—but that is simply not true. It's rather a question of adapting our work to our personality so that we can best use our positive traits and conceal the negative ones. No one is born with a recipe for success.

## WHAT TYPE OF "BUSINESS" TEMPERAMENT DO YOU HAVE?

You will be more successful at running your business if you better understand your own temperament first. Determine what type of temperament you have. Are you an entrepreneur, a manager, or a technician? Most small business owners need to fill multiple roles. Most people are not skilled at all three but may have to act in all three roles initially, even though they are most likely a technician or someone who knows how to do the work of the business but not necessarily how to have a vision for that business.

### Entrepreneurs

People with entrepreneurial skills are visionaries with the initiative to take advantage of opportunities when they come along. They usually have a clear view of what they can do to add value to their customers' lives. They work in the future and see opportunities before they materialize. Examples of entrepreneurial skills include:

- The ability to see the big picture
- Risk taking
- High self-motivation
- Thinking, often of ways to improve things
- Getting energized by talking to people about ideas

List below entrepreneurs you know and why they are successful (including yourself if you are one).

| NAMES OF ENTREPRENEURS | REASONS WHY THEY ARE SUCCESSFUL |
|---|---|
|  |  |
|  |  |
|  |  |
|  |  |
|  |  |
|  |  |
|  |  |

### Managers

People with managerial skills are usually good at creating order and managing resources, time and information. They are good at tracking income and expenses and making decisions based on information. They are good at dealing with the past and the present. Examples of managerial skills include:

- Good organizational skills
- Good time-management and planning skills
- Knowledge about where every penny goes
- Good decision-making skills
- Good inter-personal skills

List below managers you know and why they are successful (including yourself if you are one).

| NAMES OF MANAGERS | REASONS WHY THEY ARE SUCCESSFUL |
|---|---|
|  |  |
|  |  |
|  |  |
|  |  |
|  |  |
|  |  |
|  |  |
|  |  |

## TECHNICIANS

Technicians are people with highly refined skills and abilities they can use to produce products or services others will buy from them. People with such skills work in the present and use their knowledge and experience to refine their skills regularly. Examples of technical skills include:

- Knowing how to cut hair, bake delicious pies, or run mechanical equipment, etc.
- Having good communication skills
- Having good technical skills (computer, Internet, etc.)
- Having the ability to do the work required to produce or create a product or service on time

List below technicians you know and why they are successful (including yourself if you are one).

| NAMES OF TECHNICIANS | REASONS WHY THEY ARE SUCCESSFUL |
|---|---|
|  |  |
|  |  |
|  |  |
|  |  |
|  |  |
|  |  |
|  |  |
|  |  |

Note: the following congruency graph demonstrates the need for possessing all three characteristics as shown by the three overlapping white sections in the graph. Although you may possess the characteristics of one primary temperament, you must work to develop the characteristics of all three temperaments (or hire those with such characteristics) to be successful in your business.

| ENTREPRENEUR | MANAGER | TECHNICIAN |
|---|---|---|
| • Manages future opportunities<br>• Envisions market opportunities<br>• Surrounded with talent<br>• Seeks to improve products | • Studies past to manage present.<br>•. Creates procedures and order<br>• Organizes personnel<br>• Manages time and resources | • Manages present tasks<br>• Highly skilled<br>• Enjoys hands-on work<br>• Gets Things done on times |

# CHAPTER 7

# THE CONCEPT OF ANTS IN BUSINESS

We often find ants mentioned in the Bible as a symbol of collaboration, assiduity, and devotion to all their endeavors. There are many references to ants in the Bible, and these insects are emblems of teamwork and community. Ants working together are the perfect examples of men to follow. Ants teach us the value of hard work. Laziness does nothing but encourages us to procrastinate and remain in a state of lack and apathy. Ants are never lazy! Neither are they poor nor hungry!

What does the Bible say about the wisdom of ants? The Bible says, "The ants are a people not strong, yet they prepare their food in the summer" (Proverbs 30:25, NKJV). No one tells them, but with their wisdom, they can do that. The wisdom of ants has intrigued many people like me and scientists. If Kingdom Entrepreneurs embrace the wisdom of the ants in their business operation with collaboration, assiduity, devotion, and teamwork, they will surely be successful. Other Bible verses about hard work and preparedness are shown below:

> **Proverbs 6:6-8 (NKJV)**
> Go to the ant, O sluggard; consider her ways, and be wise. Without having any chief, officer, or ruler, she prepares her bread in summer and gathers her food in harvest.

**Proverbs 30:24-25 (NKJV)**

Four things on earth are small, but they are exceedingly wise: the ants are a people not strong, yet they provide their food in the summer.

**Proverbs 30:24-28 (NKJV)**

Four things on earth are small, but they are exceedingly wise: the ants are a people not strong, yet they provide their food in the summer; the rock badgers are a people not mighty, yet they make their homes in the cliffs; the locusts have no king, yet all of them march in rank; the lizard you can take in your hands, yet it is in kings' palaces.

**Proverbs 6:9 (NKJV)**

How long will you lie there, O sluggard? When will you arise from your sleep?

**Matthew 6:26 (NKJV)**

Look at the birds of the air: they neither sow nor reap nor gather into barns, and yet your heavenly Father feeds them. Are you not of more value than they?

**Proverbs 24:30-34 (NKJV)**

I passed by the field of a sluggard, by the vineyard of a man lacking sense, and behold, it was all overgrown with thorns; the ground was covered with nettles, and its stone wall was broken down. Then I saw and considered it; I looked and received instruction. A little sleep, a little slumber, a little folding of the hands to rest, and poverty will come upon you like a robber, and want like an armed man.

**Romans 12:9-21 (NKJV)**

Let love be genuine. Abhor what is evil; hold fast to what is good. Love one another with brotherly affection. Outdo one another in showing honor. Do not be slothful in zeal, be fervent in spirit, serve the Lord. Rejoice in hope, be patient in tribulation, be constant in prayer. Contribute to the needs of the saints and seek to show hospitality. ...

**Proverbs 21:25 (NKJV)**
The desire of the sluggard kills him, for his hands refuse to labor.

## 4 LESSONS WE CAN LEARN FROM THE ANT

"Go to the ant thou sluggard. Consider its ways and be wise" (Proverbs 6:6, NKJV). The ant is an industrious creature, small, but wise in its ability to optimize its time, skills and resources. Here are some important characteristics of the ants:

1. **Diligent and hardworking.** Ants teach us the value of hard work. Laziness does nothing but encourages us to procrastinate and remain in a state of lack and apathy. Ants are never lazy! Neither are they poor nor hungry! Their efforts and hard work sustain them! If we strive to be diligent and work hard, our lives will be blessed physically, spiritually, and financially!

2. **Can-do attitude.** Ants exemplify what it means to be self-motivated. Size, lack, and location are not limiting factors for them. They make no excuses and continue with the business of getting things done. No one must whip them to move, do their work, or work together. They work for the common good. Moreover, they do not need a captain or a leader as they are disciplined and natural self-starters.

3. **Excellent strategic planning, precision, and organization skills.** Ants teach us the necessity to plan and look ahead. They store their food during seasons of plenty, so that they will have adequate amounts in times of scarcity. They also plan seasons of work and rest to prevent burnout.

4. **Teamwork and unity.** Ants know that they can accomplish more by working together than by working alone. They set goals and work together to achieve it.

**THE WISDOM OF ANTS IN FOCUS**

**Wisdom** is not sold and so no one can buy it. The wisdom of ants in focus: it is one precious thing unique to humans but when a man becomes too lazy to reason up in life, he becomes less sensitive and reasonable compared to the ants.

These creatures have a lot of potentials and if you watch them closely, they can awe you to the max. King Solomon, the richest and the wisest man ever to live, places emphasis on the wisdom of ants and tells us to go to the ants and learn their ways.

"Go to the ants; You sluggard, observe its ways and be wise" (Proverbs 6:6, NKJV). Solomon identified the ants as astonishing creatures and he tried to understand their ways and wisdom. Today many of us are chasing celebrities and big men in our societies and countries to learn their ways but the Bible says we should go to the ants. In the few lines below, I will share with you how ants use their wisdom to organize themselves and prepare for the future.

You and I should also go to the ants and learn their ways for there is nothing more precious than acquiring wisdom free of charge from the ants. You can go to the woods, your backyard, kitchen, garden, or anywhere you think you can find ants, observe them, know how they organize themselves, march, transport items, and how they build ant cities. You can spend months to fully understand their ways.

**WHAT DOES THE BIBLE SAY ABOUT THE WISDOM OF ANTS?**

The Bible says, "The ants are a people not strong, yet they prepare their meat in the summer" (Proverbs 30:25, NKJV).

When you observe very well, you will see that the ants march in two different directions (inwards and outwards) and as they move together in lines to carry pieces of food items, pay attention to the fact that some could be food crumbs left by people or little bones of fish and other items discarded by humans. They gather all this food in their storage house during summer. And when winter or rainy season comes, they stay indoors and enjoy their labor. The most amazing part is how they get to know it's summer and so they should store up some food to face winter or rainy seasons. No one tells them, but with their wisdom, they can do that.

The wisdom of ants has intrigued many people like scientists and myself. They can count the number of their eggs and range them in order of age. As the ants march to find food, they leave tracks for their friends to trace and find the food source and return home. If you destroy their path or direction, quickly they will know that there is a breach; so they will form another path by changing direction. Nobody directs them. The ants are also very sensitive to the aroma of their food, and they can figure out where food lies within a certain distance.

Ants are very disciplined. Although they have no central leader, they love themselves, care for each other, and are ready to die for themselves. There is nothing like greed among them. Together, they work, and, together, they enjoy the fruits of their works. The wisdom of ants is hard to comprehend by people.

Though they have tiny bodies at least they can carry food items ten times heavier than their bodies.

Personally, I have been observing their movements since I was a kid. Tracing where they are moving to and from is very interesting and as they march and bypass each other, they seem to exchange greetings. Together, they can carry dead insects like cockroaches, ants, spiders, and other dead flies into their storehouse. Recently, I found myself reading the book of Job in the Bible and to my dismay, I got to know that God deprived the peacock and the ostrich of wisdom. What an amazing God? He gave the peacock beautiful wings and yet no wisdom. The peahen's lack of wisdom sometimes leads her to step on her own babies and kill them.

"She is hardened against her young ones, as though they were not hers; Her labor is in vain without fear; Because God hath deprived her of wisdom, neither had He imparted unto her understanding" (Job 39:16-17, NKJV).

God who made all animals knows them very well in terms of their abilities, reasoning capacity, understanding, and everything. As for the horse, he gave them the courage to run fiercely in battlegrounds without fearing javelins, swords, arrows, and other war weapons.

## LESSONS FROM THE WISDOM OF ANTS

Now let us focus on what the Bible teaches us about ants. God himself is wisdom. I mean He is the source of wisdom, He is the one who gives to anyone who deserves it and deprives anyone or any creature that doesn't deserve it. Every Kingdom believer must know that the fear of the Lord is the beginning of wisdom (see Proverbs 28:28 (NKJV).

So, if you fear the Lord then automatically you are wise or full of wisdom. This in no small way means the ants fear the Lord and so they are one of the wisest creatures on earth. Scientists have found out that they make use of the moonlight and the sunlight for navigation in their nests. So movement is never difficult for them.

1. **Caring**

The second ants lesson is how they care for each other (see Philippians 2:4, NKJV). We must learn from the ants, how they want each other to be successful by showing support to help anyone who is in need. If you wish good things for your friend, then surely good things shall come unto you as well.

2. **Love**

Again, the next Bible lesson about ants is how they show love to each other to the extent of laying down their lives for others. They are ever ready to die for each other and the Bible tells us that there is no love greater than laying down your life for your friends (see John 15:13, NKJV).

3. **Investments**

The next ants lesson is how they invest in the future. They are wise enough to know that a time will come that would be difficult for them to get food or march searching for food, building ants cities, and so forth so they prepare themselves by storing up food in their room. In the future when winter comes, or rainy seasons come, they wouldn't be in any trouble.

So, you and I must know that it is good to invest our future lives into something profitable to help us feel secure in the future. We shouldn't wait for a catastrophe to hit us before we take a step. We can invest in the future by acquiring health insurance, life insurance, car insurance and all the good insurances you can think of. We should also be futuristic by planning for the future.

Finally, lessons from the ants tell us that we should share what we have with everyone who deserves the profits of our labor. Here it is good for us to avoid cheating if we are to share something among ourselves. The ants share the food they have stored in their nest without discrimination.

## MORE TO LEARN FROM ANTS

I like almost every movement of the ants with the exception that:

1. **They sting:** when they encounter your body, they feel threatened, so they defend themselves and they sting. When they sting, it's very painful and the pains could last for a couple of minutes or hours.

2. **They can invade your house for food:** just like I said earlier, they are very sensitive; so if you leave food crumbs in your room, they can show up as uninvited guests marching around your room. They like food items like sugar, bread, roasted groundnut, dead insects, etc. In conclusion, as human beings, we are God's greatest creation. We are worth more than everything God created because he made us in his own image.

And for God to tell us to go to the ants to learn wisdom, it sounds a little satirical because the kind of wisdom God gave us to take care of all creatures surpasses that of the ants. But why then should we go to the ants to learn from them? God said that because some of us are too lazy to the extent that we feel bossy or lazy to sweat and earn from our sweat. A lazy man shouldn't eat, but today, in our world lazy people are eating and enjoying more than those who are working, and they do this through illegal means by indulging in fraud, bribery and corruption, lies, and many more. These people lack wisdom and they should go to the ants and learn wisdom.

We must love one another, care for one another, obey rules, even if there are no rulers or leaders in our societies, workplaces, and countries. The wisdom of human beings should put things in order for the benefits of everyone.

## 13 ATTRIBUTES OF ANTS

The 13 attributes of the worker ants' life we should focus on are listed below. Here you will see how scripture lines up with the ants' wisdom attributes.

There are however many more to show you which will be covered later. There are much scriptural evidence about the wisdom of ants that we can learn from.

When considering the attributes of the different types of ants, you will, without a doubt, soon realize that their good and awesome attributes, accurately, reflect the finest properties of true Kingdom living.

These also include how spiritually, in scripture, the Church, the Body of Christ, and man should be operating in comparison. God profoundly uses the small ant, as a clear mirror, so that we may consider, looking at ourselves, comparatively, in the process.

Here are a few specific parallels and comparative facts between ants and the Kingdom walk in the Word as follows:

1. They work together (see Eccl 4:9-12, Heb 10:24-25, NKJV).
2. They care for one another (see 1 Timothy 5:8, 1 Cor 12:25-26, NKJV).
3. They are always looking out for one another (see Phil 2:4, NKJV).
4. They love one another. We are the light that reveals Christ on the Earth and our light shines when we walk and live. Just as the ant's dwell in dark places, in general, they emerge from the nest into the light (see John 12:35-36, Eph 5:8, John 13:34, NKJV).
5. They are faithful to one another, and the Queen (see Heb 13:4, 1Sam 12:24, Eph 5:25, NKJV).
6. The life of the ant is to break bread with one-another. They have a doctrine, an "operating system" within the nest that God ordained right from the beginning of time when God created them. He spoke once and they have been doing what they were told to do ever since. Man, on the other hand, has been disobedient in what God originally instructed him to do (see Acts 2:42, NKJV).
7. They defend and die for one another (see John 15:13, NKJV).
8. They build and repair together (see 1 Thes. 5:11, Math 18:20, Eccl 4:9-12, Zep 3:9, NKJV)
9. They have constant fellowship with each other (see Heb 10:25, 1 John 1:3, NKJV).

10. They obey God's Word right from the beginning. When God created them, they have just kept on doing what He spoke (see John 14:15, Is 1:19, 2 Cor 2:9, NKJV).
11. They adopt one another whenever the opportunity arises (see Eph 1:5, Esther 2:7, NKJV).
12. They dwell in peace with one another within the nest (see James 2:8, Rom 15:2, Gal 5:14, NKJV).
13. They protect their Queen and each other with their lives (see Rom 12:10-13, John 15:13, John 13:38, NKJV).

Just like the ants, Christians should be able to use these heavenly wisdoms to operate on earth. In like manner, the true Kingdom entrepreneur can learn and apply these habits that are eternally enduring from these simple, yet profound, 13 attributes of the ants.

## 5 IMPORTANT LESSONS FROM ANTS

Ants are fascinating creatures! If you ever get an opportunity to see a Discovery channel show on them, check it out. These little guys can carry up to seven times their own body's weight! They also set up complex communities where each ant plays a role. They're incredible!

Proverbs 6:6-8 (NKJV) says, "Go to the ant, thou sluggard; consider her ways, and be wise: Which having no guide, overseer, or ruler, provided her meat in the summer, and gathered her food in the harvest."

This is a verse I memorized years ago and it is still convicting me every time I read it or think about it. And of course, I think about it every time I see an ant.

## 5 LESSONS ENTREPRENEURS CAN LEARN FROM ANTS:

a. Ants take the shortest path possible. As an entrepreneur, don't wander—be intentional.

b. Ants communicate with each other to reach a desired goal. As an entrepreneur, communicate—don't assume.
c. Ants cooperate with one another. As an entrepreneur, be friendly and helpful.
d. Ants aren't lazy. As an entrepreneur, don't be slothful.
e. Ants plan. If ants plan and they only have somewhere near a 60-day lifespan, shouldn't we also plan?

The ants pictured above were making their way across my porch earlier this week and every time I went outside, I was reminded that the Bible calls me a sluggard, quite accurately, I might add. Sure, I could make the defense that I'm always busy because I am. Or that my mind never slows down because it doesn't. However, the truth is I'm quite lazy.

I avoid doing things that I dislike doing or things that require more effort. Whether that's ironing clothes or having an uncomfortable but needed conversation. I procrastinate and stay busy with other things. Right now, I need to be planning VBS that is happening way too soon! Could I have done it earlier? Yes. Did I over the past few months ever have an uninterrupted two-hour block of time during the day where I could sit down and do it? Of course not. But I could have done it. I should have done it, but I chose the easy road.

You want to know a secret? The easy road always looks easy but once you get on it, it turns into the hard road. The hard road on the other hand looks hard but once you get on it, it turns out to be easy. The easy road is deceptive. It's a liar. It's the way of destruction, poverty, starvation, and desperation. It's the way to financial ruin, wasted days, wasted weeks, wasted months, wasted years, and well, wasted lives. The hard road which seems to be difficult is the road to prosperity, blessing, fulfillment, happiness, and personal satisfaction. The hard road is the bumpy path that leads you to the top while the easy road is a slippery slope that leads you to the bottom. The only road that goes to the top is the hard road. It's tough at first but it's the only road that will get you to where you want to be.

I'm not saying you should be a work-aholic, to spend yourself till there's nothing left, or to work 80+ hours a week. As a mom, I know it's easy to feel defeated at the end of a very hard day. I feel like with each day that passes, I'm a little more behind on laundry, or housework, or corresponding with loved ones, etc. That's a whole other story, but the point I'm trying to make is don't waste your life.

## DON'T WASTE YOUR LIFE!

Don't waste your life, especially on the things that won't matter one iota next year. Get up and do something with the opportunities that God has placed before you. Whatever you do, do it to the glory of God (see 1 Cor. 10:31, NKJV). Use your intelligence, your passions, your gifts, your resources, and do something. Do it with all you might! In the words of my third-grade teacher, Mrs. Franklin, "Don't just twiddle your thumbs!" Dear friend, life is happening, don't let it pass you by.

# CHAPTER 8

# BASIC BOOKKEEPING SKILLS

**INTRODUCTION TO BOOKKEEPING**

The term bookkeeping means different things to different people:

- Some people think that bookkeeping is the same as accounting. They assume that keeping a company's books and preparing its financial statements and tax reports are all part of bookkeeping. Accountants do not share this view.
- Others see bookkeeping as limited to recording transactions in journals or daybooks and then posting the amounts of accounts in ledgers. After the amounts are posted, the bookkeeping has ended and an accountant with a college degree takes over. The accountant will make adjusting entries and then prepare the financial statements and other reports.
- The past distinctions between bookkeeping and accounting have become blurred with the use of computers and accounting software. For example, a person with little bookkeeping training can use the accounting software to record vendor invoices, prepare sales invoices, etc. and the software will update the accounts in the general ledger automatically. Once the format of the financial statements has been

established, the software will be able to generate the financial statements with the click of a button.
- At mid-size and larger corporations, the term bookkeeping might be absent. Often corporations have accounting departments staffed with accounting clerks who process accounts payable, accounts receivable, payroll, etc. The accounting clerks will be supervised by one or more accountants.

Our explanation of bookkeeping attempts to provide you with an understanding of bookkeeping and its relationship with accounting. Our goal is to increase your knowledge and confidence in bookkeeping, accounting, and business. In turn, we hope that you will become more valuable in your current and future roles.

### BOOKKEEPING: PAST AND PRESENT

**BOOKKEEPING IN THE OLD DAYS**
Prior to computers and software, the bookkeeping for potential businesses usually began by writing entries into journals. Journals were defined as the books of original entry. To reduce the amount of writing in a general journal, special journals or daybooks were introduced. The special or specialized journals consisted of a sales journal, purchases journal, cash receipts journal, and cash payments journal.

The company's transactions were written in the journals in date order. Later, the amounts in the journals would be posted to the designated accounts located in the general ledger. Examples of accounts include Sales, Rent Expense, Wages Expense, Cash, Loans Payable, etc. Each account's balance had to be calculated and the account balances were used in the company's financial statements. In addition to the general ledger, a company may have had subsidiary ledgers for accounts such as Accounts Receivable.

Handwriting the many transactions into journals, rewriting the amounts in the accounts, and manually calculating the account balances would likely result in some incorrect amounts. To determine whether errors had occurred, the bookkeeper prepared a trial balance. A trial balance is an internal report that lists 1) each account's name, and 2) each account's balance in the appropriate debit column or credit column. If the total of the debit column did not equal the total of the credit column, there was at least one error occurring somewhere between the journal entry and the trial balance. Finding one or more errors often meant spending hours retracing the entries and postings.

After locating and correcting the errors, the bookkeeping phase was completed and the accounting phase began. It began with an accountant preparing adjusting entries so that the accounts reflected the accrual basis of accounting. Adjusting entries were necessary for the following reasons:

- Additional revenues and assets may have been earned but were not recorded.
- Additional expenses and liabilities may have been incurred but were not recorded.
- Some of the amounts that had been recorded by the bookkeeper may have been prepayments which were no longer prepaid.
- Depreciation and other non-routine adjustments needed to be computed and recorded.

After all the adjustments were made, the accountant presented the adjusted account balances in the form of financial statements.

After each year's financial statements were completed, closing entries were needed. The purpose of closing entries is to get the balances in all of the income statement accounts (revenues, expenses) to be zero before the start of the new accounting year. The net amount of the income statement account balances would ultimately be transferred to the proprietor's capital account or to the stockholders' retained earnings account.

## BOOKKEEPING TODAY

The electronic speed of computers and accounting software gives the appearance that many of the bookkeeping and accounting tasks have been eliminated or are occurring simultaneously. For example, the preparation of a sales invoice will automatically update the relevant general ledger accounts (Sales, Accounts Receivable, Inventory, Cost of Goods Sold), update the customer's detailed information, and store the information for the financial statements as well as other reports.

The accounting software has been written so that every transaction must have the debit amounts equal to the credit amounts. The electronic accuracy also eliminates the errors that had occurred when amounts were manually written, rewritten, and calculated. As a result, the debits will always equal the credits and the trial balance will always be in balance. No longer will hours be spent looking for errors that occurred in a manual system.

While the accounting software is amazingly fast and accurate in processing the information that is entered, the software is unable to detect whether some transactions have been omitted, have been entered twice, or if incorrect accounts were used. Fraudulent transactions and amounts could also be entered if a company fails to have internal controls.

After the sales invoices, vendor invoices, payroll and other transactions have been processed for each accounting period, some adjusting entries are still required. The adjusting entries will involve:

- Revenues and assets that were earned, but not yet entered into the software.
- Expenses and liabilities that were incurred, but not yet entered into the software
- Prepayments that are no longer prepaid.
- Recording depreciation expense, bad debts expense, etc.

The adjusting entries will require a person to determine the amounts and the accounts. Without adjusting entries, the accounting software will be producing incomplete, inaccurate, and perhaps misleading financial statements.

After the financial statements for the year are released, the software will transfer the balances from the income statement accounts to the sole proprietor's capital account or to the stockholders' retained earnings account. This allows for the following year's income statement accounts to begin with zero balances. (The balance sheet accounts are not closed as their balances are carried forward to the next accounting year.)

## RECORDING TRANSACTIONS

Bookkeeping (and accounting) involves the recording of a company's financial transactions. The transactions will have to be identified, approved, sorted, and stored in a manner so they can be retrieved and presented in the company's financial statements and other reports.

Here are a few examples of some of a company's financial transactions:

- The purchase of supplies with cash.
- The purchase of merchandise on credit.
- The sale of merchandise on credit.
- Rent for the business's office.
- Salaries and wages earned by employees.
- Buying equipment for the office.
- Borrowing money from a bank.

The transactions will be sorted into perhaps hundreds of accounts including Cash, Accounts Receivable, Loans Payable, Accounts Payable, Sales, Rent Expense, Salaries Expense, Wages Expense Dept 1, Wages Expense Dept 2, etc. The amounts in each of the accounts will be reported on the company's financial statements in detail or in summary form.

With hundreds of accounts and perhaps thousands of transactions, it is clear that once a person learns the accounting software, there will be efficiencies and better information available for managing a business.

## ACCRUAL METHOD

There are two main methods of accounting (or bookkeeping):

- Accrual method
- Cash method

The accrual method of accounting is the preferred method because it provides:

1. A more complete reporting of the company's assets, liabilities, and stockholders' equity at the end of an accounting period, and
2. A more realistic reporting of a company's revenues, expenses, and net income for a specific time interval such as a month, quarter or year.

As a result, US GAAP (General Accounting Accepted Practices) requires most corporations to use the accrual method of accounting.

The following table compares the accrual and cash methods of accounting:

| Accrual method | Cash method |
| --- | --- |
| Receivables are reported as assets when they are earned. | Receivables are not reported as assets. |
| Revenues are reported when they are earned. | Revenues are reported when cash is received. |
| Payables are reported as liabilities when they are incurred. | Payables are not reported as liabilities. |
| Expenses are reported when they best match revenues or when they are used up. | Expenses are reported when cash is paid. |
| Net income is based on revenues earned and expenses incurred during an accounting period. | Net income is based more on cash receipts and cash disbursements rather than the revenues earned and expenses incurred during the accounting period. |
| The balance sheet is more complete as far as the reporting of assets, liabilities and the amount of stockholders' equity. | The balance sheet omits certain assets, liabilities. The amount of stockholders' equity will also be affected. |
| The accrual method is required by generally accepted accounting principles. | The cash method is likely to violate the matching principle in accounting. |

Note: Some potential companies may be allowed to use the cash method of accounting and in turn may experience an income tax benefit. Since our website does not provide income tax information, you should seek tax advice from a tax professional or from IRS.gov.

## REVENUES AND RECEIVABLES

'Under the accrual method, revenues are to be reported in the accounting period in which they are earned (which may be different from the period in which the money is received).

To illustrate the reporting of revenues under the accrual method, let's assume that the hypothetical business Servco provides a service to a customer on December 27. Servco prepares a sales invoice for the agreed upon amount of $1,000. The invoice is dated December 27 and states that the amount is due in 30 days.

Under the accrual method, on December 27 Servco:

- Has earned revenue of $1,000, and
- Has earned a receivable of $1,000.

If Servco uses accounting software to prepare the invoice, the following will be recorded automatically as of December 27:

- The income statement account Service Revenues will be increased by $1,000, and
- The asset Accounts Receivable will be increased by $1,000.

In addition to updating the general ledger accounts (which are used in preparing the financial statements), the software will update and store the customer's information for generating an aging of accounts receivable and a statement of each customer's activity.

## EXPENSES AND PAYABLES

Under the accrual method, expenses should be reported on the income statement in the period in which they best match with the revenues. If a cause-and-effect relationship is not obvious, the expense should be reported on the income statement when the cost is used up or expires. In any event, the payment of cash is not the primary factor for determining the accounting period in which an expense is reported on the income statement.

To illustrate, let's assume that Servco uses a temporary help agency at a cost of $200 in order to assist in earning revenues on December 27. The invoice from the temp agency is received on December 27, but it will not be paid until January 4.

Under the accrual method, on December 27 Servco:

- Has incurred an expense of $200, and
- Has incurred a liability of $200.

If accounting software is used to record the temp agency's invoice, the following will occur automatically as of December 27:

- The income statement account Temporary Help Expense will be increased by $200, and
- The liability Accounts Payable will be increased by $200.

When Servco issues its check on January 4:

- The asset Cash will be decreased by $200, and
- The liability Accounts Payable will be decreased by $200.

**NET INCOME**

If Servco had only the two transactions described above, its net income under the accrual method for the day of December 27 will consist of the following:

- Earned revenue of $1,000.
- Incurred an expense of $200.
- Earned a net income of $800 ($1,000 of revenues minus $200 of expenses).

  [The cash method of accounting would have reported a much different picture:
  - No revenue, expense or net income would have been reported on the December income statement.

- The revenues of $1,000 might be reported in February if the customer paid in 35 days.
- The expense of $200 will be reported in January when Servco pays the temp agency.]

Obviously, the accrual method does a better job of reporting what occurred on December 27, the date that Servco provided the services and incurred the expense.

## DOUBLE-ENTRY, DEBITS AND CREDITS

### DOUBLE-ENTRY

Except for some very potential companies, the standard method for recording transactions is double entry. Double-entry bookkeeping or double-entry accounting means that every transaction will involve at least two accounts. To illustrate, here are a few transactions and the two accounts that will be affected:

| Transaction | Account #1 | Account #2 |
| --- | --- | --- |
| Company borrows money | Cash | Loans Payable |
| Company pays its rent | Cash | Rent Expense |
| Sale of merchandise on credit | Accounts Receivable | Sales |
| Purchase of goods on credit | Inventory | Accounts Payable |
| Receives money from a customer who had purchased goods or services on credit | Cash | Accounts Receivable |

Note: Double-entry bookkeeping means that every transaction will involve a minimum of two accounts.

### DEBITS AND CREDITS

The words debit and credit have been associated with double-entry bookkeeping and accounting for more than 500 years. Here are the meanings of those words:

**Debit:** an entry on the left side of an account

**Credit:** an entry on the right side of an account

The debit and credit rule in double-entry bookkeeping can be stated in several ways:

- For each transaction, the total amount entered on the left side of an account (or accounts) must be equal to the total amount entered on the right side of another account (or accounts).
- For each transaction, the total of the debit amounts must be equal to the total of the credit amounts.
- Debits must equal credits.

In short:

> Debit amounts = Credit amounts
> Debits = Credits

Dependable accounting software will be written/coded to enforce the rule of debits equal to credits. In other words, a transaction will be accepted and processed only if the amount of the debits is equal to the amount of the credits.

The accuracy of accounting software will also ensure that the accounts and the trial balance will always be in balance. Here is an example of a partial trial balance:

**Servco**
**Trial Balance (Partial)**
**December 31, 2020**

|  | Debits | Credits |
|---|---|---|
| Cash | $ 895.24 |  |
| Accounts receivable | 499.58 |  |
| Accounts payable |  | $ 225.00 |
| Common stock |  | 500.00 |
| Retained earnings |  | 234.21 |
| Service revenues |  | 7,500.00 |
| Rent expense | 6,000.00 |  |
| *Some accounts and amounts are omitted* |  |  |
| Totals | $ 13,444.32 | $ 13,444.32 |

Even though the accounting software has eliminated the clerical errors that occurred because amounts were handwritten and the account balances were calculated manually, some other errors can still occur. Here are some errors that will not be detected by the accounting software:

- An entire transaction (both the debit amount and the credit amount) was omitted.
- An entire transaction was entered twice.
- An incorrect amount was entered both as a debit and as a credit.
- An incorrect account was debited.
- An incorrect account was credited.

Even with the above errors, the trial balance will remain in balance. The reason is that the total of the debit balances will still be equal to the total of the credit balances.

## T-ACCOUNTS

To assist in visualizing the effect of recording a debit or credit amount and the resulting balances of general ledger accounts, it is helpful to draw a T-account, as shown here:

Debit amounts will be entered on the left side of the T-account, and credit amounts will be entered on the right side. The title of the account will appear at the top of each "T".

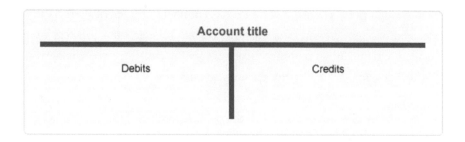

Since every transaction will involve at least two accounts, we recommend that you always begin by drawing two T-accounts. For example, if a company pays its rent of $2,000 for the current month, the transaction could be depicted with the following T-accounts:

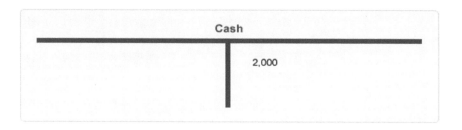

Note that one T-account (Rent Expense) has a debit of 2,000 and that one T-account (Cash) has a credit amount of 2,000. Hence, the transaction had debits equal to credits.

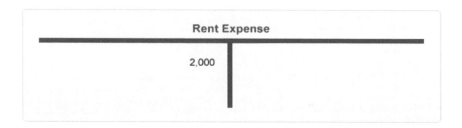

## GENERAL LEDGER ACCOUNTS

The accounts that are used to sort and store transactions are found in the company's general ledger. The general ledger is often arranged according to the following seven classifications. (A few examples of the related account titles are shown in parentheses.)

- Assets (Cash, Accounts Receivable, Land, Equipment)
- Liabilities (Loans Payable, Accounts Payable, Bonds Payable)
- Stockholders' equity (Common Stock, Retained Earnings)
- Operating revenues (Sales, Service Fees)
- Operating expenses (Salaries Expense, Rent Expense, Depreciation Expense)
- Non-operating revenues and gains (Investment Income, Gain on Disposal of Truck)
- Non-operating expenses and losses (Interest Expense, Loss on Disposal of Equipment)

## BALANCE SHEET ACCOUNTS

The first three classifications are referred to as balance sheet accounts since the balances in these accounts are reported on the financial statement known as the balance sheet.

- Balance sheet accounts
  - Assets
  - Liabilities
  - Stockholders' (or Owner's) equity

The balance sheet accounts are also known as permanent accounts (or real accounts) since the balances in these accounts will not be closed at the end of an accounting year. Instead, these account balances are carried forward to the next accounting year.

## INCOME STATEMENT ACCOUNTS

The four remaining classifications of accounts are referred to as income statement accounts since the amounts in these accounts will be reported on the financial statement known as the income statement.

- Income statement accounts
    - Operating revenues
    - Operating expenses
    - Non-operating revenues and gains
    - Non-operating expenses and losses

The income statement accounts are also known as temporary accounts since the balances in these accounts will be closed at the end of the accounting year. Each income statement account is closed to begin the next accounting year with a zero balance.

The year-end balances from all the income statement accounts will be combined and entered as a single net amount in Retained Earnings (a balance sheet account within stockholders' equity) or in a proprietor's capital account.

Note: If an account has not had any activity in the current or recent periods, it is often omitted from the current general ledger.

## CHART OF ACCOUNTS

The chart of accounts is simply a list of all of the accounts that are available for recording transactions. This means that the number of accounts in the chart of accounts will be greater than the number of accounts in the general ledger. (The reason is that accounts with zero balances and no recent entries are often omitted from the general ledger until there is a transaction for the account.)

The chart of accounts is organized similar to the general ledger: balance sheet accounts followed by the income statement accounts. However, the chart of accounts does not contain any entries or account balances.

The chart of accounts allows you to find the name of an account, its account number, and perhaps a brief description. It is important to expand

and/or alter the chart of accounts to accommodate the changes to an organization and when there is a need for improved reporting of information.

In some accounting software, the chart of accounts is also used to designate where an account will be reported in the financial statements.

## DEBITS AND CREDITS IN THE ACCOUNTS

If you already understand debits and credits, the following table summarizes how debits and credits are used in the accounts.

| Type of account | Normal balance | To increase | To decrease |
| --- | --- | --- | --- |
| Assets | Debit | Debit | Credit |
| Liabilities | Credit | Credit | Debit |
| Stockholders' equity | Credit | Credit | Debit |
| Operating revenues | Credit | Credit | Debit |
| Operating expenses | Debit | Debit | Credit |
| Non-operating revenues & gains | Credit | Credit | Debit |
| Non-operating expenses & losses | Debit | Debit | Credit |

If you are not familiar with debits and credits or if you want a better understanding, we will provide a few insights to help you. We will also provide links to our visual tutorial, quiz, puzzles, etc. that will further assist you.

## ACCOUNTING EQUATION CAN HELP

The accounting equation is a central part of bookkeeping and accounting. It can also provide insights into debits and credits. The basic accounting equation is:

**Assets = Liabilities + Stockholders' equity** (if a corporation)

or

**Assets = Liabilities + Owner's equity** (if a sole proprietorship)

With double-entry accounting, the accounting equation should always be in balance. In other words, not only will debits be equal to credits, but the amount of assets will be equal to the amount of liabilities plus the amount of owner's equity.

The accounting equation is also the framework of the balance sheet, one of the main financial statements. Hence the balance sheet must also be in balance.

We will use the accounting equation to explain why we sometimes debit an account and at other times we credit an account.

**Assets are on the left side of the accounting equation.**
**Asset account balances should be on the left side of the accounts.**

In the accounting equation you can see that assets are on the left side of the equation:

Earlier you learned that debit means left side. Recall our T-account that showed debits on the left side:

Hence, asset accounts such as Cash, Accounts Receivable, Inventory, and Equipment should have debit balances.

**Liabilities are on the right side of the accounting equation.**
**Liability account balances should be on the right side of the accounts.**

In the accounting equation you can see that liabilities are on the right side of the equation:

> Assets = **Liabilities** + Stockholders' Equity

Earlier you learned that credit means right side. Recall our T-account that showed credits on the right side:

Thus liability accounts such as Accounts Payable, Notes Payable, Wages Payable, and Interest Payable should have credit balances.

**Stockholders' equity is on the right side of the accounting equation. Stockholders' equity account balances should be on the right side of the accounts.**

In the accounting equation you can see that stockholders' equity is on the right side of the equation:

> Assets = **Liabilities** + Stockholders' Equity

Again, credit means right side and our T-account showed credits on the right side. This means that stockholders' equity accounts such as Common Stock, Retained Earnings, and M J Smith, Capital should have credit balances.

Example

To demonstrate the debits and credits of double entry with a transaction, let's assume that a new corporation is formed, and the stockholders invest $100,000 in exchange for shares of common stock. There are two effects of this transaction:

1. The corporation receives cash, which is recorded as a corporation asset.
2. The corporation issues share of common stock. The amount received for the shares will be recorded as part of the corporation's stockholders' equity.

Here's how the transaction will impact the accounting equation and the company's balance sheet:

**Assets = Liabilities + Stockholders' equity**
+ 100,000 =                           + 100,000

Here is what will occur in the general ledger accounts:

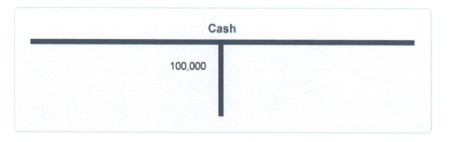

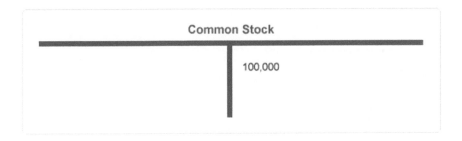

If this transaction is entered in a general journal, it would appear as follows:

| Debit: | Cash | 100,000 | |
|---|---|---|---|
| Credit: | Common Stock | | 100,000 |

**Revenues increase stockholders' equity (which is on the right side of the accounting equation).**

**Therefore the balances in the revenue accounts will be on the right side.**

To illustrate, let's assume that a company provides a service and bills the customer $400 with the amount due in 30 days. Two things occur:

1. Revenues of $400 are earned and that causes stockholders' equity to increase.
2. The company earns the right to receive $400. This increases the company's asset account Accounts Receivable.

Here's the effect on the accounting equation and the company's balance sheet because of earning the revenues:

**Assets = Liabilities + Stockholders' equity**
+ 400 =                              + 400

Here is what occurs in the general ledger accounts:

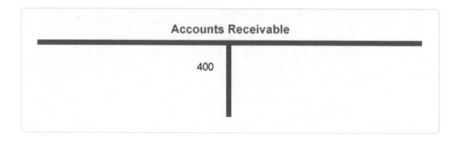

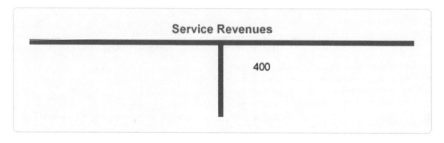

Note: Even though stockholders' equity will increase, the transaction is recorded in the account Service Revenues. The reason is that we want the amount of revenues to be reported on the current period's income statement. (In other words, we temporarily credit Service Revenues instead of crediting the stockholders' equity account Retained Earnings. At the end of the accounting year, the balances in all of the income statement accounts will be closed/transferred to Retained Earnings.)

If this transaction were entered in a general journal, it would appear as follows:

| | | | |
|---|---|---|---|
| Debit: | Accounts Receivable | 400 | |
| Credit: | Service Revenues | | 400 |

Expenses decrease stockholders' equity (which is on the right side of the accounting equation).

Therefore expense accounts will have their balances on the left side.

To reduce the normal credit balance in stockholders' equity accounts, a debit will be needed. Hence, the accounts such as Rent Expense, Advertising Expense, etc. will have their balances on the left side.

For example, when a company pays cash of $150 for advertising materials that are distributed immediately at a local event, two things occur:

1. An expense of $150 occurred and the expense will cause stockholders' equity to decrease.
2. The company has reduced its asset Cash by $150.

The effect on the accounting equation and the company's balance sheet is:

**Assets = Liabilities + Stockholders' equity**
- 150 =                                   - 150

The effect on the company's general ledger accounts is shown here:

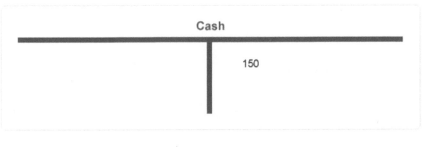

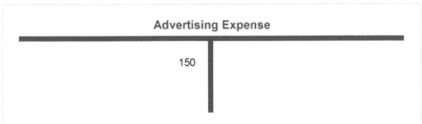

Note: Even though this expense causes stockholders' equity to decrease, the transaction is recorded in the account Advertising Expense. The reason is that we want the current period's income statement to report this expense. (In other words, we temporarily debit Advertising Expense instead of debiting the stockholders' equity account Retained Earnings. At the end of the accounting year, all the balances in the income statement accounts will be closed/transferred to Retained Earnings.)

If this transaction were entered in a general journal, it would appear as follows:

| | | |
|---|---|---|
| *Debit:* | Advertising Expense | 150 |
| *Credit:* | Cash | 150 |

## A FEW TIPS ABOUT DEBITS AND CREDITS:
- When cash is received, debit Cash.
- When cash is paid out, credit Cash.
- When revenues are earned, credit a revenue account.
- When expenses are incurred, debit an expense account.

**Here are some common transactions with the appropriate debits and credits:**

| | |
|---|---|
| If a company pays $900 for the current month's rent... | |
| Debit the account Rent Expense $900. | *Expenses get debited.* |
| Credit the asset account Cash for $900. | *When cash is paid, credit Cash.* |
| | |
| If a company performs services for $100 cash... | |
| Debit the asset account Cash for $100. | *When cash is received, debit Cash.* |
| Credit Service Revenues for $100. | *Revenues get credited.* |
| | |
| If a company purchases equipment for $5,000 in cash... | |
| Debit the asset account Equipment for $5,000. | *Assets are increased with a debit.* |
| Credit the asset account Cash for $5,000. | *When cash is paid, credit Cash.* |
| | |
| If a company borrows $10,000 from its bank... | |
| Debit the asset Cash for $10,000. | *When cash is received, debit Cash.* |
| Credit the liability Loans Payable for $10,000. | *Liabilities are increased with a credit.* |
| | |
| If a company repays $4,000 of its bank loan... | |
| Debit the liability Loans Payable for $4,000. | *Liabilities are decreased with a debit.* |
| Credit the asset Cash for $4,000. | *When cash is paid, credit Cash.* |

## ASSET ACCOUNTS

Asset accounts are one of the three major classifications of balance sheet accounts:

- Assets
- Liabilities
- Stockholders' equity (or owner's equity)

The ending balances in the balance sheet accounts will be carried forward to the next accounting year. Hence the balance sheet accounts are called permanent accounts or real accounts.

The asset accounts are usually listed first in the company's chart of accounts and in the general ledger. In the general ledger the asset accounts will normally have debit balances.

The balances in some of the asset accounts will be combined and presented as a single amount when the balance sheet is prepared. For example, if a company has ten checking accounts, the balances will be combined, and the total amount will be reported on the balance sheet as the asset Cash.

Assets include the things or resources that a company owns, that were acquired in a transaction, and have a future value that can be measured. Assets also include some costs that are prepaid or deferred and will become expenses as the costs are used up over time.

Here are some examples of asset accounts:

- Cash
- Short-term Investments
- Accounts Receivable
- Allowance for Doubtful Accounts (a contra-asset account)
- Accrued Revenues/Receivables
- Prepaid Expenses
- Inventory
- Supplies

- Long-term Investments
- Land
- Buildings
- Equipment
- Vehicles
- Furniture and Fixtures
- Accumulated Depreciation (a contra-asset account)

## DESCRIPTIONS OF ASSET ACCOUNTS

The following are brief descriptions of some common asset accounts.

### Cash

Cash includes currency, coins, checking account balances, petty cash funds, and customers' checks that have not yet been deposited. A company is likely to have a separate general ledger account for each checking account, petty cash fund, etc. but will combine the amounts and will report the total as Cash (or Cash and Cash Equivalents) on the balance sheet.

### Short-term Investments

Short-term or temporary investments may include certificates of deposit, bonds, notes, etc. that will mature in less than one year. It may also include investments in the common or preferred stock of another corporation if the stock can be easily sold on a stock exchange.

### Accounts Receivable

Accounts receivable is a right to receive an amount as the result of delivering goods or services on credit. Under the accrual method of accounting, Accounts Receivable is debited at the time of a credit sale. Later, when the customer pays the amount owed, the company will credit Accounts Receivable (and will debit Cash).

## Allowance for Doubtful Accounts

The Allowance for Doubtful Accounts is a contra-asset account since its balance is intended to be a credit balance (or a zero balance). When the balance in this account is combined with the balance in Accounts Receivable, the resulting amount is known as the net realizable value of the receivables. The Allowance for Doubtful Accounts is used under the allowance method of reporting bad debts expense.

## Accrued Revenues/Receivables

Under the accrual method of accounting, revenues are to be reported when goods or services have been delivered even if a sales invoice has not been generated. This account will report the amounts that a company has a right to receive but the sales invoices have yet to be prepared or entered in Accounts Receivable.

## Prepaid Expenses

These are future expenses that have already been paid. The amounts appear as assets until the costs have been used up or expired. A common example of a prepaid expense is the payment for vehicle insurance. To illustrate this, assume that on December 29, a new company pays $6,000 for the insurance covering its vehicles for the six-month period that will begin on January 1. As of December 31, the entire $6,000 will be a prepaid expense because none of the cost has expired. Since none of the cost expired in December, there is no insurance expense in December. The insurance expense will begin in January at a rate of $1,000 per month. This is depicted in the following chart:

|  | Dec | Jan | Feb | Mar | Apr | May | June |
|---|---|---|---|---|---|---|---|
| Payment | $6,000 | $    - | $    - | $    - | $    - | $    - | $    - |
| Expense* | - | 1,000 | 1,000 | 1,000 | 1,000 | 1,000 | 1,000 |
| Prepaid/asset** | 6,000 | 5,000 | 4,000 | 3,000 | 2,000 | 1,000 | - |

*The expense is the amount that is expiring during the month.
**The prepaid amounts are the unexpired amounts and should be the balance in the asset account Prepaid Expenses or Prepaid Insurance at the end of each of the months.

## Inventory

Inventory is the cost of goods that have been purchased or manufactured and have not yet been sold.

## Supplies

Supplies could be office supplies, manufacturing supplies, packaging supplies or other supplies that are on hand. The cost of the supplies that remain on hand is reported as an asset.

## Long-term Investments

This account or asset category will be reported on the balance sheet immediately following current assets. It may include investments in the common stock, preferred stock, and bonds of another corporation. It also includes real estate being held for sale and the money that is restricted for a long-term purpose such as a building project or the repurchase of bonds payable. The cash surrender value of a life insurance policy owned by a company is also reported under this asset heading.

## Land

This account represents the property portion of the balance sheet heading "Property, plant and equipment." It reports the cost of land used in a business. Since land is assumed to last indefinitely, the cost of land is not depreciated.

## Buildings

This account will report the cost of the building used in the business. The cost of buildings will be depreciated over their useful lives.

## Equipment

This account reports the cost of the machinery and equipment used in the business. The cost of equipment will be depreciated over the equipment's useful life.

### Vehicles

This account reports the cost of trucks, trailers, and automobiles used in the business. The cost of vehicles is to be depreciated over the vehicles' useful lives.

### Furniture and Fixtures

This account reports the cost of desks, chairs, shelving, etc. that are used in the business. The cost of furniture and fixtures is to be depreciated over the useful lives.

### Accumulated Depreciation

Accumulated Depreciation is known as a contra asset account because it has a credit balance instead of a debit balance that is typical for asset accounts. Whenever Depreciation Expense is debited for the periodic depreciation of the buildings, equipment, vehicles, etc. the account Accumulated Depreciation is credited. The credit balance in Accumulated Depreciation will continue to grow until an asset is sold or scrapped. However, the maximum amount of the credit balance is the cost of the asset(s).

## LIABILITY AND STOCKHOLDERS' EQUITY ACCOUNTS

### LIABILITY ACCOUNTS

A company's liability accounts appear in the chart of accounts, general ledger, and balance sheet immediately following the asset accounts. In the general ledger, the liability accounts will usually have credit balances.

Note: Liabilities are a company's obligations. They are the amounts that the company owes. Liabilities also include amounts received from customers in advance of being earned.

Here are some examples of liability accounts:

- Short-term Loans Payable
- Current Portion of Long-term Debt
- Accounts Payable
- Accrued Expenses

- Unearned or Deferred Revenues
- Installment Loans Payable
- Mortgage Loans Payable

## DESCRIPTIONS OF LIABILITY ACCOUNTS

The following are brief descriptions of some common liability accounts.

**Short-term Loans Payable**

This account will report the amount of loans which will be due within one year of the date of the balance sheet.

**Current Portion of Long-term Debt**

This account or line description reports the principal portion of a long-term debt that will have to be paid within one year of the date of the balance sheet. (The portion of the debt that is not due within one year is reported as a non-current liability.)

**Accounts Payable**

Accounts Payable is the account containing the amounts owed to suppliers for invoices that have been approved and entered for payment. The balance in this account reports the amount of those invoices which are unpaid.

**Accrued Expenses/Liabilities**

Under the accrual method, the amounts in this account are owed but have not yet been recorded in Accounts Payable. This account could include the vendor invoices awaiting processing, employee wages and benefits earned but not yet recorded, and other expenses incurred but not yet recorded.

**Unearned or Deferred Revenues**

Unearned revenues reports the amounts received in advance of having been earned. For example, if a law firm requires that a client pays $4,000 in advance for future legal work, the law firm will record the cash of $4,000 and the liability to deliver $4,000 of legal services. The law firm cannot report the $4,000 as revenue until it is earned. This liability account could have the title Unearned Revenues or Deferred Legal Fees. As the legal services are performed and therefore are earned, the law firm will reduce the liability account and will report the amount as revenues.

### Installment Loans Payable

Installment loans are loans that require a series of payments. A common example is a three-year automobile loan that requires monthly payments. The principal due within one year of the balance sheet date will be reported as a current liability and the remainder of the principal owed will be reported as a noncurrent liability. (The future interest is not recorded as a liability, since it is not due or payable as of the date of the balance sheet.)

### Mortgage Loans Payable

Mortgage loans are usually long-term loans with real estate pledged as collateral. The principal due within one year of the balance sheet will be reported as a current liability and the remainder of the principal owed is reported as a noncurrent liability. (The future interest is not recorded as a liability since it is not due or payable as of the date of the balance sheet.)

### Stockholders' Equity Accounts

The stockholders' equity accounts of a corporation will appear in the chart of accounts, general ledger, and balance sheet immediately following the liability accounts. In the general ledger, most of the stockholders' equity accounts will have credit balances. The following are brief descriptions of typical stockholders' equity accounts.

### Paid-in Capital

Paid-in capital is a subheading within stockholders' equity which indicates the amount paid to the corporation at the time that shares of stock were issued. Paid-in capital is also referred to as permanent capital. Every corporation will have common stock and a potential percentage of corporations will have preferred stock in addition to common stock.

The paid-in capital accounts report the amounts received when the corporation's stock was issued. Often there are two accounts for the common stock:

- Par value of the common stock, and
- Paid-in capital in excess of the par value of the common stock

If a corporation also issued preferred stock, there will also be two additional accounts.

**Common Stock**
If a corporation's common stock has a par value or a stated value, only the par or stated value of the shares issued will be recorded in this account. However, if a corporation's common stock has neither a par value nor a stated value, the entire amount received by the corporation at the time that the shares were issued will be recorded in this account.

**Paid-in Capital in Excess of Par Value—Common Stock**
When a corporation issues common stock, the amount received minus the par value or stated value is recorded in this account. (The par value of common stock is recorded in the account Common Stock.)

**Retained Earnings**
Generally, the amount of a corporation's retained earnings is the cumulative amount of earnings (net income) since the corporation was formed minus the cumulative number of dividends that have been declared since the corporation was formed.

The current accounting period's earnings (or net income) will be added to this account and the current period's dividends will be deducted.

Note: Revenues will cause retained earnings to increase, while expenses will cause retained earnings to decrease.

Retained earnings is a component of stockholders' equity, but it is separate from paid-in capital. Hence, the amounts reported under retained earnings are not considered to be permanent capital.

## INCOME STATEMENT ACCOUNTS

The income statement accounts are categorized in a variety of ways. Here are the classifications we will be using:

- Operating revenues
- Operating expenses
- Other revenues and gains
- Other expenses and losses

The amounts in these accounts at the end of an accounting year will not be carried forward to the subsequent year. Rather, the balances in the income statement accounts will be transferred to Retained Earnings (for a corporation) or to the owner's capital account (for a sole proprietorship). This will allow for all of the income statement accounts to begin each accounting year with zero balances. This explains why the income statement accounts are referred to as temporary accounts.

### OPERATING REVENUES

Operating revenues are the amounts earned from carrying out the company's main activities. For example, the sales of merchandise are a retailer's operating revenues.

A few examples of accounts for recording operating revenues include:

- Sales
- Sales Revenues
- Service Revenues
- Fees Earned
- Sales - Product Line #1
- Sales - Product Line #2

The revenue accounts are expected to have credit balances (since revenues cause the stockholders' or owner's equity to increase). Contra revenue accounts such as Sales Returns and Allowances and Sales Discounts will have debit balances.

Under the accrual method of accounting, revenues are reported as of the date the goods are sold or the services were performed. If a service is provided on December 27, but the customer is allowed to pay in February, the revenues are reported on the income statement that includes December 27.

At the end of the accounting year, the balance in each of the accounts for recording operating revenues will be closed to start the next accounting year with a zero balance.

## OPERATING EXPENSES

Operating expenses are the expenses incurred in earning operating revenues. For example, advertising expense is one of the operating expenses of a retailer.

A few of the many accounts used to record operating expenses include:

- Cost of Goods Sold
- Cost of Goods Sold - Product Line #1
- Salaries Expense
- Fringe Benefit Expense
- Rent Expense
- Utilities Expense
- Utilities Expense - Store #45
- Depreciation Expense - Buildings
- Depreciation Expense - Equipment
- Repairs Expense

The accounts for operating expenses should have debit balances.

Under the accrual method of accounting, the expenses should be reported in the same accounting period as the related revenues. If that is not certain, then an expense should be reported in the accounting period in which its cost expires or is used up.

Expenses are often organized by function such as manufacturing, selling, and general administrative. At other times expenses will be organized by responsibility such as Department #1, Sales Region #5, Warehouse #2, Legal Department, etc.

At the end of the accounting year, the balance in each of the accounts used for recording operating expenses will be closed to start the next accounting year with a zero balance.

## NON-OPERATING REVENUES AND GAINS

Revenues earned outside of a company's main business activities are referred to as non-operating revenues or as other revenues. For example, the interest earned by a retailer on its idle cash balances is part of non-operating or other revenues.

Gains often occur when a company sells an asset that was used in the business, and the cash received was greater than the asset's carrying amount on the company's books. For example, if a company car is sold for $10,000 and its book value is $9,000, there will be a gain of $1,000.

The accounts that report non-operating revenues, other revenues, and gains are expected to have credit balances since they cause stockholders' equity to increase.

## NON-OPERATING EXPENSES AND LOSSES

The expenses incurred to earn non-operating revenues are reported as non-operating expenses or other expenses. In addition, interest expense for a retailer is a non-operating expense or other expense. (On the other hand, the interest expense paid by a bank for the use of depositors' money is one of the bank's operating expenses.)

Losses are reported when a company disposes of a long-term asset for the cash, and the amount of cash received is less than the book value of the asset. For example, if a company car is sold for $7,500 and its book value is $9,000, a loss of $1,500 will be reported. Another example of a loss is the loss from a lawsuit.

The accounts for non-operating expenses and losses will have debit balances since they cause stockholders' equity to decrease.

## RECORDING TRANSACTIONS

With sophisticated accounting software and inexpensive computers, it is no longer practical for most businesses to manually enter transactions into journals and then to post to the general ledger accounts and subsidiary ledger accounts. Today, software such as QuickBooks* will update the relevant accounts and provide more information with a minimum of data entry.

In this section we will highlight how the accounting software will capture financial transactions and then automatically update the general ledger and store the information for management's future use.

## ACCOUNTS PAYABLE

When accounting software is used to enter the invoices received from suppliers (vendor invoices), the software will update Accounts Payable and will require that the account or accounts that should be debited be entered as well. The accounting software's vendor files also allow a company to prepare purchase orders, receiving tickets and to pay the vendors' invoices.

A company should have internal controls so that only legitimate invoices are recorded and paid.

## CHECK WRITING

When the accounting software is used to write checks, the software will automatically credit the Cash account and will require that another account be designated for the debit. An additional benefit is that the amounts will move electronically, and the account balances will be automatically calculated with speed and accuracy.

Again, a company should have internal controls to ensure that only legitimate payments are processed.

## SALES ON CREDIT

When the accounting software is used to prepare a sales invoice for a customer who purchased on credit, the customer's detail will be updated, the general ledger account Sales will be credited, and the general ledger account Accounts Receivable will be debited. Statements for each customer and an aging of all the accounts receivable can be printed with the click of a button.

## PAYROLL

Another source of financial transactions is the company's payroll. While many companies process payroll on their accounting software, others opt to outsource payroll to companies such as ADP, Paychex, Intuit, or local firms.

## BANK RECONCILIATION

The purpose of the bank reconciliation is to be certain that the financial statements are reporting the correct amount of cash and the proper amounts for any related accounts (since every transaction affects a minimum of two accounts).

The bank reconciliation process involves:

1. Comparing the following amounts
   - The balance on the bank statement
   - The balance in the company's general ledger account. (The account title might be Cash - checking.)
2. Determining the reasons for the difference in the amounts shown in 1.

The common reasons for a difference between the bank balance and the general ledger book balance are:

- Outstanding checks (checks written but not yet cleared in the bank)
- Deposits in transit (company receipts that are not yet deposited in the bank)
- Bank service charges and other bank fees
- Check printing charges
- Errors in entering amounts in the company's general ledger

The outstanding checks and deposits in transit do not involve errors by either the company or the bank. Since these items are already recorded in the company's accounts, no additional entries to the company's general ledger accounts will be needed.

Bank charges, check printing fees and errors in the company's accounts do require the company to make accounting entries. The company should make the entries before the financial statements are prepared since a minimum of two accounts have the incorrect balances (due to double-entry accounting). Here is an entry for a bank service charge that was listed on the bank statement:

|  |  |  |
|---|---|---|
| Bank Fees Expense | 34.00 |  |
| Cash - Checking Account |  | 34.00 |

If the reconciliation reveals that an incorrect amount has been recorded in the company's Cash account, perhaps the easiest way to correct the error is to remove the incorrect amount and then enter the correct amount.

## ADJUSTING ENTRIES

### WHY ADJUSTING ENTRIES ARE NEEDED

For a company's financial statements to be complete and to reflect the accrual method of accounting, adjusting entries must be processed before the financial statements are issued. Here are three situations that describe why adjusting entries are needed:

### Situation 1

Not all a company's financial transactions that pertain to an accounting period will have been processed by the accounting software as of the end of the accounting period. For example, the bill for the electricity used during December might not arrive until January 10. (The reason for the 10-day lag is that the electric utility reads the meters on January 1 in order to compute the electricity actually used in December. Next the utility has to prepare the bill and mail it to the company.)

## Situation 2

Sometimes a bill is processed during the accounting period, but the amount represents the expense for one or more future accounting periods. For example, the bill for the insurance on the company's vehicles might be $6,000 and covers the six-month period of January 1 through June 30. If the company is required to pay the $6,000 in advance at the end of December, the expense needs to be deferred so that $1,000 will appear on each of the monthly income statements for January through June.

## Situation 3

Something like Situation 2 occurs when a company purchases equipment to be used in the business. Let's assume the equipment is acquired, paid for, and put into service on May 1. However, the equipment is expected to be used for ten years. If the cost of the equipment is $120,000 and will have no salvage value, then each month's income statement needs to report $1,000 for 120 months to report depreciation expense under the straight-line method.

These three situations illustrate why adjusting entries need to be entered in the accounting software to have accurate financial statements. Unfortunately, the accounting software cannot compute the amounts needed for the adjusting entries. A bookkeeper or accountant must review the situations and then determine the amounts needed in each adjusting entry.

### Steps for Recording Adjusting Entries

Some of the necessary steps for recording adjusting entries are:

- You must identify the two or more accounts involved.
    - One of the accounts will be a balance sheet account.
    - The other account will be an income statement account.
- You must calculate the amounts for the adjusting entries.
- You will enter both accounts and the adjustment in the general journal.
- You must designate which account will be debited and which will be credited.

## TYPES OF ADJUSTING ENTRIES

We will sort the adjusting entries into five categories.

| | | |
|---|---|---|
| 1. | Accrued revenues | Revenues (and the related receivables) have been earned, but the sales invoices have not yet been processed. |
| 2. | Accrued expenses | Expenses (and the related payables) have been incurred, but the vendors' invoices have not been completely processed. |
| 3. | Deferred revenues | Money was received in advance of having been earned. |
| 4. | Deferred expenses | Money was paid for a future expense. |
| 5. | Depreciation expense | An asset was purchased in one period, but its cost must be allocated to expense in each of the accounting periods of the asset's useful life. |

### 1. Accrued Revenues

Under the accrual method of accounting, a business is to report all of the revenues (and related receivables) that it has earned during an accounting period. A business may have earned fees from having provided services to clients, but the accounting records do not yet contain the revenues or the receivables. If that is the case, an accrual-type adjusting entry must be made in order for the financial statements to report the revenues and the related receivables.

If a business has earned $5,000 of revenues, but they are not recorded as of the end of the accounting period, the accrual-type adjusting entry will be as follows:

| | | |
|---|---|---|
| Accrued Receivables | 5,000 | |
| Service Revenues | | 5,000 |

### 2. Accrued Expenses

Under the accrual method of accounting, the financial statements of a business must report all of the expenses (and related payables) that it has incurred during an accounting period. For example, a business needs to report an expense that has occurred even if a supplier's invoice has not yet been received.

To illustrate, let's assume that a company utilized a worker from a temporary personnel agency on December 27. The company expects to receive an invoice on January 2 and remit payment on January 9. Since the expense and the payable occurred in December, the company needs to accrue the expense and liability as of December 31 with the following adjusting entry:

| | | |
|---|---|---|
| Temporary Help Expense | 200 | |
| Accrued Liabilities | | 200 |

## 3. Deferred Revenues

Under the accrual method of accounting, the amounts received in advance of being earned must be deferred to a liability account until they are earned.

Let's assume that Servco Company receives $4,000 on December 10 for services it will provide at a later date. Prior to issuing its December financial statements, Servco must determine how much of the $4,000 has been earned as of December 31. The reason is that only the amount that has been earned can be included in December's revenues. The amount that is not earned as of December 31 must be reported as a liability on the December 31 balance sheet.

If $3,000 has been earned, the Service Revenues account must include $3,000. The remaining $1,000 that has not been earned will be deferred to the following accounting period. The deferral will be evidenced by a credit of $1,000 in a liability account such as Deferred Revenues or Unearned Revenues.

The adjusting entry for this deferral depends on how the receipt of $4,000 was recorded on December 10. If the receipt of $4,000 was recorded with a credit to Service Revenues (and a debit to Cash), the December 31 adjusting entry will be:

| | | |
|---|---|---|
| Service Revenues | 1,000 | |
| Deferred Revenues | | 1,000 |

If the entire receipt of $4,000 had been credited to Deferred Revenues on December 10 (along with a debit to Cash), the adjusting entry on December 31 would be:

| | | |
|---|---|---|
| Deferred Revenues | 3,000 | |
| Service Revenues | | 3,000 |

## 4. Deferred Expenses

Under the accrual method of accounting, any payments for future expenses must be deferred to an asset account until the expenses are used up or have expired.

To illustrate, let's assume that a new company pays $6,000 on December 27 for the insurance on its vehicles for the six-month period beginning January 1. For December 27 through 31, the company should have an asset Prepaid Insurance or Prepaid Expenses of $6,000.

In each of the months January through June, the company must reduce the asset account by recording the following adjusting entry:

| | | |
|---|---|---|
| Insurance Expense | 1,000 | |
| Prepaid Insurance | | 1,000 |

## 5. Depreciation Expense

Depreciation is associated with fixed assets (or plant assets) that are used in the business. Examples of fixed assets are buildings, machinery, equipment, vehicles, furniture, and other constructed assets used in a business and having a useful life of more than one year. (However, land is not depreciated.)

Depreciation allocates the asset's cost (minus any expected salvage value) to expense in the accounting periods in which the asset is used. Hence, office equipment with a useful life of 5 years and no salvage value will mean monthly depreciation expense of 1/60 of the equipment's cost. A building with a useful life of 25 years and no salvage value will result in a monthly depreciation expense of 1/300 of the building's cost.

## REVERSING ENTRIES

The first two categories of adjusting entries that we had discussed above were:

1. Accrued revenues
2. Accrued expenses

These categories are also referred to as accrual-type adjusting entries or simply accruals. Accrual-type adjusting entries are needed because some transactions had occurred, but the company had not entered them into the accounts as of the end of the accounting period. In order for a company's financial statements to include these transactions, accrual-type adjusting entries are needed.

In all likelihood, an actual transaction (that required an accrual-type adjusting entry) will get routinely processed and recorded in the next accounting period. This presents a potential problem in that the transaction could get entered into the accounting records twice: once through the adjusting entry and also when it is routinely processed in the subsequent accounting period. The purpose of reversing entries is to remove the accrual-type adjusting entries.

Reversing entries will be dated as of the first day of the accounting period immediately following the period of the accrual-type adjusting entries. In other words, for a company with accounting periods which are calendar months, an accrual-type adjusting entry dated December 31 will be reversed on January 2.

To illustrate, let's assume that the company had accrued repairs expenses with the following adjusting entry on December 31:

| | | |
|---|---|---|
| Repairs Expenses | 6,000 | |
| Accrued Liabilities | | 6,000 |

This accrual-type adjusting entry was needed so that the December repairs would be reported as 1) part of the expenses on the December income statement, and 2) a liability on the December 31 balance sheet.

On January 2, the following reversing entry is recorded in order to remove the accrual-type adjusting entry of December 31:

| | | |
|---|---|---|
| Accrued Liabilities | 6,000 | |
| Repairs Expense | | 6,000 |

The reversing entry removes the liability established on December 31 and also puts a credit balance in the Repairs Expense account on January 2. When the vendor's invoice is processed in January, it can be debited to Repairs Expenses (as would normally happen). If the vendor's invoice is $6,000 the balance in the account Repairs Expenses will show a $0 balance after the invoice is entered. (The $6,000 credit from the reversing entry on January 2, plus the $6,000 debit from the vendor's invoice equals $0.) Zero is the correct amount because the expense of $6,000 belonged to December and was reported in December as the result of the December 31 adjusting entry.

Some accounting software will allow you to indicate the adjusting entries you would like to have reversed automatically in the next accounting period.

## BALANCE SHEET

The balance sheet is one of the four main financial statements of a business:

- Balance Sheet
- Income Statement
- Cash Flow Statement
- Statement of Stockholders' Equity

The balance sheet reports a company's assets, liabilities, and stockholders' equity as of a moment in time. (The other three financial statements report amounts for a period such as a year, quarter, month, etc.) The balance sheet is also known as the statement of financial position, and it reflects the accounting equation:

Assets = Liabilities + Stockholders' Equity.

Bankers will look at the balance sheet to determine the amount of a company's working capital, which is the amount of current assets minus the amount of current liabilities. They will also review the assets and the liabilities and compare these amounts to the amount of stockholders' equity.

When a balance sheet reports at least one additional column of amounts from an earlier balance sheet date, it is referred to as a comparative balance sheet.

## BALANCE SHEET CLASSIFICATIONS

Typically, companies issue a classified balance sheet. This means that the amounts are presented according to the following classifications:

```
ASSETS
    Current assets
    Investments (long-term)
    Property, plant and equipment
    Intangible assets
    Other assets
        Total assets

LIABILITIES & STOCKHOLDERS' EQUITY
LIABILITIES
    Current liabilities
    Noncurrent liabilities
        Total liabilities
STOCKHOLDERS' EQUITY
        Total liabilities and stockholders' equity
```

## DESCRIPTIONS OF THE BALANCE SHEET CLASSIFICATIONS

The following are brief descriptions of the classifications usually found on a company's balance sheet.

### Current Assets

Generally, current assets include cash and other assets that are expected to turn to cash within one year of the date of the balance sheet. Examples of current assets are cash and cash equivalents, short-term investments, accounts receivable, inventory and prepaid expenses.

**Investments**
This classification is the first of the noncurrent or long-term assets. Included are long-term investments in other companies, the cash surrender value of life insurance, bond sinking funds, real estate held for sale, and cash that is restricted for construction of plant and equipment.

**Property, Plant, and Equipment**
This category of noncurrent assets includes the cost of land, buildings, machinery, equipment, furniture, fixtures, and vehicles used in the operations of a business. Except for land, these assets will be depreciated over their useful lives.

**Intangible Assets**
Intangible assets include goodwill, trademarks, patents, copyrights and other non-physical assets that were acquired at a cost. The amount reported is their cost to acquire minus any amortization or write-down due to impairment. Valuable trademarks and logos that were developed by a company through years of advertising are not reported because they were not purchased from another person or company.

**Other Assets**
This category often includes costs that have been paid but are being expensed over a period greater than one year. Examples include bond issue costs and certain deferred income taxes.

**Current Liabilities**
Current liabilities are obligations of a company that are payable within one year of the date of the balance sheet (and will require the use of a current asset or will be replaced with another current liability).

Current liabilities include loans payable that will be due within one year of the balance sheet date, the current portion of long-term debt, accounts payable, income taxes payable and liabilities for accrued expenses.

**Noncurrent Liabilities**

These are also referred to as long-term liabilities. In other words, these obligations will not be due within one year of the balance sheet date. Examples include portions of automobile loans, portions of mortgage loans, bonds payable, and deferred income taxes.

**Stockholders' Equity**

This section of the balance sheet consists of the following major sections:

- Paid-in capital (the amounts paid by investors when the original shares of a corporation were issued)
- Retained earnings (the earnings of the corporation since it began minus the amounts that were distributed in the form of dividends to the stockholders)
- Treasury stock (a subtraction that represents the amount paid to repurchase the corporation's own stock)

## INCOME STATEMENT

The income statement is also known as the statement of operations, the profit and loss statement, or P&L. It presents a company's revenues, expenses, gains, losses and net income for a specified period of time such as a year, quarter, month, 13 weeks, etc.

## INCOME STATEMENT FORMATS

There are two formats for presenting a company's income statement:

- Multiple step
- Single step

The difference in formats has to do with the number of subtractions and subtotals that appear on the income statement before getting to the company's bottom line net income.

## Multiple-step Income Statement

Note that in the following multi-step income statement, there are three subtractions:

1. The first subtraction results in the subtotal gross profit.
2. The second subtraction results in the subtotal operating income.
3. The third subtraction provides the bottom-line net income.

*(Heading omitted)*

| | |
|---|---:|
| Sales | $ 85,000 |
| Cost of goods sold | 61,000 |
| **Gross profit** | 24,000 |
| Selling, general and admin expenses | 13,000 |
| **Operating income** | 11,000 |
| Nonoperating income | |
| Investment income | 500 |
| Interest expense | (800) |
| **Net income** | $ 10,700 |

## Single-step Income Statement

In the single-step format, the income statement will have only one subtraction—all of the expenses (both operating and non-operating) are subtracted from all of the revenues (both operating and non-operating). In this format, there is no subtotal for gross profit or operating income. The bottom line, net income, results from a single subtraction (a single step) as shown here:

(Heading omitted)

| | |
|---|---:|
| **Revenues** | |
| Sales | $ 85,000 |
| Investment income | 500 |
| **Total revenues** | **85,500** |
| | |
| **Expenses** | |
| Cost of goods sold | 61,000 |
| Selling, general & admin expenses | 13,000 |
| Interest expense | 800 |
| **Total expenses** | **74,800** |
| **Net income** | **$ 10,700** |

## BALANCE SHEET AND INCOME STATEMENT ARE LINKED

As we had discussed earlier, revenues cause stockholders' equity to increase while expenses cause stockholders' equity to decrease. Therefore, a positive net income reported on the income statement (which is the result of revenues being greater than expenses) will cause stockholders' equity to increase. A negative net income will cause stockholders' equity to decrease.

The income statement accounts are temporary accounts because their balances will be closed at the end of each accounting year to the stockholders' equity account Retained Earnings. (The balances in a sole proprietorship's income statement accounts will be closed to the owner's capital account.)

The link between the balance sheet and income statement is helpful for bookkeepers and accountants who want some assurance that the amount of net income appearing on the income statement is correct. If you verify the ending balances in the relatively few balance sheet accounts, you can have confidence that the income statement has the proper net income. Hence, you are wise to establish a routine to verify all of the balance sheet amounts.

Note: This technique does not guarantee that the details within the income statement are perfect.

Here is our suggestion for reviewing the balance sheet amounts.

| Balance Sheet Amounts | How to Verify the Amounts |
|---|---|
| Cash – checking account | Compare to the bank reconciliation |
| Accounts receivable | Compare to and review the aging of accounts receivable |
| Inventory | Compare to and review the physical inventory records |
| Property, plant, equipment | Compare to and review the fixed asset records |
| Accounts payable | Compare to and review the aging of accounts payable |
| Loans payable | Compare to the principal balance shown by the lender |
| …and so on. | |

## ADDITIONAL REVIEW

Another review that should be done routinely is to compare each item on the income statement to the same item on an earlier income statement. For example, the amounts for the 5-month period of the current year should be compared to the 5-month period of the previous year. If budgets are prepared, also compare this year's 5-month period to the budgeted amounts for the 5-month period.

The same holds for the balance sheet: compare the recent amounts to the amounts on the balance sheets from a year earlier and from a month earlier.

## CASH FLOW STATEMENT

While the balance sheet and the income statement are the most frequently referenced financial statements, the statement of cash flows or cash flow statement is a very important financial statement.

The cash flow statement is important because the income statement and balance sheet are normally prepared using the accrual method of accounting. Hence the revenues reported on the income statement were earned, but the company may not have received the money from its customers. (Many times, companies allow customers to pay in 30 days or 60 days and often customers pay later than the agreed upon terms.) Similarly, the expenses that are reported on the income statement have occurred, but the company may not have paid for the expense in the same period. To understand how cash has changed, and because many believe that "cash is king" the cash flow statement should be distributed and read at the same time as the income statement and balance sheet.

## FORMAT OF THE CASH FLOW STATEMENT

Within the cash flow statement, the cash receipts or cash inflows are reported as positive amounts. The cash paid out or cash outflows are reported as negative amounts.

The following table provides various ways for you to think of the positive and negative amounts that are shown on the cash flow statement:

| Think of **positive amounts** as... | Think of **negative amounts** as... |
|---|---|
| Cash received | Cash paid out |
| Having a positive effect on cash | Having a negative effect on cash |
| A source of cash | A use of cash |
| Good for the cash balance | Not good for the cash balance |
| Increasing cash | Decreasing cash |

The net total of all the positive and negative amounts reported on the cash flow statement should equal the change in the amount of the company's cash and cash equivalents. (The company's cash and cash equivalents are reported on its balance sheets.)

The cash inflows and cash outflows which explain the change in a company's cash and cash equivalents are reported in three main sections of the cash flow statement:

1. Operating activities
2. Investing activities
3. Financing activities

In addition to the three main sections, the cash flow statement requires the following disclosures:

- The amount of interest paid
- The amount of income taxes paid
- Exchanges of major items that did not involve cash (such as ex-

changing land for common stock, converting bonds into common stock, etc.).

1. **Operating Activities**

The cash flows reported in the operating activities section of the cash flow statement can be presented using one of two methods:

- Direct method
- Indirect method

The direct method is recommended by the FASB. However, a survey of 500 annual reports of large U.S. corporations revealed that only about 1% had used the recommended direct method. Nearly all the U.S. corporations in the survey used the indirect method. Hence, we will limit our discussion to the indirect method.

When the indirect method is used, the first section of the cash flow statement, Cash Flows from Operating Activities, begins with the company's net income (which is the bottom line of the income statement). Since the net income was computed using the accrual method of accounting, it needs to be adjusted to reflect the cash received and paid.

The very first adjustment involves depreciation. The amount of Depreciation Expense reported on the income statement had reduced the company's net income, but the depreciation entry did not involve cash. (The journal entry for the current period's depreciation was a debit to Depreciation Expense and a credit to Accumulated Depreciation. Cash was not used.) Since the depreciation expense reduced net income, but did not use any cash, the amount of depreciation expense is added back to the net income amount.

| | |
|---|---|
| Net income | $19,000 |
| Add back: Depreciation expense | + 9,000 |

So far, the Cash Flows from Operating Activities is $28,000

Any amortization or depletion expense is also added back.

Next, the operating activities will adjust the net income to reflect the changes in the amounts of current assets and current liabilities during the accounting period. For example, if accounts receivable increased from $9,500 to $9,800 during the period, we conclude that the company did not collect cash for all of the sales revenues shown on the income statement. Not collecting all of the sales amounts (or seeing accounts receivable increase) is viewed as negative for the company's cash. Hence the $300 increase in accounts receivable is shown as a negative adjustment of $300:

| | |
|---|---|
| Net income | $19,000 |
| Add back: depreciation expense | 9,000 |
| Increase in accounts receivable | (300) |

So far, the Cash Flows from Operating Activities is $27,700.

If accounts payable increased from $3,100 to $3,350 during the period, it indicates that the company did not pay all its expenses. Not paying the bills is good for the company's cash. Hence, the $250 increase in accounts payable will be shown as a positive amount:

| | |
|---|---|
| Net income | $19,000 |
| Add back: depreciation expense | 9,000 |
| Increase in accounts receivable | (300) |
| Increase in accounts payable | 250 |

So far, the Cash Flows from Operating Activities is $27,950

The changes in the current asset and the current liability accounts are reported as adjustments to the company's net income in the operating activities section except that the change in short-term notes payable will be reported in the financing activities section.

## 2. Investing Activities

The purchasing and selling of long-term assets are reported in the second section of the cash flow statement, investing activities.

The cash flows that involve long-term assets include:

- The cash received from selling long-term assets. These are reported as positive amounts.
- The cash used to purchase long-term assets. These are reported as negative amounts.

## 3. Financing Activities

The changes in the noncurrent liabilities, stockholders' (or owner's) equity, and short-term loans are reported in the financing activities section of the cash flow statement.

The positive amounts in the financing activities section could indicate that cash was received from:

- Issuing bonds payable
- Borrowing through other long-term loans
- Issuing shares of stock
- Borrowing through short-term loans

The negative amounts indicate that cash was used for:

- Retiring (paying off) long-term debt
- Purchasing shares of the company's stock (treasury stock)
- Paying dividends to stockholders
- Repaying short-term loans

## OTHER

At the bottom of the cash flow statement, the net totals of the three sections are reconciled with the change in the cash and cash equivalents that are reported on the company's balance sheet.

The reporting requirements for the cash flow statement also include disclosing the amounts paid for interest and income taxes and significant noncash investing and financing activities. (Two examples of noncash investing and financing activities are converting bonds to common stock and exchanging bonds payable for land.)

## STATEMENT OF STOCKHOLDERS' EQUITY

The fourth financial statement is the statement of stockholders' equity. This statement lists the changes to the stockholders' equity section of the balance sheet during the current accounting period.

ABC Corporation
Statement of Stockholders' Equity
For the Year Ended December 31, 2020

|  | Common Stock - par | Common Stock - excess of par | Retained Earnings | Accumulated Other Comprehensive Income | Treasury Stock | Total |
|---|---|---|---|---|---|---|
| Balance, Dec 31, 2019 | xxx | xxxx | xxxxx | xxx | (xxx) | xxxxxx |
| Net earnings |  |  | xxxx |  |  | xxx |
| Other comprehensive income |  |  |  | xx |  | xx |
| Treasury stock purchases |  |  |  |  | (x) | (x) |
| Dividends |  |  | (xx) |  |  | (xx) |
| Balance, Dec 31, 2020 | xxx | xxxx | xxxxxx | xxxx | (xxxx) | xxxxxx |

*See accompanying notes to the financial statements.*

A common format of the statement of stockholders' equity is shown here:

To see additional examples of the statement of stockholders' equity we recommend that you identify a few U.S. corporations with stock that is publicly traded. On each corporation's website, select Investor Relations and then select each corporation's Form 10-K (the annual report to the Securities and Exchange Commission). Go to the section of the 10-K which presents the corporation's financial statements and view the statement of stockholders' equity.

## CLOSING CUT-OFF

At a minimum of once per year, companies must prepare financial statements. In addition, companies often prepare quarterly and monthly financial statements which are referred to as interim financial statements.

For any of the financial statements to be accurate it is necessary to have a proper cut-off. This means including all a company's business transactions in the proper accounting period. For example, the electricity bill arriving on January 10 might be the cost of the electricity that was used in December. (The time lag resulted from the utility company reading the electric meters and preparing and mailing the bill.) Hence under the accrual method of accounting, the bill received on January 10 needs to be included in December's expenses and must also be reported by the company as a liability as of December 31.

Similarly, the hourly payroll processed during the first few days in January and paid on January 6 is likely to include the cost of employees working during the last few days in December. The cost of the hours worked through December 31 must be included in the company's December expenses and, in the liabilities, as of December 31.

As you read the previous paragraph, you may have been reminded of our discussion of adjusting entries. That's because the adjusting entries are part of each period's closing process. The adjusting entries are prepared to report a company's revenues and expenses in the proper accounting period.

## THE CLOSING PROCESSES

To achieve a proper cut-off and to distribute the financial statements in a timely manner, it is helpful to have a timeline (or PERT chart) that indicates the necessary steps in the closing process. The timeline will indicate what needs to be done and the sequence in which things need to occur. It will also reveal what is preventing the financial statements from being distributed sooner.

In addition, a checklist of the closing tasks should be prepared and distributed to the appropriate employees as to what is required, who is responsible, and the day it is due.

If some journal entries must be written every month, it is helpful to assign journal entry numbers to these standard journal entries or recurring journal entries. For example, a company may designate JE33 (Journal Entry #33) to be the recurring accrual of expenses that have occurred but have not yet been recorded in Accounts Payable as of the end of a month. Perhaps the timeline/checklist will indicate that JE33 must be submitted by the accounts payable clerk six days after each month ends. The company may also have its computer automatically prepare JE34 which is the entry that automatically reverses the previous month's accrual entry JE33.

Some recurring journal entries will have the same amount each month. For example, a company's JE10 might be $10,800 every month of the year for the company's depreciation expense. (Some companies will refer to the entries that have the same amounts and accounts every month as standard entries.)

Another recurring entry may involve the same accounts each month, but the amounts will vary from month to month. For example, a company's JE03 might be the recurring monthly entry for bad debts expense. The company has determined in advance that the amount of JE03 will be 0.002 of the company's monthly credit sales. Since the amount of sales is different every month, the amounts on JE03 will be different each month.

Having entry numbers and standard entries should help to make the monthly closings more routine and efficient.

**IMPORTANCE OF CONTROLS**

The use of accounting software has eliminated some of the tedious tasks previously associated with bookkeeping. This could result in fewer people involved in the bookkeeping, accounting, and administrative tasks. A side effect of fewer people handling more tasks is the potential for concealing some dishonest activity. For example, if the person who processes the cash receipts is also the person that records the amounts in customers' accounts, stealing some cash will be easier than if the tasks were separated. Having a third person mailing statements to customers with instructions to report any discrepancies to a fourth person will further safeguard the company's assets.

Accountants refer to the practices and policies for safeguarding assets as internal controls. Very large corporations may have a staff of internal auditors that ensure there are controls in place (including the separation of duties) so that fraud and misappropriation will not occur. Potential companies or organizations with a potential staff are therefore at a disadvantage. Nonetheless owners and managers of even the smallest companies and organizations must be aware of the need for internal controls. Here is a partial list of some internal controls that smaller organizations can implement:

- Separate the handling of cash from the person processing accounts receivable.
- Have the bank statement reconciled by someone who does not process the receipts or record the amounts in the general ledger cash account.
- Have the owner of a potential company approve all purchase orders.
- Have the owner of a potential company review all payments and sign all checks.
- Have all credit memos to customers be approved by the owner.

We are not experts in internal controls, but we realize their importance. We strongly recommend that you seek assistance from your professional accountant regarding internal controls that are appropriate for your business or organization.

# CHAPTER 9

# TAXES

Did you ever wonder why taxes are so often mentioned in the same sentence as death? They're both unpleasant, and you can't, in the end, avoid either of them. But that doesn't have to get you down! Your business is killing it and your customers are being served. You just need to keep Uncle Sam and the KGB oops . . . the IRS off your back. And to do that, you need to know what the potential business tax rates are.

So, let's walk through it together.

## WHAT IS A BUSINESS TAX?

The taxes you pay and how you pay them depend on how you set up your business, but there are three general types of business taxes.

### 1. Income Taxes

All businesses must file an annual income tax return. C corporations pay income tax at the corporate rate, while all other businesses are considered "pass-through" entities and are taxed at the individual rate (we'll dig in on these in a minute).

2. **Estimated Taxes**

Freelancers, independent contractors, and potential business owners who expect to owe at least $1,000 in taxes need to estimate and pay quarterly taxes. If you don't pay them, or don't pay enough, you can be hit with penalties and interest, and open yourself up to all kinds of unpleasantness. So, you need to be sure that you know the due dates and the payment period for the estimate.

| WHEN YOU GET PAID | TAX DUE DATE |
| --- | --- |
| Jan. 1–March 31 | April 15 |
| April 1–May 31 | June 15 |
| June 1–Aug. 31 | September 15 |
| Sept. 1–Dec. 31 | January 15 of the following year |

3. **Employment Taxes**

People who are self-employed have to pay self-employment taxes, which are Social Security and Medicare taxes.

You must pay self-employment taxes if:

- Your net earnings are $400 or more
- You work for a church or a qualified church-controlled organization that elected an exemption from Social Security and Medicare taxes, and you make $108.28 or more in wages.[3] This does not apply to ministers or members of a religious order (such as nuns).

If you have employees, you must pay employment taxes, which include:

- Social Security and Medicare taxes
- Federal income tax withholdings (this is technically paid by your employee, but you're responsible for making sure Uncle Sam gets it)
- Federal unemployment (FUTA) tax

There are also various excise taxes depending on the type of business. Often called sin taxes, these could be anything from taxes on purchasing heavy-duty trucks to sales of alcohol and tobacco.

## WHAT IS THE BUSINESS TAX RATE FOR 2020?

Now that we know what kinds of taxes businesses pay, what are the rates? It depends on how you set your business up. There are basically two ways to do it.

### C Corporations

This one is easy-peasy (sort of). The Tax Cuts and Jobs Act of 2018 aka the tax reform bill cut the income tax rate to a flat 21% for all businesses that are set up as C corporations. Simple enough, right? But there's one more thing.

If the corporation pays dividends, shareholders pay taxes on those on their personal tax returns. So, C corporation profits are taxed twice. There are two types of dividends: qualified and unqualified. Let's look at those:

- Qualified: if you've owned the stock for longer than 60 days, that dividend is qualified. Qualified dividends get favorable tax rates and are taxed at long-term capital gain rates.
- Unqualified: also known as ordinary dividends, these are taxed at the shareholder's regular income tax rate (more on that below!).

### Pass-Through Entities

The tax rate for pass-through entities is the same as the owner's personal income tax rate.[4] There is also an alternative minimum tax (AMT). The AMT only applies to certain high-income earners who may otherwise avoid paying any individual income taxes.[5]

So, which types of businesses are pass-through entities?

- Sole Proprietorship: a business where you are the only owner. You are the boss and totally responsible for everything that happens. It's really important to keep your personal finances and business finances separate so you don't get into any tax trouble.

- Partnership (Limited and Limited Liability): a business owned by two or more people. Limited partnerships (LPs) have a greater potential for personal conflict between the partners, since only one of the partners has unlimited liability meaning they're on the hook for any debts or bills if the business goes belly-up. The partners with limited liability also tend to have limited control of the business. In a limited liability partnership (LLP), however, all partners are protected from debts and obligations against the partnership.

- Limited Liability Company (LLC): LLCs help separate personal assets and liabilities from business ones, reducing your personal risk if your business is unable to pay its bills. In an LLC, your profits and losses can pass through to your personal income without facing corporate taxes, but members of an LLC are considered self-employed and must pay self-employment taxes.

- S Corporation: An S corporation is structured to avoid the double taxation that happens in a C corporation. S corporations allow profits, and some losses, to pass directly through to the owners' personal income without being subject to corporate tax rates. But there are some limits to S corporations: You can't have more than 100 shareholders, and all shareholders must be U.S. citizens. Plus, S corporations still have to follow strict filing and operational processes.

**TAX PLANNING**

This process evaluates options to determine when, whether, and how to conduct business and personal transactions for minimal taxes. As an individual taxpayer, and as a business owner, you generally can complete a taxable transaction by multiple methods, choosing whichever results in the lowest legal tax liability. While tax avoidance is expected, tax evasion—reducing tax through deceit or concealment is not.

## CHOOSING TAX YEAR AND ACCOUNTING METHODS

As a potential business owner, your decisions often have tax implications—whether or not you realize it. Suppose you buy a car for business use, rather than lease it. You can't deduct the purchase price (as you can a lease payment), but you can deduct a portion of the cost annually as depreciation. Some tax-related choices have a more general effect on your business income, namely:

**Tax year:** this determines the time period for which your taxable income will be computed. All the income received or accrued within a single year is reported on that year's return, along with expenses paid or accrued. The end of the tax year is the cut-off point for many tax-saving strategies.

**Accounting method:** whether you're a sole proprietor filing Schedule C or a partnership or LLC filing Form 1065, you must report your accounting method to the IRS. There are two basic methods available to most potential businesses: Cash and Accrual. In some cases, you may be able to use a hybrid that combines elements of both. Also, owners of certain types of businesses can use special accounting methods under the tax law.

**Determining business income and deductions:** calculating your income tax requires computing your business income. This means taking your gross business receipts or sales and subtracting your cost of goods sold to arrive at your gross profit, then deducting your other business expenses. Generally, any income you receive connected with your business is "business income" and should be reported on your business tax return. Income is "connected with your business" if the payment would not have been made if you did not have the business. Other considerations:

> *Gross income from sales:* in most cases, this will be the bulk of the income you receive from operating your business.
>
> *Miscellaneous business income:* this topic can get complicated, since different business-related types of income must be reported on different parts of your tax return.

*Cost of goods sold:* this must be computed if your business uses inventory, in order to complete the business income portion of your tax return.

*Deductions:* digging up every legitimate deduction is usually your best bet for reducing your taxable income and tax bill. Capital expenditures, start-up, travel (notably vehicles), meal and entertainment expenses, business gifts, compensation, home office deduction, casualty losses and vehicle expenses are all common business deductions.

Potential businesses can write off several expenses as tax deductions to help lower the amount they owe on their income tax. The top potential business tax deductions include:

1. *Business meals.* As a potential business, you can deduct 50 percent of food and drink purchases that qualify. To qualify, the meal needs to be related to your business and you need to keep the following documentation related to the meal:

   - Date and location of the meal
   - Business relationship of the person or people you dined with
   - The total cost of the meal

   The easiest way to track business meal expenses is to keep your receipt and jot down notes on the back about the details of the meal.

2. *Work-related travel expenses.* All expenses related to business travel can be written off at tax time, including airfare, hotels, rental car expenses, tips, dry cleaning, meals and more. You can reference the IRS website for a full list of deductible business travel expenses. To qualify as work-related travel, your trip must meet the following conditions:

   - The trip must be necessary to your business.

- The trip must take you away from your tax home, i.e., the city or area in which your company conducts its business.
- You must be travelling away from your tax home for longer than a normal workday and it must require you to sleep or rest on route.

3. *Work-related car use.* If you use your car strictly for work-related purposes, you can write off all costs associated with operating and maintaining it. If your car use is mixed between business and personal reasons, you can only deduct costs that are related to the business usage of the vehicle. You can claim the mileage you use for business driving, either by deducting the actual miles traveled for business, or by using the standard mileage deduction of $0.545 per mile driven.

4. *Business insurance.* You can deduct the cost of your business insurance on your tax return. If you have a home office or use a portion of your home to run your business, you can deduct your renter's insurance costs as part of your home office write-offs.

5. *Home office expenses.* Under new simplified IRS guidelines for home office expenses, home-based potential businesses and freelancers can deduct five dollars per square foot of your home that is used for business purposes, up to a maximum of 300 square feet. To qualify as a tax deduction, your work area has to be used exclusively for business (i.e., you can't write off the square footage of your dining room if you do your work at the table during the day) and you need to use the home office regularly as your principal place for conducting business.

6. *Office supplies.* You can write off office supplies including printers, paper, pens, computers and work-related software, as long as you use them for business purposes within the year in which they were purchased. You can also deduct work-related postage and shipping costs. Be sure to file all receipts for office supply purchases, for documentation.

7. ***Phone and internet expenses.*** If using the phone and internet is vital to running your business, you can deduct these expenses. If, however, you use the phone and internet for a mix of work and personal reasons, you can only write off the percentage of their cost that goes toward your business use. For example, if roughly half of your internet usage is business related, you can write off 50% of your internet expenses for the year.

8. ***Business interest and bank fees.*** If you borrow money to fund your business activities, the bank will charge you interest on the loan. Come tax season, you can deduct the interest charged both on business loans and business credit cards. You can also write off any fees and additional charges on your business bank account and credit card, such as monthly service fees and any annual credit card fees.

9. ***Depreciation.*** When you deduct depreciation, you're writing off the cost of a big-ticket item like a car or machinery over the useful lifetime of that item, rather than deducting it all in one go for a single tax year. Businesses usually deduct depreciation for long-term business investments that are more costly, so they are reimbursed for the expense over the entire useful lifetime of the item. Here's how to calculate depreciation:

Depreciation = Total cost of the asset / Useful lifetime of the asset

10. ***Professional Service Fees.*** Any professional service fees that are necessary to the functioning of your business, such as legal, accounting, and bookkeeping services, are deductible for tax purposes. If you use accounting or bookkeeping software for your business, that will also qualify as a tax deduction. If you are having trouble determining whether a particular professional service expense is for work or personal use, these guidelines for legal and professional fees from the IRS can help you judge the nature of the expense.

*11. **Salaries and Benefits.*** If you are a potential business owner with employees, you can write off their salaries, benefits and even vacation pay on your tax returns. There are a few requirements for writing off salary and benefit expenses:

- The employee is not a sole proprietor, partner, or LLC member in the business.
- The salary is reasonable and necessary.
- The services delegated to the employee were provided.

*12.* Charitable Contributions. You can deduct charitable donations that you make to qualifying organizations. If your business is set up as a sole proprietorship, LLC or partnership, you can claim these expenses on your personal tax forms. If your company is a corporation, you claim charitable donations on your corporate tax return.

*13.* Education. Any educational expenses you incur to bring value to your business are fully deductible for tax purposes. The requirements for education-related expenses are that the course or workshop must improve your skills or help maintain your professional expertise. Educational expenses that qualify for deductions include:

- Courses and classes related to your field of work
- Seminars and webinars
- Trade publication subscriptions
- Books related to your industry

*14.* Child and Dependent Care. Costs you incur for caring for children or adult dependents is tax deductible. If your own children are twelve years old or younger, you can write off costs associated with their care. Adult dependents also qualify for deductions, including spouses and some other related adults who are unable to care for themselves because of physical or mental disability.

15. Energy Efficiency Expenses. Upgrades that you make to your home to ensure it is more energy efficient can qualify for tax credits. You can claim 30 percent of the cost of alternative energy equipment for your home, including solar panels, solar water heaters and wind turbines. The IRS site offers further details on the home energy tax credits.

16. Investments. If you borrow money to make investments, you can write off the interest paid on the loan. You can deduct the interest up to the point that it matches what you earned in investment income.

17. Foreign-earned Income Exclusion. American citizens with businesses based abroad can, under certain circumstances, leave the foreign income they have earned off their tax return. To qualify for the exclusion, your tax home must be based abroad. This article can help you better understand the requirements for foreign-earned income exclusion.

18. Medical Expenses. You can claim both insurance premiums and medical care expenses, including doctor's fees, prescription drugs and home care. If you're self-employed and pay for your own health insurance, then you can deduct your health and dental care insurance premiums.

19. Real Estate Taxes. Real estate taxes paid at the state and local levels can be deducted on your income taxes. Property taxes are included in these deductions, and you can claim up to a total of $10,000.

20. Mortgage interest. You can deduct interest payments made toward mortgage loans to buy, construct or improve your home if you use your home for business purposes. If you take out loans against your home equity, you can also deduct the interest on those loans.

*21.* Moving Expenses. If you move, and the main reason for doing so is work related, you might be able to fully deduct the costs associated with the move. To qualify, your move has to pass the distance test. To pass the distance test your new job location must be at least 50 miles farther from your former home than your old job location was from your previous home.

*22.* Retirement Contributions. If you contribute to an Individual Retirement Account, doing so helps reduce your taxable income for the year. Your total IRA contributions can't exceed the total income you earned that year, or it can't exceed the annual maximum contribution, whichever one is less.

*23.* Advertising and Promotion. You can fully deduct expenses related to promoting your business, including digital and print advertising, website design and maintenance and the cost of printing business cards.

*24.* Client and Employee Entertainment. If you take business clients out, you can deduct the expense if you discuss business during the meeting and the entertainment takes place in a business setting for business purposes. You can deduct 50 percent of the cost of these entertainment expenses. You can also deduct as much as 100 percent of the cost of social events held for your employees.

*25.* Startup Expenses. If you launched a new business venture in the latest tax year, you could deduct as much as $5,000 in startup expenses you incurred in the lead up to your business launch. That can include costs associated with marketing your new business, travel, and training costs.

## CAPITAL ASSETS AND DEPRECIATION.

Almost every business must invest in major equipment, vehicles, machinery, or furniture in order to operate. Some require land, a building or franchise rights. Major assets used in your business for more than a year are known as "capital assets" and subject to special tax treatment. You generally can't deduct the entire cost of them in the same year you acquire them, with some notable exceptions for first-year expensing. Here's how it works: an asset's cost is deducted over the number of years it will be used, according to the asset's estimated drop in value each year. You could subtract all depreciation claimed to date from the cost of the asset, to get the asset's "book value" (theoretically equal to its market value). At the end of the asset's useful life for the business, any un-depreciated portion represents the salvage value. Since the actual drop in value is difficult and time-consuming to compute, accountants use various conventions to standardize the process: the straight-line method assumes assets depreciate by an equal percentage for each year used, while the declining balance method assumes they depreciate more in earlier years. The IRS has specific rules governing how you are allowed to deduct depreciation for tax purposes.

### NET PROFIT, LOSS, AND SELF-EMPLOYMENT TAXES

Once you have computed your gross business income and deducted your cost of goods sold to arrive at your gross profit, subtract your other business expenses for the year to calculate your net business income. This amount is your net profit for tax purposes. There are two important issues to consider when computing your net profit: self-employment taxes. For sole proprietors, your net business income is the amount on which you must pay self-employment taxes. If your business is a partnership, LLC, or corporation, you must follow somewhat different rules. Net operating losses. Owning a business is full of surprises. Some years, your expenses exceed your gross income, translating into a loss for the year. You may be able to deduct this loss against any other income you have or carry it back to offset prior years' taxable income or carry it over to offset income in future years.

### CLAIMING TAX CREDITS

Beyond tax deductions, minimize your income tax bill by claiming tax credits—they are generally preferable because they're subtracted directly from your tax bill. Deductions, in contrast, are subtracted from the income on which your tax bill is based. As great as tax credits can be, they are only available for certain situations or industries (e.g., research and development, home-buying, car buying, or alternative energy production). And credits come with a set of very complicated rules, which you or your tax pro must follow in order to claim.

## DEALING WITH THE IRS

As a potential business owner, be aware of your tax payment obligations and when they are due even if you use a tax adviser or accountant. There's no worse feeling than watching your cash surplus disappear because of an impending IRS payment. Worse yet is discovering that funds have been spent elsewhere because you didn't realize a tax payment was due. With a good awareness of your filing and payment obligations, you can avoid unexpected payments or penalties.

## STATE AND LOCAL TAXES ON BUSINESSES

Depending on where you live, you may also have to pay state and local taxes. The types and amounts of taxes you'll pay are different depending on your location. This is where a tax pro can really come in handy. Our small-business tax Endorsed Local Providers (ELPs) focus on the local. They live in your community and can guide you through complex state, county or city tax laws.

There are three big state and local taxes to be aware of:

- **State income taxes:** unless you live in one of the states that doesn't have them, you will owe state income taxes.
- **Property taxes:** if you own commercial property, you will have to pay property taxes, which are typically assessed at the county or city level.
- **Sales taxes:** if you sell things, you'll be responsible for collecting sales taxes. If you sell things online, this can get complicated, because some states charge based on where the seller is located, while other states charge taxes based on where the buyer is located.

It's one of Benjamin Franklin's most famous quotations: "In this world nothing can be said to be certain, except death and taxes" (p. 1). While business taxes are a certainty, the actual tax rates you pay are anything but certain in the current political climate.

As politicians continue to wrangle about tax rates on large corporations and potential businesses, the types of taxes a potential business owner will be reporting and paying are pretty stable. They include federal and state income taxes, employment taxes and sales taxes. But before you can pay your share, you need a tax ID.

### WHAT'S AN EIN NUMBER AND DO I NEED ONE?

Typically, most businesses need an Employer Identification Number (EIN), also known as a Federal Tax Identification Number. This nine-digit number, expressed as XX-XXXXXXX, is used to identify your business on all business tax reporting returns and forms.

You will need an EIN if you answer YES to any of the following questions:

- Do you have employees?
- Is your business a corporation or a partnership?
- Do you file employment, excise, or Alcohol, Tobacco and Firearms returns?
- Do you withhold wages on income, other than wages paid to a non-resident alien?
- Do you have a qualified retirement plan?

And a bank will want your EIN before you open a business bank account.

You can apply for a new EIN online. There is no charge for this service so beware of any private website that charges a fee to supply an EIN. You can also apply by phone, fax, or mail. Simply complete and return Form SS-4, which you can download from the IRS website or request by calling 1-800-TAX-FORM. If you apply online or by phone, you can get your EIN quickly. A faxed application may take one to two weeks to be processed and a mailed application could take up to four weeks. Make sure you have your EIN before you need to file a return or make a tax deposit.

## 3 STEPS TO FILING EMPLOYMENT TAXES

Running a business with employees adds several line items to your tax responsibilities. Specifically, you're required to report and deposit employment taxes, which include federal income taxes, Social Security and Medicare taxes, and Federal Unemployment (FUTA) taxes. Here is a list of employment tax due dates.

## DEPOSITING EMPLOYMENT TAXES

According to the IRS website, you must deposit any federal income tax withheld, plus both the employer and employee Social Security and Medicare taxes. The IRS has monthly, and semi-weekly deposit schedules and you can determine which schedule applies to your business by reviewing either IRS Publication 15 or 51.

FUTA tax deposits are required for any quarter in which the tax is more than $500 and must be made by the end of the month following the end of the quarter. The FUTA tax is paid entirely by you, the employer, and is not withheld from your employees' wages.

All federal tax deposits must be made electronically through the Electronic Federal Tax Payment System (EFTPS). To enroll, visit the website or call 1-800-555-4477.

## REPORTING EMPLOYMENT TAXES

Generally, you must report wages, tips and other compensation paid to your employees by filing Form W2 with the IRS at the end of the year. This is in addition to reporting the taxes you deposit. The reporting of income, Social Security and Medicare taxes is done each quarter using Forms 940, 941 (for most businesses) and 944 on paper or through e-file. FUTA tax is reported annually using Form 940.

## MAINTAINING TAX RECORDS

You should keep all records associated with your employment taxes, including amounts and dates of all wage and pension payments made to all employees, for at least four years.

Consult with your tax professional (3mb Management Consultants) to make sure you're taking full advantage of the federal and state tax laws, and for general guidance as you work through tax-related issues.

## HOW TO FILE SELF-EMPLOYMENT TAXES

The IRS considers you self-employed if any of the following applies to you:

- You are in a trade or business as a sole proprietor or independent contractor.
- You are a member of a partnership or limited liability company (LLC) that carries on a trade or business (limited partners are usually exempt; LLC members may be treated as employees if the business makes an election).
- You are otherwise in a business for yourself, including a part-time business.

If you are self-employed earning $400 or more per year, you will need to pay self-employment taxes, which consists of Social Security and Medicare taxes, in addition to income taxes. Since you don't have an employer withholding these taxes from your wages, you must estimate them and pay them quarterly. Use Form 1040-ES for this.

To report your Social Security and Medicare taxes, file Schedule SE on Form 1040.

## HUSBAND AND WIFE VENTURES

There may be some tax advantages for a business run exclusively by a husband and wife. The Potential Business and Work Opportunity Act of 2007 allows a husband-and-wife business to avoid being treated as a partnership for federal tax purposes. Instead, each spouse is treated as a sole proprietor and all income, gains, losses, credits, and deductions are divided between the spouses based on their respective interests in the venture. This may give each spouse credit for individual Social Security earnings. Like everything involving tax laws, it gets complicated, so consult with your tax advisor to see if you qualify.

**Note: 3mb Management Consultants can help you navigate both your personal and self-employed tax situation**

## UNDERSTANDING STATE BUSINESS TAXES
Your business tax obligations don't stop at the federal level. State and local government agencies want slices of your revenue, too.

## STATE INCOME TAXES
Nearly every U.S. state has a business or corporate income tax on their books and your tax requirement depends on the legal structure of your business. For example, a Limited Liability Company (LLC) is taxed separately from the business owners, while sole proprietors use the same tax form to report personal and business income taxes.

## STATE EMPLOYMENT TAXES
In addition to federal employment taxes, you must pay certain state employment related taxes as well. All states require payment of state workers' compensation insurance and unemployment insurance taxes. The following states or territories also require businesses to pay for temporary disability insurance:

- California
- Hawaii
- New Jersey
- New York
- Rhode Island
- Puerto Rico

## WHAT YOU NEED TO KNOW ABOUT COLLECTING SALES TAXES
As a consumer, you're familiar with paying sales tax whenever you purchase goods from a retailer (unless you live in one of the five states that do not have a general sales tax). The sales tax is collected from the buyer by the seller, who then forwards it on to the state.

As a businessperson, you are the seller, so it's your responsibility to collect, report and pay sales tax on almost everything sold to a customer in a state where your business has a physical presence. That means the state where your physical building sits, where your employees are living or working, or where you warehouse inventory.

But sales tax rates and regulations are set by each state and the rules are as different as the weather in Minnesota versus California. Adding to the complexity, local municipalities such as cities and counties may tack on additional sales taxes. To find the general sales and use tax rates and regulations for your area, go online and search your state's department of revenue or taxation.

**DOING THE PAPERWORK**

Generally, to collect sales tax you'll need a license or seller's permit from your state, which assigns you a special identification number. You keep track of sales transactions and taxes collected, then file a return and pay the taxes to the state. Filings and payments might be done monthly, quarterly or annually depending on the dollar amount of your sales.

**INTERNET SALES: TO COLLECT OR NOT TO COLLECT?**

Internet sales have added yet another layer of confusion. There continues to be debate about whether a business must collect sales tax on products purchased online and shipped to states where they have no physical presence. Some states have passed laws requiring the collection of sales taxes regardless of physical presence. And the federal government is considering legislation that would affect how this works on a national level. To learn more about how this may apply to your business, go online and search for "[Your State] Internet sales tax."

**Note:** Spend some time on your state's department of revenue or taxation website to learn about specific state tax requirements for your business and how to apply for a sales tax permit. For help in understanding how you should handle Internet sales, go online and search for "[Your State] Internet sales tax."

## USE TAX DEDUCTIONS TO LOWER YOUR TAX BILL

New potential business owners must stretch their financial resources.

Potential businesses have business expenses that include vehicle expenses, wages, business travel, contract labor (i.e., hiring freelancers and independent contractors), supplies, equipment, depreciation of assets, rent on business property, utilities, insurance (i.e., property, business, health insurance, etc.), and repairs.

Fortunately, as a potential business owner, you can minimize your business taxes by writing off a lot of those operational expenses come tax season.

## WRITE OFF YOUR STARTUP COSTS

Many brand-new startups make the mistake of thinking initial business expenses aren't deductible until their businesses are fully operational. However, the IRS allows potential business owners to deduct a wide array of startup expenses before beginning business operations.

The IRS allows you to deduct up to $5,000 in business startup costs and up to $5,000 in organizational costs, but only if your total startup costs are $50,000 or less. With the help of your tax software or a tax expert, you can write off typical costs associated with setting up a business during tax filing.

Typical costs to set up a business include business insurance, office space, real estate, office supplies, business cards, business assets, professional fees (i.e., hiring accountants), and potential business loan fees. If you're operating your business from a home office, you can qualify for a home office deduction.

Additional costs can also include employee training, locating suppliers, and advertising to potential clients. While companies cannot deduct licensing and incorporation fees as startup expenses, these costs may be deductible as organizational expenses.

It's important to remember that startup founders can only deduct those expenses leading to the creation of a viable business entity. If you decide against forming your business, the above costs will be labeled as personal expenses, and you may not be able to deduct any of your costs.

## PAY QUARTERLY TAXES

According to the IRS, individuals, including sole proprietors, partners, and S corporation shareholders, must make quarterly estimated tax payments if they expect to owe taxes of $1,000 or more when their federal returns or state tax returns are filed.

You can figure out your estimated tax payments as a business owner using Form 1040-ES. It may be helpful to use last year's income, deductions, and tax credits as a starting point. You can also use your previous year's federal tax return as a guide.

Once you've figured out the number and e-file, you can pay the IRS in several ways. These include IRS Direct Pay, which takes money owed out of your checking or savings account, and IRS Pay by Card, which allows you to pay with a credit or debit card online. Another option is paying by phone.

Quarterly estimated tax payments for each respective quarter are due every April 15, June 15, September 15, and January 15 (of the following tax year).

The self-employed and sole-proprietor business owners almost always have to pay estimated quarterly taxes unless their business loses money. Unlike a salaried employee — where their employer withholds a certain amount with each paycheck—sole proprietors, freelancers, and business owners assume the full tax burden.

Additionally, people who are partners in a business, a corporation, or an S Corporation often pay quarterly taxes if they expect to owe at least $500 in taxes.

Business owners who fail to submit at least 90% of the taxes they owe are subjected to severe penalties, so working with a tax professional can be very helpful to double check if the amount owed is correct.

## SOME BUSINESS TAXES YOU MIGHT NEED TO PAY

Keeping track of the amount of taxes you're responsible for can come as a great surprise when you own your business. Here are the most common types of taxes to account for as a business owner.

### Self-Employment Tax

If you've never owned a business before, then you are likely unaccustomed to paying self-employment taxes. Businesses pay a 15.3% FICA tax, which is used to fund Social Security and Medicare. Employees pay 7.65%, and employers pay the other 7.65%.

As a self-employed individual, you're responsible for the full 15.3%, which is sometimes called "self-employment tax." However, you can deduct half of the self-employment tax on your personal tax return (Form 1040). Additionally, it's important to take advantage of all possible startup and operating business expenses to maximize tax deductions.

### Payroll Tax

If you have employees, you'll be responsible for paying payroll taxes on their wages. Payroll taxes include federal income tax withholding, Social Security and Medicare taxes, and federal and state unemployment taxes. Many businesses hire a payroll service to file their tax forms and manage their payroll tax liabilities on their behalf.

### Excise Tax

Depending on the nature of your business and industry, you might be responsible for paying excise taxes. Excise taxes are indirect taxes that are not paid directly by the consumer of a product.

Often the tax is included within the price of the product itself, such as with cigarettes, gasoline, and liquor. Businesses that sell products subject to excise taxes are responsible for collecting the taxes and sending them directly to the IRS.

### Sales Tax

Although a federal sales tax doesn't exist in the United States, the majority of states levy sales taxes. Customers pay a sales tax on goods and services at the point of purchase. Business owners are responsible for collecting and reporting sales taxes to local and state governments. As a potential business owner, it's also important to understand state and local tax rules with respect to sales taxes.

**Property Tax**

If you own commercial property, you'll have to pay property taxes to the city or county where your business is located.

## MAXIMIZE YOUR FLEXIBILITY AS A POTENTIAL BUSINESS OWNER

Setting up and operating a potential business can come with significant initial costs. Whether you're flying solo or working with partners, the tax system is set up to help offset those potentially high costs for self-employed professionals at tax season. Maximizing tax deductions by writing off startup and operating costs can limit your tax liability in relation to your business income.

Having quality potential business tax software can guide you. As a new business owner, it also helps to work with a tax professional to avoid common pitfalls like underreporting your business expenses or ignoring an important tax form that can save you money.

# CHAPTER 10

# BASIC MARKETING MIX [5PS]

Also called the Marketing Mix, the 5 P's of marketing (place, price, product, promotion and now people) are the five pillars of a successful marketing strategy. Combined, they get your product or service in front of the right audience at the right time.

Originally known as the 4 P's, this concept was developed by Edmund Jerome McCarthy, a Notre Dame marketing professor. Rather than studying marketing from a functional standpoint, McCarthy's approach focused on the challenges and problem-solving marketers faced.

It was a revolutionary concept starting in the Mad Men era. Instead of just defining what marketing was, McCarthy developed a model that classified the essential marketing activities into four dimensions. This format was able to have marketers improve best practices by incorporating sociology and psychology to gain insight into consumer behavior.

As a marketer, to be successful in the execution of your marketing campaigns and put your brand above other competitors, you need to have the perfect combination of supplying a desirable product or service, sold at an attractive price, positioned in the right location, using attention-grabbing and conversational promotional tactics. That is, the 5 P's.

The 5 P's of Marketing—Product, Price, Promotion, Place, and People—are key marketing elements used to position a business strategically. The 5 P's of Marketing, also known as the marketing mix, are variables that managers and owners control to satisfy customers in their target market, add value to their business, and help differentiate their business from competitors.

| | | Marketing Mix | | |
|---|---|---|---|---|
| **Product** | **Price** | **Promotion** | **Place** | **People** |
| Functionality | Selling Price | Sponsorships | Distribution Channels | Service Provided |
| Appearance | Discounts | Advertising | Logistics | Attitude |
| Warranty | Payment Arrangements | Public Relations Activities | Services Levels | Customer Service |
| Quality | Price Matching Services | Message | Location | Appearance |
| Packaging | Credit Terms | Media | Market Coverage | Employee Portrayal |

## PRODUCT

A product can be either a tangible good or an intangible service that fulfills the needs or desires of consumers. It is imperative for companies to determine which aspects of the product itself are important and will influence customers' perception (emotionally, physically, and mentally) and purchase intentions. The benefits offered by the product or services need to be understood by the consumer and the unique selling proposition of the product need to be studied. In addition, the potential buyers of the product need to be identified and understood.

Product refers to the products and services offered by a business. Product decisions include function, packaging, appearance, warranty, quality, etc. Customers need to understand the features, advantages, and benefits that can be enjoyed by buying goods or services. When thinking about a product, consider the key features, benefits, and the needs and wants of customers.

A product can be anything like a physical product, a service, information, etc., that benefits and satisfies the needs of customers. To begin with, you first need to tell your audience what your product is. And how your product differs from your competitors. Before you showcase products to the prospects, you have to be clear and specific about the benefits you're offering.

For that, you need to really ask some critical questions to yourself, such as:

- Is your product suitable for today's market?
- How does your product solve a specific problem?
- Are there any physical attributes of the product that customers should know?
- Compared to your competitors, does your product offer more benefits?

## PRICE

Once an understanding of the product offering is established, pricing decisions can come into effect. Price determinations impact profit margins, supply, demand, and overall marketing strategy. It is important for this to be linked to what the perceived value of the product is to the customer rather than an objective cost. Determining a pricing strategy is imperative to understand how a customer sees and can clearly differentiate your product from what other companies are selling.

Price refers to the pricing strategy for products and services and how it will affect customers. Pricing decisions do not include just the selling price, but also discounts, payment arrangements, credit terms, and any price-matching services offered. When determining a pricing strategy, it is important to consider the business's position in the current marketplace. For example, if the business is advertised as a high-quality provider of mechanical equipment, the product pricing should reflect that.

Determining your product's price is the most crucial part because it has a direct impact on your product's success. To stand alone in the market, make sure you're offering competitive prices and not undervalue the product. You must reexamine your product's price continuously to validate that the cost is appropriate to the current market.

Below are some of the questions that you should consider before finalizing the price of your product.

- Does the price match the quality of your offering?
- What's the ongoing price for the same product in the marketplace?
- What are the margins for everyone in the distribution channel?
- Are customers ready to pay for the extra benefits you're providing?
- Are you generating enough profits to sustain in the market?
- Can you provide a promotional offer or discounts on your product?

**PROMOTION - OFFLINE TO ONLINE**

Once you've optimized the previous three P's in your marketing plan, it's time to promote your offer. Promotion includes elements like advertising, public relations, social media marketing, email marketing, search engine marketing, video marketing, and more. The best way to visualize how a customer interacts with a business is by mapping it. Most customer journey maps outline key events, customer motivations, and areas of friction within the user's experience. Then, this information is combined into a comprehensive vision that describes an average experience with your business. Each touchpoint must be supported by properly positioning a brand to truly maximize return on investment. Developing a customer journey map is that brands should leverage channels.

Promotion refers to the activities that make the business more known to consumers. It includes items such as sponsorships, advertising, and public relations activities. Since promotion costs can be substantial, it is essential to conduct a break-even analysis when making promotion decisions. It is important to understand the value of a customer and whether it is worth conducting promotions to acquire them. Your promotional strategy will be part of your marketing plan.

Your product is top-notch, has the best location and competitive price, but without promotion, you won't reach out to customers. Start spreading a message about your company's vision and values, and the customers' problem you're solving. The promotion may include various distribution channels such as offline marketing, sales promotions, telemarketing, online advertising, and more.

To craft the perfect promotional campaign, you need to figure out the following:

- Does your competitor do promotions?
- Can you promote your products more than the competitors?
- Do your promotional messages entice prospects to buy your product?
- Are you going to promote your brand everywhere (both offline and online)?

**THINGS TO CONSIDER BEFORE PROMOTING YOUR BUSINESS**

**MARKETING AND BUSINESS PLANS**

Consider what you want to achieve with your advertising or promotional campaign? Does it align with your brand and your business goals and objectives?

Before you start any promotion, write down your goals and objectives. You'll then be able to track and evaluate your success after the campaign. This will help you decide whether to take this approach or to try different promotions in the future.

**YOUR TARGET CUSTOMERS**

If you've been in business for a while, you should have a good understanding of who your target customers are. These are the people who you expect will buy most of your products or services. If you're not sure who your target customers are, then have a look at who is currently buying your products and services. Look for ways to make sure your promotional activities are reaching them.

**WHERE TO ADVERTISE OR PROMOTE**

How do your customers normally find you? Through the internet, social media, word of mouth, flyer, ad in a publication, online, on radio or TV? Find out how your current customers find you, then target your advertisements and promotions in these areas.

## YOUR BUDGET

Advertising and promotion can be expensive. Pick options that will give you the best value for money, while still reaching your target customers. Remember, the cheapest option is not always the best. The best option will be whatever is most effective for your business. Some budget-friendly advertising options include flyers, posters, social media and newsletters.

## PLACE

As they say in marketing, it's all about location, location, location. Place is a huge influence because consumers aren't actively shopping for your product or service. When consumers want something, they are strongly influenced by what's currently available to them. Getting the place and timing right is an essential part of success. The placement strategy will help assess what channel is the most suited to a product.

Place refers to where the product/service of the business is seen, made, sold, or distributed. In essence, place decisions are associated with distribution channels and ways of getting the product to targeted key customers. It is important to consider how accessible the product or service is and ensure that customers can easily find you. The product or service must be available to customers at the right time, at the right place, and in the right quantity. For example, a business may want to provide their products over an e-commerce site, at a retail store, or through a third-party distributor.

The place is the location or channel where your product can be found. So, you should make your product more accessible and visible to the prospects. Nowadays, your virtual place is more important than that of a physical location as people tend to buy online more.

To identify the ideal location for your product, you must determine the following questions.

- What is the geographic location of your target audience?
- In how much time can you provide your product to customers?
- Is your product available on both offline stores and online platforms?

- Do you distribute products yourself or use third-party platforms such as Amazon?

## PEOPLE

The fifth P, and perhaps the most important one, is people. We all know that your customer is fundamental to your strategic success as a marketer. At the heart, everything you do and everything your organization does should be an all-encompassing consideration of your target audience to encompass customer needs and ensure customer satisfaction. But we also need to be aware that people don't also mean "customer". It includes staff, salespeople, customer service teams, and anyone involved in the marketing and sales processes. You want your employees to be effective and perceived positively by customers.

People refer to the staff, salespeople, and those who work for the business. People's decisions are usually centered around customer service. How do you want your employees to be perceived by customers? The final and most important P in the 5 P's of marketing is People. To be successful in business, you always must build relationships with your customers first and provide a great user experience.

You need to understand your customers concerning:

- Demographics – Age, Gender, Education, Occupation, and Life Events
- Geographics – Location segmented into cities, regions, states, countries, and continents

## INTERESTS AND BEHAVIORS

Suppose you're an owner of a vegan restaurant, then promoting it among the non-veg society will drown your business in no time. That's why understanding your people (or audience) is crucial. While focusing on customers, don't forget your internal people, as they are also essential to grow your business. In many cases, businesses fail to grow because they don't put the right people in the right position in the company.

## EXAMPLE OF THE 5 P'S OF MARKETING

John is considering operating a jet ski shop catering to travelers and tourists. To position his business, John may consult the 5 P's of marketing in the following manner:

- **Product:** By-the-hour jet ski rentals for people who are in the city for a short duration of time. A limited liability form to be signed by people who participate in the service and a monetary deposit in case of damages.
- **Price:** Cheap jet ski trips to cater to the budget constraints of travelers and tourists. A 10% discount on jet ski trips when referred by a travel agency.
- **Promotions:** A Facebook page, Instagram page, and a Twitter handle to promote the business. Also, paid promotions on travel agency websites.
- **Place:** An easy to access location from existing transit systems.
- **People:** Friendly staff members who love meeting travelers and offer exceptional customer service.

## CHAPTER 11

## SEPARATE YOURSELF FROM THE BUSINESS

Separating business and personal finances is a multi-step process that many first-time business owners are unfamiliar with. To help you get started, we've created step-by-step instructions. No matter what kind of business you operate, you're going to want to do these things to ensure your business and personal finances stay separate.

The most important thing you need to start separating business and personal finances is a business bank account. It's up to you whether you decide to open a business checking or savings account. But we'd recommend starting with a business checking account, since it's the cornerstone of any company's financial foundation.

With a dedicated business checking account, you can pay bills, deposit cash, collect invoice payments, and buy equipment without having to run a cash-only operation, or by having to pull from your personal bank account. Here are three fantastic options to kick things off.

Business checking is a top business bank account that can be opened very quickly and easily online. Not only that, but business checking offers unlimited transactions, two free checkbooks, a free business debit card, mobile and online banking and all without monthly service fees.

In addition, this account has no NSF fees, no minimum opening deposit requirement, no minimum balance requirement, no ACH fees, and no incoming wire fees. The only fees you'll pay are for outgoing wires $15. That said, the business checking account also gives you the opportunity to earn interest on your account 1% on any balance over $1,000.

So, even if you don't have a $1,000 balance to start, you can start earning interest the minute your balance reaches that threshold, and there is no penalty or fee for having an account balance under $1,000. Moreover, this bank account gives you access to over 38,000 fee-free ATMs around the U.S., as well as over 90,000 Green Dot locations where you can deposit cash something that's not always an option for online-based business checking accounts.

Finally, you can manage all your account online, pay vendors and bills, make transfers to and from other accounts, schedule one-time and recurring payments, and more. Perhaps you do deal in some cash, though, or would prefer a brick-and-mortar bank that you can walk into for services like sending wire transfers. If that's the case, business bank accounts are some of the bests out there.

For a first account, most Business Complete Banking is a strong offering. There's a low monthly fee, which can be waived multiple ways such as if you keep a $2,000 minimum daily balance. With unlimited fee-free electronic transactions and $5,000 of cash deposits per month, this account suits most small business owners' needs.

**GET A BUSINESS CREDIT CARD**

You might be all set with a business bank account. But if you're also putting business expenses on a personal credit card, then you're not done yet. The same principle applies here if you're not separating your company's expenses on a dedicated card, then you're not distinct. Having a business credit card also allows you to build your business credit score.

You likely know all about your personal credit score, which helps you get credit cards, loans, mortgages, etc. But as an entrepreneur, you get a separate business credit score for your commercial operation. And it serves much the same function: a numerical history of your responsibility with debt as a business, measured on a different scale.

This is a substantial thing for a business owner to build, especially if you see your business getting any bigger whether that's expanding to a larger space, opening more locations, getting a higher line of credit, and doing any of this with business financing. A business credit card is the absolute best place for you to begin building that business credit score. Here are a couple of ideas where to start with your first card.

The American Express Blue Business Plus is a great fit as a first business credit card for many business owners and it truly might be the only business credit card you'll need. First, the Amex Blue has a 12-month 0% introductory APR period, which means no interest on purchases for a year. After that, a variable interest rate sets in depending on the market Prime Rate and your creditworthiness. In addition, the card has no annual fee, and you can earn reward points redeemable for travel, gift cards, and lots more. It's a great, versatile card but especially for that 0% intro APR offer, which could allow you to make some big investments into your business without being on the hook for them immediately.

## LINE OF CREDIT

A line of credit is a financial product that allows you to borrow money repeatedly. You can borrow up to a certain limit, and then you repay what you owe. You can continue drawing on the line of credit as long as the amount you owe doesn't go over your limit. You pay interest on the money you borrow, and you may be charged a fee each time you use a credit line.

A business credit card is a popular and flexible tool for those times when business owners need quick access to cash. There are few restrictions on what you can purchase with a credit card and many small business owners use credit cards for purposes that include purchasing inventory, paying bills, or to cover travel expenses. In fact, according to the Small Business Administration (SBA), roughly 65 percent of small business owners use credit cards on a regular basis. A business line of credit could also be a good option for your business.

There Are Benefits to Using a Business Credit Card

In addition to being a flexible financing and purchasing tool, there are other benefits associated with business credit cards, which include more sophisticated reporting and expense tracking, the ability to issue multiple cards to employees on the same account, more flexible payment options, and often larger credit limits compared to personal credit cards.

Many business credit cards report your transaction history to the business credit bureaus instead of the personal credit bureaus, which is important for business owners interested in building their business credit and protecting their personal credit. Maxing out your personal credit cards on business expenses (even if you pay the entire balance at the end of every payment cycle) may still negatively impact your personal credit score.

## WHY A BUSINESS LINE OF CREDIT COULD MAKE SENSE IN ADDITION TO A BUSINESS CREDIT CARD

Although business credit cards are convenient and flexible, there are some things you just can't do with a credit card. For example, you may not be able to make certain payments, including your property lease, payroll, and invoices from vendors; but you can use a business line of credit. Additionally, while some business credit cards come with lower credit limits, and line of credit is between $5,000 and $100,000.

## WHEN TO USE A BUSINESS LINE OF CREDIT VS. A BUSINESS CREDIT CARD

As a business owner, one of your most valuable tools is access to credit. And like any job, you'll be much better off when you select the right tool for your needs. Two of the most popular ways that a business can access credit is through a small business line of credit and a small business credit card. Take a look at how each type of credit works.

## BUSINESS LINE OF CREDIT

You can apply for a small business line of credit from your local bank or from an online provider. A line of credit can be unsecured, or it can be secured by a lien on your assets or another financial instrument such as a certificate of deposit. Once established, you can draw from this line of credit by making a direct deposit to your checking account, or by using a debit card linked to the account. Your minimum monthly payment will be for interest charges only, which will be based on your average daily balance. You are free to pay off your balance and borrow again as often as you'd like.

### The Best Time to Use a Business Line of Credit
Business lines of credit can be the best tool for the job when you need to make payments to suppliers who won't accept credit cards, or who impose additional fees for credit card use. A business line of credit can also be used to pay existing bills by check or by cash, or when you simply don't have a sufficient line of credit on your business credit cards.

### Pros
- Ability to write checks to pay billers that don't accept credit cards.
- Interest-only payments.
- No cash advance fees.
- Helps to build a credit history for your business.

### Cons
- No interest-free grace period.
- Smaller lines of credit for new businesses.
- No rewards or benefits.
- May require collateral.

### Cost Range
A small business line of credit may have an opening fee of $150 or more. Some also have annual renewal fees or monthly maintenance fees. Interest will accrue only when you make purchases, generally about 8% to 35%, depending on the provider.

### Credit Considerations
You can qualify for a small business line of credit based on your personal credit, or you can use your personal credit along with your company's income, provided it has been in business for over two years.

### How to Qualify
You can apply online or at your local bank. If using your business income or collateral, you will have to provide documentation.

## BUSINESS CREDIT CARD

A small business credit card will work almost exactly like a personal credit card does. You will use your personal credit to qualify, and it will represent an unsecured loan. As with your personal credit cards, you can avoid interest charges by paying your statement balances in full, giving you as long as 55 days of interest-free float on your charges (your 30-day statement period plus a grace period of up to 25 days; however, check with your issuer for specifics on your due date and grace period). Otherwise, you will incur interest charges on your average daily balance.

And just like your personal cards, you can receive rewards for your business spending in the form of points, miles, and cash back. In fact, a business credit card is more likely to offer bonus rewards for the types of purchases that businesses tend to make most, such as those from office supply stores, telecommunications service providers, and advertisers. Business credit cards can also offer a range of purchase protection and travel insurance benefits that can be valuable.

### Best Times to Use a Small Business Credit Card

A small business credit card is an entirely different type of financial instrument than a line of credit, but there can be many advantages to using them. First, many business owners use their credit cards to earn valuable travel rewards or cash back. These rewards are considered a refund on a purchase and are not taxable income.

Also, business travelers can be protected by polices such as trip delay and cancellation insurance as well as lost luggage insurance, so long as they purchase their tickets with the business card. When making equipment purchases, your business credit card could offer you damage and theft protection, extended warranty coverage, and even a price protection policy that can refund the difference if your purchase goes on sale later. And when you are able to pay your entire statement balance in full each month, you can receive the equivalent of an interest-free, short-term line of credit.

### Pros

- Easy application process.

- Earn valuable rewards.
- Receive travel insurance and purchase protection benefits.
- The option to have an interest-free grace period.

## Cons

- Cash advances are very expensive.
- Not all billers accept credit cards.
- Relies on your personal credit, not your company's.

### Cost Range

Some business credit cards have no annual fee, while premium reward cards can have fees of up to $450. Most cards have annual fees of $95 or less.

### Credit Considerations

You must have good or excellent credit to obtain a small business credit card.

### How to Qualify

You can apply for a small business credit card online in just a few minutes.

## SOME OF THE BEST BUSINESS CREDIT CARD FOR BUILDING OR REBUILDING CREDIT

Even if you're in a position in which you need to build or rebuild credit, you still don't have an excuse not to be putting your business purchases on a separate card. The Capital One Spark Classic for Business card has a lower barrier to approval than the Amex Blue (580+ credit score), but still allows you to both build business credit and earn a flat 1% cash back on all spending. And with no annual fee, this card is an easy choice for so many.

## PAY YOURSELF A SALARY

Paying yourself a salary from your business creates a more formal boundary between your business finances and your personal finances. Simply take money from your business bank account and transfer it to your personal checking account once or twice per month, just as if you were working for somebody else.

By paying yourself a salary, you establish when and how you will take money out of your business, rather than just pulling from your business finances whenever you need to.

## SEPARATE RECEIPTS

Make sure that you're not combining where you store business receipts and where you store personal receipts. If you were to be audited, the IRS would want to look at your business receipts, and if you can't separate them from your personal receipts, you're in trouble. Keep in mind that having a business bank account and business credit card (that you only use for business purposes) will make the whole process of separating receipts a lot easier.

## IDENTIFY WHEN YOU'RE USING PERSONAL ITEMS FOR BUSINESS PURPOSES

If you have a home office, use your personal vehicle to attend client meetings, or talk to customers on your personal phone, you need to take note of these scenarios. Being able to track when you use personal items for business purposes will allow you to write off some or all those expenses come tax season. So, educate yourself on what are qualified business expenses and what aren't. Then take notes and give them to your accountant when it comes time to file.

## EDUCATE OTHER MEMBERS OF THE BUSINESS

Our last step to separating business and personal finances is to make sure all business stakeholders are on the same page. If you're separating business and personal finances, but other members of your business aren't, it's not going to make any difference. It needs to be a collaborative effort. So, make sure everyone understands what the difference is between a business expense and a personal expense, and then work out a system to ensure that separating business and personal finances is as easy as possible.

## WHY IT'S IMPORTANT TO SEPARATE PERSONAL AND BUSINESS FINANCES

We've explained to you how business and personal finances can be kept separate, but we haven't really touched on why personal and business finances should be kept separate. The short answer is: many reasons. Let's list all the issues you're exposing yourself to when you choose not to separate business and personal finances.

### LEGAL IMPLICATIONS

You've likely gone through the semi-arduous process of filing a lot of paperwork to become an LLC, partnership, S-Corp, or C-corp. And one of the reasons you did that? For the legal protections that establishing a distinct, separate business entity affords you as a business owner.

But if your personal and business finances are muddled, those legal protections aren't in effect (what's called "piercing the corporate veil") there literally isn't a way to delineate between you, the business owner, and you, the private citizen. So, if, for instance, a client brings a lawsuit against your company and a judgment goes against you, you're now personally exposed for damages.

### PERSONAL ASSET EXPOSURE

This brings us into the second point. Say you do lose that lawsuit. If you don't have that protection in place by dividing your business finances, you risk opening your personal finances to seizure when that judgment goes against you.

Similarly, in cases of business bankruptcy in which you don't have a separately established business entity, your personal credit score will tank along with your business credit score.

### BOOKKEEPING AND TAX HEADACHES

If you haven't gotten a slap on the wrist from your bookkeeper or accountant yet for your commingled finances, it's coming. Certain business entities are required to file entirely distinct business tax returns. And even pass-through business entities that pay taxes passed through to personal returns require certain types of distinct, detailed documentation come tax time, especially if you're considering writing off any kind of business expenses.

If your accountant needs to dig through your personal records to identify business purchases from a year ago, it's not only an arduous waste of time, but also potentially inaccurate. That could lead to an IRS audit on your tax returns, which is something you don't want.

## BUSINESS LENDING EFFECTS

Your business might be so new that the thought of applying for a business loan right now seems next to impossible. But there might be a time when you want to finance a great opportunity and, if that happens, you'll be expected to submit both your personal and business tax returns for lenders to evaluate.

But if you've filed both together since you have commingled finances, that's a red flag for a potential business lender. With only one return, they won't be able to get a pulse on your business to make important judgments about your cash flow, revenue, and other factors essential to determining your potential to pay back your loan. Which goes to show why it's so much harder to get approved for a loan as a sole proprietor, which files only one tax return.

## GENERAL SANITY PRESERVATION

If all of this sounds maddening, overwhelming, and potentially a little frightening, it is. If you're a serious entrepreneur or even a casual one there's no reason to put your personal assets, credit score, and precious time at risk. Especially when creating a distinct home for your business finances, as we've explained, is simple.

## WHEN TO SEPARATE BUSINESS AND PERSONAL FINANCES

You should know by now that you'll want to separate business and personal finances as soon as possible. And it's never too late. Here's how to get started.

## PARSE OUT YOUR CASH IF IT'S ALL LUMPED TOGETHER

If things are all tied up, you can separate them and start fresh. Once you've set up a separate bank account, download your bank statements for the year into a CSV or Excel format. Then, go through the statements line by line, and note next to each deposit and expense whether the transaction was business or personal. Doing this in a CSV or Excel file will let you quickly group all your business and personal transactions together, and your accountant can use this information to make the necessary adjustments to your tax return or bookkeeping file.

## SET UP A RECURRING TRANSFER TO HELP WITH STRUCTURE
Grigg also says that discipline is the other key piece to making sure you keep up the good work; meaning don't sway the opposite direction and start dipping into the business account for personal matters. She recommends clients "reverse-engineer a 'paycheck' (for sole proprietors, this is in the form of a draw from the business) based on their household financial needs" (p 5).

Even if it's only a little bit, it'll help prevent you from paying for personal expenses from the business.

## DOES EVERY BUSINESS NEED TO SEPARATE PERSONAL AND BUSINESS FINANCES?
We've talked a lot about why separating business and personal finances makes sense, but we haven't addressed whether it's required.

The answer is, separating business and personal finances is required for LLCs and corporations, but not for sole proprietorships. Sole props don't need to separate finances because they're considered an unincorporated legal entity. This means all the sole proprietorship's profits, losses, and liabilities are tied to the owner.

Ironically, this means it's even more important for a sole proprietorship to be separating business and personal finances. If you're audited by the IRS, the burden of proof is on you to disclose your business expenses and income. Therefore, sole proprietors, more than anyone, should prioritize separating business and personal finances.

## EASY WAYS TO SEPARATE YOUR PERSONAL AND BUSINESS FINANCES
Certain things don't mix well like your personal finances and your business's. Keeping these things separate not only helps you reduce problems; it also greatly simplifies things and makes it easier to manage your finances.

You don't know where to start with separating out your personal and business finances? Let's look at some easy ways to do it.

1. **Put your business on the map.** If you haven't already, establish a separate legal entity for your business, such as an LLC, C Corp, or S

Corp. The Small Business Administration has tips on what structure may work for you, but it's always best to get advice from a legal expert. You also need to apply for an Employer Identification Number (EIN) via the IRS's website. Don't worry, it only takes a few minutes. Establishing a separate legal entity for your business has many advantages, including the ability to protect your personal assets from business debts, losses, and lawsuits.

2. **Get a business debit or credit card.** Opening a business debit card or credit card allows you to stop using personal accounts for business transactions, and it's an easy way to draw a clear line between personal and business expenses.

    Square now offers a small business debit card. It provides real-time access to your Square Balance so you can access your funds as soon as you make a sale. Labels for business and personal expenses in your Square app also make it easy to track your business expenses and to keep them separate from your personal expenses.

    A business credit card may help you build stronger business credit scores, if you pay your bills on time. A strong business credit profile may boost your borrowing power and help you qualify for small business loans with lower interest rates. Read more about establishing business credit.

3. **Open a business checking account.** If you're serious about keeping your personal and business finances separate, opening a checking account strictly for your business is a no-brainer. If you're strict about using it (along with your business debit card) for business needs and business needs alone, then getting a clear and complete picture of these expenditures when tax time rolls around become a simple matter of reviewing your bank statements.

4. **Pay yourself a salary.** You're your own boss! Make it official and write yourself a check each month from your business checking ac-

count. Transfer this to your personal checking account, and then behave as you would if you were working for someone else. That is, once the money runs out, tighten your belt, and wait patiently for the next payday. Regarding personal needs, treat your business checking account and your business credit card as you'd treat a former employer's hands off.

5. **Separate your receipts and keep them.** What better way to demonstrate your commitment to keeping your personal and business expenses separate than by physically separating your respective receipts? Think good old-fashioned folders, or separate folders in your email for digital receipts. This simple practice helps you sleep easier knowing that if the IRS ever comes knocking, you're prepared.

6. **Track shared expenses.** One advantage of being a small business owner is that many business expenses are tax deductible. Taking a prospective partner to a nice lunch to talk things over? Stocking up on coffee for your employees? Write it off. At the same time, avoid the temptation to use the business card for personal needs.

    You can ask a cashier to ring up purchases as separate transactions every time. Or you can use a business debit card, such as Square Debit Card, that allows you to label your personal and business expenses. Not only will separating expenses make things easier for your accountant come tax time, but you also protect yourself by (1) keeping a spotless financial record and (2) continuing the keep-the-receipts-separate discipline that can save you so much headache down the road as your company grows.

7. **Keep track of when you use personal items for business purposes.** We all wish we could drive a company car and fly a company jet. But for most small business owners, the car that gets you to the gym in the morning is also what gets you to that big marketing convention in another state. The same thing goes for your cellphone, and

any item that you use regularly for both personal and business purposes. Any expenditure that you can legally write off should be written off to save you money come tax time. Your tax advisor can help you figure out what's deductible, what's not, and how to keep the right records.

8. **Educate your employees and partners.** You know the difference between a personal and business expense; now make sure that the other people involved in your business do, too. Get everybody on the same page, committed to the same goals. Staying disciplined is easier if others are doing it with you.

At first, it may not be easy to keep things neat and tidy. But even if you can work on a few of these tips in the years to come, you'll save both time and money during the next tax season, an audit, or even while looking for financing. Strong businesses grow by careful, incremental improvements, and learning to keep your personal and business finances separate is the perfect place to start.

# CHAPTER 12

# CUSTOMER RELATIONSHIP

In today's business culture, customer satisfaction should always be a priority. Customers today are more knowledgeable and have higher expectations than ever before. To achieve success, businesses need to have an exceptional plan in place to be able to adequately manage customer expectations. It can often be the defining factor that makes or breaks a business. Quality customer relations practices are crucial to the success of any company. Many facets go into having a good plan for managing customer expectations.

Customer expectations management can be very challenging indeed. Your clients and customers will all have their own expectations of your business or organization, and these can be enormously varied. What's more, their expectations will change over time, often becoming more demanding.

Today's customers are more knowledgeable and more critical than ever before. To meet their expectations, businesses and organizations need to understand their changing needs and demands and they need to have effective strategies in place that will ensure high levels of customer satisfaction into the future. Ideally, businesses should be anticipating and exceeding customer expectations before they are even expressed.

## PRIORITIZE

To adequately manage customer expectations, it is important to prioritize the needs of the client. Everyone should be on the same page with regards to what the client expects of the business and what the business can promise to deliver. Every client will be different. Asking lots of questions is a great way to find out what the client is prioritizing as the most important required service. It is also good for the client representative to ask the customer what he/she expects from the business relationship. One of the best ways to make prioritizing easier is to get to know the client/customer. Customer services managers should try and understand the ins and outs of the client. They should understand the values of the client, what they are buying, and why they are buying it.

## REVIEWS AND WORD OF MOUTH

The internet is a magnificent research tool; so you can expect your customers to have researched before making their purchase. They will have read reviews of your product or service, and they will have potentially read reviews of your business. They may also have read what people are saying in forums and on social media. What they derive from these sources will influence their expectations, so you need to be aware of what's being said.

## PREVIOUS EXPERIENCE WITH OTHER COMPANIES

People's experiences with other companies and organizations greatly influence their expectations. Regardless of whether other companies are in the same niche as yours, these days customers expect the same high levels of great customer service from all businesses and organizations.

## EFFECTIVE COMMUNICATION

Communication is key when it comes to effective customer expectation management. Having poor communication can be extremely frustrating for both the customer and the business. One great way to stay on top of communication is by establishing a set schedule in which the client can expect to hear from the business representative. The customer should know in advance how often the business will be in contact and during which times it is most convenient to be in touch. Changes in the schedule should be noted to the client promptly. Having good communication between customers and business ensures that everyone is always on the same page, and it eliminates the possibility of negative surprises. It is also important to always be honest with the client. Even in circumstances where the service provided by the business has run into a flaw, representatives should always be upfront with the client. Owning up to mistakes and communicating a solution with the client is a way to establish trust. In some cases, establishing a call center is a great way to be available for the client.

As noted, your customer expectations will have been influenced by what they have read and possibly seen. Since you have complete control over how you communicate with your customers, you should ensure that the information you provide is clear, consistent, complete, and honest. Lack of clarity in communications has been widely cited as a significant issue that negatively affects the customer experience. Here are some fundamental guidelines:

- Ensure that the information provided from your website is accurate, complete, consistent, and always up to date.
- The language used on your website and in all communications must be appropriate for your customers. Don't bamboozle them with technical jargon. Engage them using the right language and tone of voice.
- Your social media communications need to be responsive and timely. What's stated needs to be accurate, honest and positive.
- Advertising and promotion must not be misleading or dishonest.
- Any printed documentation such as brochures, pamphlets, and flyers, must be accurate, honest and clear.
- Any video and visual messaging from your organization needs to be aligned with other communications.
- Service agents and all staff involved in direct customer communications must be appropriately trained and skilled. The information they provide must be consistent with other communication channels and their style and manner must be appropriate.
- Let your customers know how long they need to wait. These days, people expect almost instantaneous responses, but this is not always

realistic, especially when dealing with a worldwide customer base. Clearly informing your customers of how long they will need to wait can effectively set their expectations and avoid disgruntlement.

## CULTIVATE LOYALTY

Fostering customer loyalty is enormously beneficial to all businesses. It costs far less to retain an existing customer than it does to create a new one. And loyal customers can be enormously helpful in identifying and defining changing customer expectations.

Some basic tactics that contribute toward developing customer loyalty include:

- Always personalizing communications by using their names.
- Ensuring that each customer is made to feel special.
- Always thanking them for their custom and their loyalty.
- Regularly and routinely communicating with them.
- Paying attention to the details which can affect customer expectations.

## MONITOR YOUR MARKET AND BEYOND

The expectations of your clients and customers will be greatly influenced by what they may have experienced from other businesses in your sector and elsewhere. If a customer has previously used an online 'chat' facility on another website to get some customer support and they received a response within maybe 30 seconds, then they are likely to expect the same from you when you implement an online chat tool. Similarly, if a customer has previously received a fast response via social media from an unrelated organization or business then they are likely to expect the same level of response from your social media channels.

You need to be aware of these expectations and ideally endeavor to match or beat them. If this is not possible then you need to clearly communicate with your customers to realistically set their expectations.

## BE AN EXPERT

Your people need to be recognized as experts in what they do and what they are providing. Every member of staff involved in direct customer communications, from front-line service personnel to switchboard operators and sales professionals, needs to be adequately trained and highly confident in their skills and their ability to manage even the most demanding customer expectations.

### ALWAYS FOLLOW UP

Customer experience can be greatly influenced by whether or not an organization follows up after initial contact. For example, if a customer has contacted a service desk, via telephone, or maybe via an online chat facility, and a resolution to their issue was provided, this should be followed up, possibly via email, to confirm the recommendations provided and that the solution was successful.

Similarly, after purchase, it's good practice to contact customers to verify that they are satisfied. Simple, easy-to-complete customer satisfaction surveys are a great way to follow up and derive some potentially valuable customer feedback.

### DISCOVER AND EXCEED

By establishing a rapport with your customers you're in a great position to discover their anticipated expectations. What are they looking forward to in the future? What do they expect of the products or services provided by your industry? What are they experiencing elsewhere that is influencing what they expect from you?

### CONSISTENCY

Consistency is something that all customers expect. When services or goods change on a whim, the client can be left feeling dazed and confused. It is also a surefire way to lose any gained trust that has already been established. Maintaining consistency in client relations also helps the customer to manage their own expectations because they will always know what to expect. Listening to customer concerns and complaints will help to determine where inconsistencies occur and what the shortcomings are. Consistency builds trust and trust leads to long-lasting business relationships.

### REALISTIC PROMISES

Companies should not offer goods/services that they cannot deliver. A business must understand how to say no to a customer. It is important to explain why the answer is no and communicate the reasoning behind the answer. The company does far more damage to trust and reputation by agreeing to provide a service that cannot be delivered. It is far better to under-promise and over-perform to keep control of customer expectations. Make promises that are realistic and achievable, and then go the distance to over-deliver on the promise. The customer will feel as if the business goes above and beyond for them, rather than feeling like a promise has come up short.

### ORGANIZATION

Staying organized will make all of these other tips easier to accomplish. Have a detailed list of all clients and needs in an easy-to-access place. The list should be easy to understand and kept up to date. The more organized the business is, the easier it will be to follow up with client needs, expectations, and deliverables. The list should also be coordinated with a schedule so that agreed-upon communication contact dates and times are never missed. The schedule will also help to ensure that goods or services are delivered at the appropriate and agreed upon time.

A company's ability to provide excellent business-to-business customer support can only go as far as its ability to manage—and ultimately exceed—the expectations of its clients. The worst thing a business can do is tell a customer his or her problem will be resolved one way and then offer a contradictory solution or timeline instead.

As business owners, we all know there is a baseline expectation for high-quality customer service in today's marketplace. For example, the Institute of Customer Service found 60 percent of consumers favor a balance of price and service and are unwilling to accept poor customer service in exchange for lower prices. However, the best way to exceed the norm and maintain happy clients in the long term is to manage their expectations from start to finish. Companies can set themselves up for success by utilizing the right B2B support software and employing these five powerful strategies for managing customer service expectations:

1. **Openly discuss solutions.** Businesses that have highly knowledgeable customer support teams should be well-versed in the solutions to every potential problem and be able to speak to those possibilities quickly. One important way businesses can manage customer service expectations is by openly discussing possible solutions to a problem with the client. By listing off possible resolutions, support teams empower their clients to understand the complexity of a particular problem and engage directly with its solution. Additionally, by painting a clear picture of possible results, service teams ensure customers don't have unrealistic expectations of how simple or difficult the resolution will be.

2. **Provide clear timelines.** Glitches, errors, and bugs in B2B software can be irritating and costly to customers. However, clients will become angrier if they look forward to their problems being solved in a week, and instead wait a week and a half. Businesses can manage customer service expectations by clearly stating how long any task will take from the moment the client gets on a customer support call until the resolution is in progress. Teams should ensure customers are well-informed of not only how long a phone call will take, but how much time and work is required to get them a solution as quickly as possible.

3. **Be transparent and honest.** Transparency is crucial to managing B2B customer service expectations effectively and will affect clients' ability to trust a company. Businesses can ensure clients remain confident in their providers and have a positive experience by remaining honest in every possible situation. This means if a customer service representative doesn't have the right answer to a problem, he or she should be open about consulting with other members of the team. Regardless of the situation, support teams should avoid keeping secrets at all costs.

4. **Remain optimistic, but realistic.** While optimism is an important part of a positive customer experience, representatives must also remain

realistic about solutions. By understanding company policies, the complexities of certain problems, and the workload of their team members, support experts can gauge how a particular ticket will be solved and the time investment that is required. While it can be nerve-wracking to tell a client a problem will take longer than expected to resolve, it is more important to be realistic than set expectations that can't be met.

5. **Follow up regularly.** Finally, support teams can manage customer service expectations by following up after each stage of the resolution process. As Customer Experience Insight pointed out, most customers are not bothered by companies touching base with them. On the contrary, clients expect businesses to follow up with them to round out their customer experience. After a customer service agent communicates the potential solutions to a problem and offers realistic timelines, he or she should follow up with the client through email to reiterate what was decided. Additionally, customer support teams should always check in with clients as the resolution progresses, and once a ticket has been closed.

There are many ways businesses can optimize their customer experience strategies. However, the first step to delivering excellence is to manage expectations effectively from the get-go.

## TYPES OF CUSTOMER EXPECTATIONS

For businesses, understanding customer expectations can be crucial because it acts as the foundation of customer engagement strategies. Learning expectations also helps to increase customer satisfaction and loyalty.

Here are the different types of customer expectations:

- Implicit expectations – are based on business performance and formed by experiences such as comparison with the products or services of the competitors.

- Explicit expectations – refers to well-identified product performance standards, quality of the product, and services rendered by any company.
- Interpersonal expectations – reflect the relationship between a customer and brand across the customer lifecycle.
- Static performance expectations – refer to the front-facing elements of your brand such as accessibility, customization, dependability, etc.

## KEY FACTORS THAT INFLUENCE CUSTOMER EXPECTATIONS

A critical part of managing client expectations is understanding the factors that can influence their perceptions. Unable to meet consumers' standards translate to low conversions and customer retention rates. By analyzing the reasons, you will be able to understand your clients' expectations and how to meet their demands.

Here are some key factors that shape your customer expectations:

- **Previous experience with other brands** – The previous experience with your competitors can shape client expectations from you. They might model their preferences based on what other brands can do for them. If you fail to outshine your competitors, you cannot win your customers.
- **Communication strategy** – What you communicate to the customers through support or marketing channels shapes their expectations. And the way you communicate pertains to your customer service. So, focus on disseminating accurate information and the way you interact as it impacts your overall brand image.
- **Customer reviews and feedback** – Feedbacks and reviews greatly influence the brand image and reputation. What your customers speak about you creates your brand image. By keeping high-quality consistent performance-focused, you should take your online reputation management seriously.

## HOW TO MANAGE AND EXCEED CLIENT EXPECTATIONS

Understanding customer needs and exceeding their expectations are becoming table stakes for businesses to compete. Let us discuss the top ways you can manage the list of customer expectations.

1. **Engage customers consistently across multiple touch points.** Customers view contextualized engagement and seamless transitions between different communication channels. If the businesses engage their customers based on earlier interactions, it could act as a winning formula.

    Businesses that follow the omni-channel communication strategy have witnessed a significant 89% increase in retention **and a 9.5% year-over-year increase in annual revenue.** See picture below:

Customers expect businesses to be active across multiple channels like the web, social media, email, mobile devices, etc. Maintaining consistency among every channel improves the customer experience that impacts brand reputation positively. So, break your silos and manage your client expectations by following the tips below:

- Identify all the channels that customers choose to reach out to your business.
- Unify all your customer conversations at a single place to get a better understanding of your customer journey.
- Use the insights to engage your customers throughout their journey across all touch-points.

As a business, having a strong omni-channel customer service strategy is critical to having a unified view of your customers and be able to take necessary actions before they churn.

Key takeaways:

- You can map your customer journey to understand their behavior and know the areas where they need your assistance. You can offer proactive assistance across the behavior stages via the right channels such as live chat, chatbot.
- You can acquire customer feedback and improve your support process to learn and exceed your customer expectations.
- Following an omnichannel approach reduces the number of customer complaints as you can reach out to them across various channels.

2. **Provide faster real time solutions 24×7.** Real time engagement is what every customer expects when they approach a brand. Most of the customers leave frustrated if they fail to receive instant support.

The core idea behind real-time customer engagement is the ability to recognize and interact with your customers promptly and cadence that matters to them. In contact study found that customers are satisfied and positive with proactive customer service.

Live chat software empowers the agents to proactively engage with customers and offer them the right solutions. You can also use visual engagement tools like video & voice chat and co-browsing solutions, to make the conversation effective and offer faster solutions. The live customer engagement tools ensure faster resolution in the first touchpoint.

Chatbots are the best solution to automate repetitive business tasks to engage customers with instant answers 24×7. They are the best way of managing customer expectations when the customers' queries are simple, or your support team is busy or not available. Bots can be easily scalable when there is a sudden rise in traffic.

Key takeaways:
- You can use live chat software to gain valuable insights about customers' profiles and trigger the right message at the right time to deliver the best customer service experience.
- With the help of customer engagement, collaborate with your customers in real time and deliver faster solutions in the first contact.
- Deploy chatbots to engage customers 24×7, handle the FAQs, and increase customer satisfaction. This reduces the number of tickets and improves team productivity
- You can provide hybrid support to your customers. Bots will handle general queries and complex queries will be transferred for humanized support.

3. **Keep your communication transparent.** Customers expect transparent communication. Businesses lose potential customers because they fail to implement transparency practices.

Being transparent is good not only for your customers but also for your business. In addition to attracting new customers, transparency allows you to better serve your existing ones, ensuring they stick with you. Here's how transparency has helped our business:

- **Build a successful business** – Being more open about your products, prices, terms and conditions will set you up for success. Potential customers respond well to straightforward talk about what we can and can't do for them.
- **Increase your brand value** – Becoming more transparent can improve your business's efficiency. By spending time talking about your customers' concerns and embellishing your results, you can save time for more productive work.
- **Build trust and loyalty** – The trust that you build with your customers is invaluable. Transparency is a key way of creating trust because it helps eliminate any suspicions or anxieties your customers might have about the value of what you're offering.

Key takeaways:

- You should propel authentic information about your product or services to avoid future confusion among customers.
- Make sure that you don't make fake commitments and set customer expectations that will break their trust and loyalty.
- You should know your brand offers and discounts prior to offering customers to maintain brand efficiency.

4. **Focus to cultivate customer loyalty.** Customers always demand high levels of customer service. Such customer service expectations are what ultimately inform their level of satisfaction, leaving brands with a difficult question: how can you possibly meet your customers' needs while staying ahead of the competition? The answer is customer loyalty.

PR Newswire says that the loyalty management market will grow from $1.4 billion in 2015 to $4.0 billion by 2021. Businesses are building strategies in focus to increase customer loyalty

Loyalty is the perfect tool for managing and exceeding customer expectations with every purchase. But to address them with loyalty, it is important to understand the types of client expectations and what they mean in the context of retention and reward marketing.

Key takeaways:

- Loyal customers have a positive impact on business by recommending your brand to friends and family with good word of mouth.
- When customers are satisfied, they become loyal and have higher customer lifetime value.

5. **Collect customer feedback.** As per the Andrews of HubSpot study, "A full 42% of companies don't survey their customers or collect feedback" (p. 1). Eventually, these companies fail to understand customer expectations. Customer feedback is vital for all businesses to get an overall transparent performance picture and improve your products and services.

Once you understand what customers need, it becomes relatively easy to provide those features in your product. It also becomes relatively easy to retain customers—since they won't have to go elsewhere when you're doing what they expect from you.

Customer feedback helps to measure customer satisfaction. There is a close connection between customer satisfaction and business performance. Therefore, you need to make sure your customers are happy with your products and services.

Naturally, the best way to find out if you meet their expectations is by their feedback. By using CSAT and NPS surveys and ratings, you can easily measure the satisfaction level and consequently predict your company's financial condition in the future.

Key takeaways:

- Customers expect brands to respond to their feedback promptly, but if the time gap is slightly poor, they churn and talk negatively about your brand.
- By asking for customer feedback, you communicate that their opinion is important to you. You involve them in shaping your business, so they feel more attached to your company. This is the best way to gain valuable brand ambassadors who will spread positive word-of-mouth for you.

6. **Meet your client expectations by going the extra mile.** Basically, to go the extra mile comes down to doing more than is expected by the customers, trying a little harder, and going above the norm. And, that excellent customer service is a key attribute that many customers value more than the price or quality of the product.

   For example, it's the extra time a sales agent spends helping customers to make the right selection or the customer support rep who takes a few minutes extra to ensure you have all of your questions answered and won't need to call back.

   What can you do to show you value your customers? Here are some ways you can make your customers feel valued or important:

   - Try to know your customers and identify their needs. Customers love the personalization and attention you give them.
   - Implement the feedback collected from customers and offer improved products or services that align their expectations.
   - Give promotional offers and discounts with their purchase.

   Going the extra mile will not only result in a much happier customer, but it can also go a long way in terms of keeping your business growing as well as staying on their radar for future opportunities and business.

Perfect example on how to exceed customer expectations

Business XXX is known for going the extra mile to fulfill customer expectations and delight them. Once a business XXX team member who was traveling noticed that the passenger seated next to him was browsing the tool's pricing page on the product's website, the team member instantly informed the CEO. Within a few minutes of reporting, business XXX's programmers added a banner on the pricing tab. And the person got a 15% discount on any subscription plan.

7. **Use social media to understand customer expectations.** Gartner et al. say, **"Businesses that do not respond to social media messages encounter a 15% increase in customer churn"** (p. 1).

Social media has become one of the most preferred platforms by customers for instant assistance. According to Insights Guide, Facebook reported that more than 1 billion messages are sent from customers to businesses, every year.

Practice social listening to monitor social conversations related to your brand. By actively listening to the conversations, you can understand their expectations and behavior. You can manage client expectations and build good relationships with them. You can promptly respond to customer service expectations on social media.

It encourages customers to spend more with the company. Your business is able to gain a competitive advantage and make your business stand out of the box.

Key takeaways:

- Practicing social media listening helps you to understand customer service psychology that further helps to know customer needs and wants.
- Identifying customer needs empowers you to serve them better and boost customer satisfaction.

8. **Conduct market research.** Conducting market research is a great way of identifying potential customers. Once you know your target audience you can plan how to exceed their expectations. The more you know about your customers, it helps you define your brand positioning around their expectations.

    Understanding customers' overall needs can benefit your business to deliver better customer service and build long-lasting relationships.

    When you identify your customer expectations, you can:

    - Offer prompt solutions – Knowing what customer expects from you helps to deliver prompt and effective support.
    - Enhance overall product – Customer research helps to understand the motives behind the buying process of the customers and improve on grey areas to create an effective USP.

    Making an effort to market research is worth it because it provides you insights on so many questions like—who the potential customers are, what they buy, why they buy it etc. Further, the research can help you to develop a more detailed picture of them and understand how to target them.

    Key takeaways:

    - Research can help you to learn about your customers' expectations across your industry. It is very important to collect the core details from your customers through regular communication and deliver service matching their expectations.
    - You can use CAST and NPS surveys to measure your customer satisfaction with the existing business products and services. Based on the answers, you can tailor your product to your client expectations.

9. **Keep your customers engaged.** Many businesses fail in meeting the expectation of keeping updated information and following up with them. This can be frustrating and end up driving customers away and negatively advocating about you.

They do so because they feel that you do not care for them and prefer to silently leave your brand. This might negatively impact your brand.

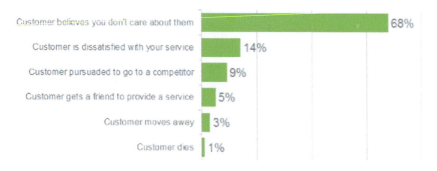

Keeping your customers up to date and making follow-ups show you care about them and that makes them feel like an integral part of your business. This develops loyalty in your customers, and they eventually become your best brand advocates.

Key takeaways:

- Make sure you provide your customers with an estimated time to reply back to keep customers informed.
- Follow up with your customers once the issue is resolved to make sure they are satisfied with the solution or not.

10. **Proactive handling of customer complaints.** The web enables customers to share their feedback in multiple channels such as forums,

social media Nexuses, and more. This indicates that you need to get proactive in handling customer complaints.

You can categorize the frequently reported complaints or analyze what sort of problem the customers might encounter and based on that, you can prepare solutions beforehand. The solutions can be in various forms such as:

- Support content
- How-to videos
- FAQs
- Tutorials

Key takeaways:

- You should never ignore your customer complaints. When you receive complaints from customers, categorize them, and share them with the relevant team or department to work on to resolve them as soon as possible.
- As you welcome customer appreciation, have a similar attitude to the complaints as they are the way to build a better product and brand.
- Customer expectations have a profound impact on every business. It has implications across the whole organization in its own way. Being customer-centric is the best way of managing clients' expectations. Once you plan and understand what your target audience expects, it becomes easy to meet and exceed them.

# CHAPTER 13

# BUSINESS GROWTH

Most small companies have plans to grow their businesses and increase sales and profits. However, there are certain methods companies must use for implementing a growth strategy. The method a company uses to expand its business is largely contingent upon its financial situation, competition, and even government regulations. Some common growth strategies in business include market penetration, market expansion, product expansion, diversification, and acquisition.

**MARKET PENETRATION STRATEGY**

One growth strategy in business is market penetration. A small company uses a market penetration strategy when it decides to market existing products within the same market it has been using. The only way to grow using existing products and markets is to increase market share, according to small business experts. Market share is the percent of unit and dollar sales a company holds within a certain market vs. all other competitors.

One way to increase market share is by lowering prices. For example, in markets where there is little differentiation among products, a lower price may help a company increase its share of the market.

## MARKET EXPANSION OR DEVELOPMENT

A market expansion growth strategy, often called market development, entails selling current products in a new market. There are several reasons why a company may consider a market expansion strategy. First, the competition may be such that there is no room for growth within the current market. If a business does not find new markets for its products, it cannot increase sales or profits.

A small company may also use a market expansion strategy if it finds new uses for its product. For example, a small soap distributor that sells to retail stores may discover that factory workers also use its product.

## PRODUCT EXPANSION STRATEGY

A small company may also expand its product line or add new features to increase its sales and profits. When small companies employ a product expansion strategy, also known as product development, they continue selling within the existing market. A product expansion growth strategy often works well when technology starts to change. A small company may also be forced to add new products as older ones become outmoded.

## GROWTH THROUGH DIVERSIFICATION

Growth strategies in business also include diversification, where a small company will sell new products to new markets. This type of strategy can be very risky. A small company will need to plan carefully when using a diversification growth strategy. Marketing research is essential because a company will need to determine if consumers in the new market will potentially like the new products.

## ACQUISITION OF OTHER COMPANIES

Growth strategies in business can also include an acquisition. In acquisition, a company purchases another company to expand its operations. A small company may use this type of strategy to expand its product line and enter new markets. An acquisition growth strategy can be risky, but not as risky as a diversification strategy.

One reason is that the products and market are already established. A company must know exactly what it wants to achieve when using an acquisition strategy, mainly because of the significant investment required to implement it.

## QUESTIONS TO CONSIDER WHETHER YOU ARE READY FOR GROWTH

First, you should consider whether you are ready for growth. You may interject at this point: "But I thought you just said that a company has only two options, either to grow or die?"

I did say that, but you don't want to launch into a business growth plan too quickly without the proper strategy and planning. That can be just as catastrophic as choosing to try to maintain the status quo for too long. Ask yourself these seven questions before you enact any business growth strategy to see if you are ready.

1. **Workforce Supply**
   Do you have enough workers?

   Do you have the right culture-fit employees?

   Do you have the right types of skills on your team as more work is trending toward higher-skilled work?

   Maybe you need help recruiting Millennials. Discussing this with your team leaders and HR folks can be a real eye-opener. This issue is not one that will go away anytime soon as many companies are challenged with finding quality employees who are the right skills and culture fit.

2. **Orders or Service Capacity (Vendor Capacity)**
   If your orders, revenues, or sales suddenly doubled or tripled, could you handle the growth without choking?

Do you have the space, equipment, inventory, fulfillment partners, and property needed to fulfill those significantly higher orders or service requests?

Can your current vendors manage the jump in growth? Perhaps, you need to replace or supplement some of those before you get in a pickle and have to turn away or significantly delay some of this new business that you've just spent a ton of time and money getting in the door.

3. **Communications (Internal & External)**
   How are you communicating with your employees?

   What about your customers, clients, or vendors? Do your employees know what your brand stands for?

   Do they know how to communicate this to existing and potential customers? It might be a good time to chat with your team leaders and formalize your communications plan to make sure everyone is on the same page. Enacting a growth strategy without everyone on the same page can cause some miscommunication, undercutting your growth strategy.

4. **Targeted Marketing Campaigns**
   Consider doing highly targeted campaigns to grow your business, whether digital or traditional marketing. Most of your customers are bombarded with generic ads every day. Find out where your customers hang out, whether physically or digitally, and speak directly to them there.

   Not only will this make for more focused targeting, but it is also usually a better use of financial resources since you don't have to talk to the masses who aren't really that interested in your products and services.

5. **Financial Resources**

    Do you have the necessary finances it takes to buy additional equipment, inventory, or hire new staff for months or years before they will contribute to the bottom line?

While it might be tempting to think that we can just figure that out later... once growth happens, that can lead to a bad situation where you can't deliver on the promises you just made to these new customers. You can borrow money from a bank, add equity through shareholders, or use an alternative financing model like supplier financing.

6. **Competitive Outlook**

    Have you taken a survey of your competition? Are they well-heeled? Or are they struggling? Taking this into account will help you determine how aggressive you can be in your growth plans.

7. **Can Clients Grow with You?**

    As you grow, some clients won't want to adjust to their expectations to your new size. Perhaps, their account, which was once a larger one, is now smaller relative to your other new clients. Yet they still expect the same level of attention, and that just isn't possible anymore.

    Plus, you may realize that some of your clients aren't all that profitable, and you may consider respectfully declining to continue to do business with them since that would keep you from other new profitable customers. In that case, it would help lessen the blow if you can find another company willing to fulfill their requests going forward as well as giving them plenty of lead time to find another vendor.

## BUSINESS GROWTH STRATEGIES YOU CAN'T AFFORD TO IGNORE.

Most of us have heard this adage, but it cannot be emphasized enough. Each of these ten business growth strategies requires planning, preparation, and communication to those on your team who are going to implement them to have a chance at success. It would be unwise to underestimate the importance of proper setup.

> "Failing to plan is planning to fail." - Benjamin Franklin

1. **Market Share Penetration**
   How much of the market do you own?
   Perhaps, you don't know precise numbers, but with a little digging around, you can usually come up with some rough ideas. Use this to identify weaker competitors who might have significant market share that you can start to chip away at.

2. **Market Segmentation Expansion**
   Is there a part of the market currently being underserved?
   Maybe there is a niche that very few are serving well. This could be a product or service related to the one you are offering now but haven't considered how that would solve a new market's problem, sometimes even with the exact same offering.

3. **Product Development**
   New product development, product line extension, or product reformulation/retooling are a few ways you can look to expand your offerings and thus grow your sales. Get creative, but not just for its sake alone; look at what your customers really want, need, and are willing to pay for. Just another "me too" product line extension probably won't cut it against stiff market competition.

4. **Diversification**

   Who hasn't heard of diversification?

   If you have too much of your overall business sales with one or two customers or with one industry, it might be time to find other companies or industries to tap, even if they are doing well and growing. Being beholden to one company can create a scenario where they have all of the negotiating power, and they may leverage that to increase the length of their payment terms, say from 30 to 90 days, or some other distasteful decisions that you are forced to swallow. But you want to be strategic on how you diversify too. Choose wisely which industries or markets to target; it's best to select ones that can be profitable.

5. **Mergers or Acquisitions**

   What vendor, competitor, or other company can you merge with or acquire?

   Look for weaker companies to approach about merging or acquiring them. If you are living in a sea of strong industry competition, perhaps it might be best to see if one of them is willing to buy you out. Just know that in the latter scenario, you will likely have little negotiating power. But it might be the right move to allow your company and employees to grow and thrive, especially if you have limited financial firepower. And after you merge, don't forget to think about how you integrate both companies.

6. **Alternative Channels**

   Maybe you sell everything through wholesalers. Or you only have one retail store. In either case, you could add the other one you don't currently offer or perhaps even add an online shopping option. Or maybe you start selling direct in addition to your wholesale channel. The key here is communication with existing channels so there aren't hurt feelings or lost business. Or if you plan to lose business in one area, make sure that it will be more than made up for in another area, either in total sales volume or profit or both.

7. **Reducing or Increasing Prices**

   "What? Increase prices, you say? I couldn't do that; it would upset too many of my customers."

   True, it might cause you to lose a customer or two, but part of that is how well the price is communicated. Many times, customers will understand an increase if their prices haven't gone up in many years, and you remind them of this fact along with solid reasons their costs are going up. Plus, taking a personal approach of communicating this face-to-face with all, or at least, your top customers will go a long way towards assuring them that their business is important.

   Or on the flip side, perhaps a strategic price reduction for specific items is in order. This could help drive market share for a product that gets the customer in the door to sell them something else more profitable later.

8. **Steal Competitor Strategies**

   If it's working for the competition, why not borrow a page from their playbook.

   Now, I'm not advocating for doing anything illegal or unethical, but if you can gain knowledge of what they're doing on the up-and-up, then why not do so. Keep in mind that you may need to modify their strategies to your own company, but by the same token, be careful not to water it down too much, thus losing the power of what's working for them.

9. **Key Partnerships or Alliances**

   Are there other companies or influential people in your industry that you can align yourself with to grow your revenues? Typically, these aren't your industry leaders since they don't need your help in return. But if you can find a company or person that has a certain level of success and needs others to create a win-win scenario for both organizations, then do it. Check out these tips for successful partnerships and alliances.

10. Brand Differentiation

Are your brand and products you sell truly differentiated in the market?

Perhaps, you have the best quality, or maybe you have the fastest turnaround. Or you have the most advanced product on the market. Just make sure you have something genuinely unique, that sets you apart and matters to your customer, meaning they are willing to pay for it at a price you can make a profit on. And make sure to communicate that to potential customers as your main point of differentiation from the competition.

## INVESTMENTS IN SMALL BUSINESSES

Small business owners are used to taking risks, but when it comes to investing, taking risks can put your business in a dangerous position. Your business is your biggest asset and main source of income, so you don't want to take any unnecessary risks. Cash flow is the lifeblood of any small business, but while in early growth mode, survival is often the main goal. Investment is one of the safest ways to increase your money fast. With your business and personal financial stability at stake, you need to understand how to invest your capital wisely and diversify your options for optimal results. While there is a wide array of investment strategies, here are a few specific strategies designed to help small business owners enjoy a healthy and bright financial future.

## DIVERSIFY INVESTMENTS

One of the most important investment strategies for small business owners is investing back into your business. However, you need to set limits since concentrating your capital on one asset can be extremely risky. If something happens to your business, your personal finances could be at risk. Find a comfortable balance between reinvesting in your own business and investing in outside opportunities.

When looking for investment opportunities outside your business, make sure not to be single-minded when it comes to where you're investing. Often, small business owners develop a bias towards their own industry due to familiarity and comfort and only invest in their area of expertise. While you may think your knowledge of the industry can be an advantage when evaluating different opportunities, it may not be the smartest decision to put all your eggs in one basket.

Jason Yau of Canvas People says,

> Diversifying your portfolio is a smart way to protect you and your business. If problems arise in your industry, your business, and the rest of your investment portfolio could be at tremendous risk, resulting in serious financial loss. How much you invest is dependent on the amount of your initial capital but, when possible, you should put your investments in a variety of industries and sectors. (p. 1)

Investment diversification reduces your overall risk since some investments may be up while others are experiencing a downturn. A good strategy for diversification is to build a broad portfolio with limited investment in your own industry. Exchange-Traded Funds (ETFs) and mutual funds are usually better options than individual stocks. You should also consider geographic location. Investing outside your region or country can protect your investments against economic troubles specific to one area that may be hurting your portfolio.

Investing in mutual funds containing foreign securities or commodities can protect against a national recession. Educate yourself about the financial markets and learn different asset allocation strategies. Different asset classes respond differently depending on the economic environment. By finding the right asset mix, you can maximize your return on investments. Review and rebalance your portfolio at least twice a year to ensure you're not favoring certain asset categories over others.

In addition to diversifying your portfolio, it's important to start investing even if you only have a small amount of capital to invest with. According to Matt Edstrom of GoodLife Home Loans,

> Preparing adequately for investing is important. Don't follow the surprisingly common, albeit ill-advisable philoso-

phy of risking a large sum of money in investing. The more practical philosophy of allocating small amounts of what you're saving and diversifying your investments regularly provides much lower risk than risking large sums of money in one investment. The hope is that by investing small amounts regularly, one's financial portfolio can grow exponentially (p. 1).

## PIN DOWN INVESTMENTS TO SERVE AS STEADY SECONDARY SOURCES OF INCOME

When diversifying your investments, consider investing outside the stock market. While there are several ways to do this, one of the most lucrative investment opportunities can be rental properties. It's important to note that the current economic condition can largely influence the profitability of investing in real estate. If the property is affordable and trends indicate the property and its neighborhood are due to grow, rental properties can provide a substantial secondary income.

According to Sacha Ferrandi, Founder of Source Capital Funding,

> Real estate investing alone provides multiple investing options. You can purchase income-producing properties, such as an apartment complex or office building. Even if you cannot purchase a larger property like an office building or apartment complex, purchasing and renting out single dwelling homes or even a condominium can still be a smart investment. Even if you are only profiting a few hundred dollars a month after paying the mortgage, the property value will increase during ownership and real returns on your investment will occur after you sell the property. Keep in mind that you'll need to hold on to a real estate investment for at least 5-10 years to see the property appreciate and the longer you hold on to the property, the larger your earnings become. (p. 1)

## DON'T NEGLECT RETIREMENT

With no employer providing a 401(k) and match your investment, you need to open and contribute to a retirement plan. There are different types of tax-deferred retirement account options to help you set aside money. As any small business owner, you might be counting on selling or liquidating your business to fund your retirement. However, if you overestimate the cost, and you cash out your business, you put your future retirement in jeopardy. If you end up being able to sell your business for the expected amount, you'll end up having more money to use towards your retirement or other investments if you've also been saving for retirement on the side.

Start saving as soon as possible and do your best to contribute the maximum allowable amount each year. By contributing the maximum amount, you put away more money to grow your retirement fund and can also use it to offset your annual tax burden. For small business owners, a self-employed (SEP) IRA is a great, tax-free option for retirement savings. You can deposit up to $55,000 from your annual company earnings into the IRA. You can invest the money in mutual funds or ETFs. Other options include individual IRAs and annuities.

## ESTABLISH AN EMERGENCY FUND

Income can vary from month to month when you're a business owner. While your business insurance can protect you in the event of a catastrophe or disaster, you should set up an emergency fund with enough cash or liquid funds to cover your personal expenses when your income cannot. A good rule of thumb is to keep enough money to hold you over for at least six months.

### SAVING AND INVESTING WHILE OWNING A BUSINESS

**Invest in your business.** According to Hammer "One of the best things you can do is invest in is your business …It could be making the product or service better. It's going to be hard to beat the returns of your business, especially if it's increasing your cash flow" (p. 1).

**Have liquid assets.** "Savings are important for everyone, but especially if you're a small business owner. Until a business is stable, getting the business to a point where an owner can make a living doing it should be the main goal, not saving for retirement," Hammer says (p. 1).

Plan to live off personal savings for the first year, possibly two. "That's critical," says Louis Grassi, owner and managing partner of Grassi & Co, an accounting firm in New York that did $50 million in business in 2015 (p. 1). "You need to have sufficient capital because most businesses go out of business because they run out of capital. You need to have a rainy-day fund" (p. 1).

## COMPARE VETTED FINANCIAL ADVISORS MATCHED TO YOUR REQUIREMENTS

Choosing the right financial advisor is daunting, especially when there are hundreds of financial advisors near you. Wiser Advisor makes it easy by matching you to vetted advisors that meet your unique needs. You save time and gain peace of mind by knowing that the two to three matched advisors are experienced professionals and hold clean records. Compare vetted financial advisors registered with FINRA/SEC near you. Get started to compare now.

Building in the contingencies will help for multiple reasons. "I don't know if the financial benefit of that doing is as big as the physiological benefit," Hammer says (p. 1). "Just knowing I can make it and I don't have a gun to my head to make it is important, because it's hard enough. Hunger is good, but desperation isn't" (p. 1).

**Be conservative when investing in a physical space.** Once new business owners have enough cash flow, many rush to get "a fancy office to have bricks and mortar," Hammer says (p. 1). Even though the cash flow is fine, the expenses quickly become too high. Depending on the business, you probably won't need it, he says. "If you're a hairdresser you might need it," Hammer says (p. 1). "But there are ways to do it, so you're not saddled with a high fixed cost base. You want to have a high variable cost base where you can scale it up or down depending on how much demand, but not a fixed cost of building or a location that's too pricy" (p. 1).

**Give your business a stress test.** A stress test is a hypothetical situation to see how a portfolio or business responds to a downturn. "See what would happen if you lost 25 percent of your business and expenses are 50 percent higher," Grassi says (p. 1). "See what you need to support the business in the capital. Stress-test it to see what capital base you need to survive" (p. 1).

**Consider buying an existing small business.** Then expand that business as time and money allow. "It lessens the risk a bit, because you kind of know what you have," Grassi says (p. 1). "You can pay the existing owner over a couple of years because you've already mapped out the existing cash flow" (p. 1).

**Look at a business as a separate entity.** Many entrepreneurs make the mistake of looking at their business as a personal credit card instead of reinvesting in the company. "You can't just drain it like it's a funnel to you and every dollar you make you take out," Grassi says (p. 1).

**When investing, take the risk in running a business, not picking stocks.** Because owning a business is so risky, don't take the risk in your retirement account, Hammer says. "Don't bother with buying individual stocks," Hammer says (p. 1). "Keep the risk in your own business and keep it simple in your portfolio" (p. 1). Consider taking the Warren Buffett approach, who infamously set up his wife's estate with 90 percent in a low-cost Standard & Poor's index fund and 10 percent in short-term government bonds.

**A diversified portfolio reduces the risk.** The broader, the better says Hammer. He suggests Vanguard Total World Stock exchange-traded fund (ticker: VT) and any S&P 500 index fund from iShares, which offers ETFs from BlackRock (BLK) to own a large portfolio of global business. "I'd favor the U.S. because even though it's the U.S., American businesses make a lot of money overseas" (p. 2).

**Have a mix of passive and active investments.** To balance the risk-and-reward ratio, every small business owner should have a blend of investments, including a passive fund that tracks the S&P 500 index as well as international exposure through active investments where a manager is keenly managing the fund.

**Consider a Simplified Employee Pension or profit-sharing plan.** After the business begins to make money and there is enough extra, consider investing in a SEP, where a business owner can contribute 25 percent of compensation or $53,000, whatever is lower. Once employees are in the mix, the calculations become complicated because an employer must contribute to their pensions as well. That's when many small business owners will then move towards a profit-sharing plan where they can contribute based on their cash flow.

**Rein in the tax-deductible expenses.** One of the big pitfalls is expensing too much travel and entertainment through the business, Hammer says. "You tend to spend that money too freely, when you can write off a dinner, or the lease on your car," he says (p. 1). "That can get out of hand pretty quickly. You can feel like it's free money, but it's still not" (p. 1).

**Don't forget the basics**. Many business owners get so busy they don't remember to create a will and buy life insurance. "If I didn't wake up tomorrow, that ATM would shut down if I wasn't here," Hammer says, "And what would happen to my family and people who are dependent on me?" (p. 1). Instead, he recommends small business owners to take a $1,000 to get a will or small life insurance policy instead of making an IRA contribution.

**Ask for money before you need it.** If you've had a good year or two good years, consider getting a line of credit from the bank when you can, Hammer says. "Ask at the point where your business looks really great," he says. "You don't want to ask when you are in the belly of the beast and everything stinks, because the bank won't give you money or you'll have to go to some hard money lender" (p. 1).

Instead, get an equity line of credit that's not drawn, but available in reserve instead of trying go through obtaining it during a cash-flow crisis. "You want your only question to be how much do we need, when do we need to take it, not how do we find this money," Hammer says. "Typically, unless you have a family member or friend, to go the traditional channel at that point could put you out of business."

## EXPANSION

All successful small business startups eventually face the issue of handling business expansion or growth. Business expansion is a stage of a company's life that is fraught with both opportunities and perils. On the one hand, business growth often carries with it a corresponding increase in financial fortunes for owners and employees alike. In addition, expansion is usually seen as a validation of the entrepreneur's initial business startup idea, and of his or her subsequent efforts to bring that vision to fruition. But as Andrew J. Sherman observed in The Complete Guide to Running and Growing Your Business, business expansion also presents the small business owner with myriad issues that must be addressed:

> Growth causes a variety of changes, all of which present different managerial, legal, and financial challenges. Growth means that new employees will be hired who will be looking to the top management of the company for leadership. Growth means that the company's management will become less and less centralized, and this may raise the levels of internal politics, protectionism, and dissension over what goals and projects the company should pursue. Growth means that market share will expand, calling for new strategies for dealing with larger competitors.

> Growth also means that additional capital will be required, creating new responsibilities to shareholders, investors, and institutional lenders. Thus, growth brings with it a variety of changes in the company's structure, needs, and objectives. Given these realities, Sherman stated that, "the need of the organization to grow must be tempered by the need

to understand that meaningful, long-term, profitable growth is a by-product of effective management and planning" (203).

## METHODS OF GROWTH

Small businesses can expand their operations by pursuing any number of avenues. The most commonplace methods by which small companies increase their businesses are incremental in character, i.e., increasing product inventory or services rendered without making wholesale changes to facilities or other operational components. But usually, after some period, businesses that have the capacity and desire to grow will find that other options should be studied. Common routes of small business expansion include:

- Growth through acquisition of another existing business (almost always smaller in size).
- Offering franchise ownership to other entrepreneurs.
- Licensing of intellectual property to third parties.
- Establishment of business agreements with distributorships and/or dealerships.
- Pursuing new marketing routes (such as catalogs).
- Joining industry cooperatives to achieve savings in certain common areas of operation, including advertising and purchasing.
- Public stock offerings.
- Employee stock ownership plans.

Of course, none of the above options should be pursued until the business's ownership has laid the necessary groundwork. "The growth process begins with an honest assessment of strengths and weaknesses," wrote Erick Koshner in Human Resource Planning (p. 13). "Given those skills, the organization then identifies the key markets or types of future market opportunities the company is likely to capture. This, of course, raises another set of issues about how to best develop the structures and processes that will further enhance the organization's core capabilities. Once these structures and processes are identified and the long-range planning completed, the business has a view of where it will be in three to five years and agreement on key strategies for building future business" (p. 14).

## EXPANSION ISSUES IN SMALL BUSINESSES

Whatever method a company chooses to utilize to expand—and whatever guiding strategy it chooses to employ—its owners will likely face a combination of potentially vexing issues as they try to grow their business smoothly and productively. "Expanding a company doesn't just mean grappling with the same problems on a larger scale," wrote Sharon Nelton in Nation's Business. "It means understanding, adjusting to, and managing a whole new set of challenges—in essence, a very different business" (p. 3).

### GROWING TOO FAST

This is a common malady that strikes ambitious and talented entrepreneurs who have built a thriving business that meets a strong demand for a specific set of goods and/or services. Success is wonderful, of course, but rapid growth can sometimes overwhelm the ill-prepared business owner. "Companies growing at hyper-speed sometimes pay a steep price for their success," confirmed Ingram's contributor Bonar Menninger (p. 10). According to management experts, "controlling fast-track growth and the problems that come with it can be one of the most daunting tasks an entrepreneur will face" (p. 17). This problem most often strikes on the operational end of a business.

Demand for a product will outpace production capacity, for example. In such instances, the business often finds that its physical needs have outgrown its present facilities but that its lease agreement or other unanticipated factors hinder its ability to address the problem. "You may sign a five-year lease for a building, and 18 months later you're busting at the seams," one executive told Menninger (p. 12). "We had to move three times in five years. When we signed our latest lease, we signed a three-year deal. It's a little more expensive, but we can bail if we have to" (p. 12). In other cases, a business may undergo a period of feverish expansion into previously untapped markets, only to find that securing a meaningful share of that market brings them unacceptably low-profit margins. Effective research and long-range planning can do a lot to relieve the problems often associated with rapid business expansion.

## RECORDKEEPING AND OTHER INFRASTRUCTURE NEEDS

It is essential for small businesses that are undergoing expansion to establish or update systems for monitoring cash flow, tracking inventories and deliveries, managing finances, tracking human resources information, and myriad other aspects of the rapidly expanding business operation. As one business owner told Nation's Business, "if you double the size of the company, the number of bills you have goes up by a factor of six" (p. 1). Many software programs currently available in the marketplace can help small businesses implement systems designed to address these recordkeeping requirements. In addition, growing enterprises often must invest in more sophisticated communication systems to provide adequate support to various business operations.

## EXPANSION CAPITAL

Small businesses experiencing growth often require additional financing. Finding expansion capital can be a frustrating experience for the ill-prepared entrepreneur, but for those who plan, it can be far less painful. Businesses should revise their business plans on an annual basis and update marketing strategies accordingly so that they are equipped to secure financing under the most advantageous terms possible.

## PERSONNEL ISSUES

Growing companies will almost always have to hire new personnel to meet the demands associated with a new production, new marketing campaigns, new recordkeeping, and administrative requirements, etc. Careful hiring practices are always essential, but they are even more so when a business is engaged in a sensitive period of expansion. As one consultant told Ingram, "Too often, companies spend all their energy on marketing and production plans and ignore developing similar roadmaps for their personnel needs" (p. 1).

Business expansion also brings with it increased opportunities for staff members who were a part of the business in its early days. The entrepreneur who recognizes these opportunities and delegates responsibilities appropriately can go far toward satisfying the desires of employees who want to grow in both personal and professional capacities. But small business owners also need to recognize that business growth often triggers the departure of workers who are either unable or unwilling to adjust to the changing business environment. Indeed, some employees prefer the more relaxed, family-type atmosphere that is prevalent at many small business establishments to the more business-like environment that often accompanies periods of growth. Entrepreneurs who pursue a course of ambitious expansion may find that some of their most valuable and well-liked employees decide to instead take a different path with their lives.

## CUSTOMER SERVICE

Good customer service is often a significant factor in small business success, but ironically it is also one of the first things that tends to fall by the wayside when business growth takes on a hectic flavor. "When the workload increases tremendously, there's a feeling of being overwhelmed," one small business owner admitted to Menninger, "and sometimes you have a hard time getting back to clients in a timely fashion. So, the very customer service that caused your growth in the first place becomes difficult to sustain" (p. 1). Under such scenarios, businesses not only have greater difficulty retaining existing clients but also become less effective at securing new businesses. A key to minimizing such developments is to maintain adequate staffing levels to ensure that customers receive the attention and service they demand (and deserve).

## DISAGREEMENTS AMONG OWNERSHIP

On many occasions, ownership arrangements that functioned effectively during the early stages of a company's life can become increasingly problematic as business issues become more complex and divergent philosophies emerge. For example, Sherman noted that in many growing enterprises that were founded by two or more people,

> "…one or more of the cofounders are unable to keep pace with the level of sophistication or business acumen that the company now requires. Such a cofounder is no longer making a significant contribution to the business and in essence, has become 'obsolete.' It's even harder when the obsolete partner is a close friend or family member: In this case, you need to ask: Will the obsolete cofounder's ego allow for a position of diminished responsibility? Can our overhead continue to keep him or her on staff?" (201)

Another common scenario that unfolds during times of business growth is that the owners realize that they have profoundly different visions of the company's future direction. One founder may want to devote resources to exploring new marketing niches, while the other may be convinced that consolidation of the company's presence in existing markets is the way to go. In such instances, the departure of one or more partners may be necessary to establish a unified direction for the growing company.

**FAMILY ISSUES**

Embarking on a strategy of aggressive business expansion typically entails an extensive sacrifice of time and often of money on the part of the owner (or owners). But as Sherman noted, "Many growing companies, especially those founded by younger entrepreneurs, are established at a time when all of the cofounders are either unmarried or in the early stages of a marriage. As the size of the company grows, so does the size of the cofounders' family. Cofounders with young children may feel pressure to spend more time at home, but their absence will significantly cut their ability to make a continuous, valuable contribution to the company's growth" (p. 145).

Entrepreneurs pondering a strategy of business growth, then, need to decide whether they are willing to make the sacrifices that such initiatives often require.

## METAMORPHOSIS OF COMPANY CULTURE

As companies grow, entrepreneurs often find it increasingly difficult to keep the business grounded on the bedrock values that were instituted in its early days. Owners are ultimately the people that are most responsible for communicating those values to employees. But as staff size increases, markets grow, and deadlines proliferate, that responsibility gradually falls by the wayside and the company culture becomes one that is far different from the one that was in place—and enjoyed—just a few short years ago. Entrepreneurs need to make sure that they stay attentive to their obligations and role in shaping company culture.

## CHANGING ROLE OF OWNER

As businesses grow, they often encounter problems that increasingly require the experience and knowledge of outside people. Entrepreneurs guiding growing businesses must be willing to solicit the expertise of accounting and legal experts where necessary, and they must recognize their shortcomings in other areas that assume increased importance with business expansion.

## CHOOSING NOT TO GROW

Finally, some small business owners choose not to expand their operations even though they have ample opportunity to do so. "For many small business people, the greatest satisfactions in owning a business, which often includes working closely with customers and employees, inevitably diminish as the business grows and the owner's role changes," indicated Nation's Business contributor Michael Barrier. "Many entrepreneurs would rather limit growth than give up those satisfactions" (p. 287). Other successful small business owners, meanwhile, simply prefer to avoid the headaches that inevitably occur with increases in staff size, etc. And many small business owners choose to maintain their operations at a certain level because it enables them to devote time to family and other interests that would otherwise be allocated to expansion efforts.

Entrepreneurs looking to limit the pace of their business's growth need to consider the ramifications of various expansion options. For example, a small business owner may decide that he or she needs an infusion of capital. But entrepreneurs who decide to secure that capital by making a public stock offering are in essence relinquishing any claim on pursuing a course of slow growth. After all, stockholders expect to see growth in the value of their stock, and that growth is predicated on upward trends in market share, sales revenue, and other factors. Robert Tomasko, author of *Go for Growth*, indicated that business owners should make certain that they and their staff are poised to handle the pressure associated with pleasing stockholders. He pointed out that while stock offerings are an excellent way of underlining ambitious growth plans, they can put nightmarish pressure on small business owners who place greater emphasis on a relaxed business environment, improving existing products or services, travel, and/or time with family.

Analysts rush to point out, however, that the entrepreneur who chooses to pursue a philosophy of limited or slow growth is not necessarily adopting a course of management in which he or she allows the business to slowly atrophy. "Limiting growth doesn't mean refusing to change," said Barrier. "In fact, the right changes can be crucial for profitability. A store's product mix may change radically over the years even if the store itself remains the same size" (p. 201). Indeed, most companies have introduced significant technological innovations into their internal operations in recent years, whether they are during tremendous growth or operating at the same basic size from year to year.

Finally, the methodologies that small business owners can employ to limit expansion vary from industry to industry. Management experts point out, for instance, that small service businesses (carpentry outfits, dressmakers, housepainters, swimming pool cleaning services, etc.) can often restrict growth by simply turning down new businesses, if they have a sufficiently reliable, stable crop of clients already in place. Other small businesses can limit growth by raising the prices on their goods and services. This method of reining in growth needs to be studied carefully before implementation, because the firm does not want to lose too much business. But analysts contend that for many niche industries, this option not only limits growth but increases profits on the company's existing workload.

Experts warn, however, that strategies of limited expansion are not practical in many of today's highly competitive industry sectors. As one executive in the high-technology industry pointed out to Nation's Business, fast-growing companies in high-tech typically obliterate companies that do not grow as quickly: "They'll get big, their manufacturing costs will drop, they'll have three times as many R&D [research and development] people fighting against you" (p. 1). Other businesses that operate in industries in which a dominant company is eating up big chunks of market share likewise cannot afford to pursue policies of limited growth. Quite the opposite, in fact, such small businesses often have to aggressively investigate possible new areas of expansion to survive.

## ENTREPRENEURSHIP MODEL

Desire/Passion – Energy – Solving problem - Collective benefit – Serving the community – Fulfillment

Passion – Vision – Feasibility Studies – Goals – Plan – Review

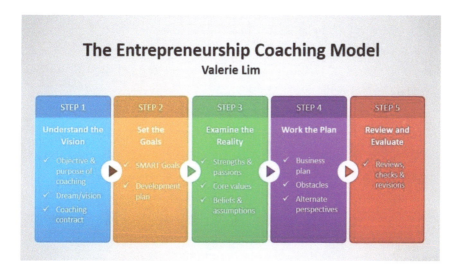

# BIBLIOGRAPHY

Andrews, Marcus. "42% Of Companies Don't Listen To Their Customers. Yikes. [New Service Data]". Blog.Hubspot.Com, 2022, https://blog.hubspot.com/service/state-of-service-2019-customer-first.

Barrier, Michael. "The animated man." The Animated Man. University of California Press, 2007.

Edstrom, Matt. "5 Tips To Building A Successful Marketing Plan For Your Start Up". Smallbiztechnology, 2022, https://www.smallbiztechnology.com/archive/2017/07/5-tips-to-building-a-successful-marketing-plan-for-your-start-up.html/.

Fajardo, A. B., Shultz, C., & Joya, J. C. M. (2019). Entrepreneurship as boundary object: Toward reintegration of Colombia's ex-militants into civil society. Journal of Macromarketing, 39(4), 368-384.

Ferrandi, Sacha. "About Source Capital - Private Hard Money Lenders". Source Capital, 2022, https://hardmoneyfirst.com/about/.

Ferrandi, Sacha. 2022, https://www.linkedin.com/in/sachaferrandi/.

Gartner, Johannes, et al. "Service quality in social media communication of NPOs: The moderating effect of channel choice." Journal of Business Research 137 (2021): 579-587.

Gartner. "Gartner | Delivering Actionable, Objective Insight To Executives And Their Teams". Gartner, 2022, https://www.gartner.com/en.

Gillespie, Rosemary. "When no means no: Disbelief, disregard and deviance as discourses of voluntary childlessness." Women's Studies International Forum. Vol. 23. No. 2. Pergamon, 2000.

Grassi, Louis. "Resources - Grassi Advisors & Accountants". Grassi Advisors & Accountants, 2022, https://grassicpas.com/resources/.

Grigg, Lyn. "Cross-disciplinary research." Australian Research Council (1999).

Hammer, Sarah. "Economic and Financial Policy Responses to the COVID-19 Pandemic: Review and Analysis." Available at SSRN 3772327 (2021).

Hayes, Andrews. 2021. What You Should Know About Entrepreneurs. Investopedia.

Helling, Brett. "What Is A Blog? Definition, Benefits & Examples In 2022". Bloggingtips.Com, 2022, https://bloggingtips.com/what-is-a-blog/.

Hoke, Steve. "Leading with a Developmental Bias: A Passionate Plea for a Return to a Biblical Perspective on People Development." Common Ground Journal 11.2 (2014).

Koshner, Erick L. "A market-focused and customer-driven approach to growth." People and Strategy 20.2 (1997): 9.

Litton, S. David, John Stallworth, J.D, Carol Pierce-Davis, (1987), www.spicewoodgroup.com

Lombardi, Vince. What It Takes To Be Number# 1: Vince Lombardi on Leadership. McGraw Hill Professional, 2001.

Menninger, Bonar, and John Hockenberry. Mortal Error: The Shot That Killed JFK. St. Martin's Press, 1992.

Nelton, Sharon. "Major shifts in leadership lie ahead." Nation's business 85.6 (1997): 56-58.

Newswire, PR. "Loyalty Management Market Worth $18.2 Billion By 2026 - Exclusive Report By Marketsandmarkets™". Prnewswire.Com, 2022, https://www.prnewswire.com/news-releases/loyalty-management-market-worth-18-2-billion-by-2026—exclusive-report-by-marketsandmarkets-301461892.html.

ORCULLO, NA. "Contemporary Entrepreneurship Accademic." (2004).

Prakash, Priyanka. "Types Of Business Entities - Nerdwallet". Nerdwallet, 2020, https://www.nerdwallet.com/article/small-business/business-entity.

Sherman, Andrew J. The complete guide to running and growing your business. Times Business, 1997.

Smith, Adam, and Stephen Copley. Adam Smith's Wealth of nations: new interdisciplinary essays. Vol. 1. Manchester University Press, 1995.

Tracey, Paul, and Nelson Phillips. "Entrepreneurship in emerging markets." Management International Review 51.1 (2011): 23-39.

Williams, Joan. Unbending gender: Why family and work conflict and what to do about it. Oxford University Press, 2001.

Yau, Jason. 2022, https://www.linkedin.com/in/yaujason.

Zomorodi, Manoush. Bored and brilliant: How spacing out can unlock your most productive and creative self. St. Martin's Press, 2017.

Phillips, Nelson, and Paul Tracey. "Opportunity recognition, entrepreneurial capabilities and bricolage: connecting institutional theory and entrepreneurship in strategic organization." Strategic organization 5.3 (2007): 313-320.

Rohn, E. James, and E. James Rohn. The treasury of quotes. Jim Rohn International, 1994.

Hill, Napoleon. Think and Grow Rich!: The Original Version, Restored and RevisedTM. SCB Distributors, 2015.

Printed in the USA
CPSIA information can be obtained
at www.ICGtesting.com
JSHW041342051123
51387JS00005B/55